Philosophy in Education

Philosophy in Education

Questioning and Dialogue in Schools

Jana Mohr Lone and Michael D. Burroughs

ROWMAN & LITTLEFIELD
Lanham • Boulder • New York • London

Published by Rowman & Littlefield
A wholly owned subsidiary of The Rowman & Littlefield Publishing Group, Inc.
4501 Forbes Boulevard, Suite 200, Lanham, Maryland 20706
www.rowman.com

Unit A, Whitacre Mews, 26-34 Stannary Street, London SE11 4AB

British Library Cataloguing in Publication Information Available

Library of Congress Cataloging-in-Publication Data
Names: Mohr Lone, Jana, 1960- | Burroughs, Michael D.
Title: Philosophy in education : questioning and dialogue in schools /
   Jana Mohr Lone and Michael D. Burroughs.
Description: Lanham, Maryland : Rowman & Littlefield [2015] | Includes bibliographical
   references and index.
Identifiers: LCCN 2015027135| ISBN 9781442234772 (cloth : alk. paper) |
   ISBN 9781442234789 (pbk. : alk. paper) | ISBN 9781442234796 (electronic)
Subjects: LCSH: Children and philosophy. | Philosophy—Study and teaching (Elementary) |
   Philosophy—Study and teaching (Secondary) | Questioning.
Classification: LCC B105.C45 M64 2015 | DDC 107.1—dc23 LC record available at
   http://lccn.loc.gov/2015027135

∞™ The paper used in this publication meets the minimum requirements of American National
Standard for Information Sciences—Permanence of Paper for Printed Library Materials, ANSI/
NISO Z39.48-1992.

Printed in the United States of America

Contents

Acknowledgments

My interest in writing this book came both from the significant growth in the field of precollege philosophy over the past decade and from my own experience working with elementary, middle, and high school students around Seattle and elsewhere in the United States. I am inspired by and indebted to all of the young people who share with me their philosophical insights and questions, and particularly the children at John Muir, Thurgood Marshall, and Whittier Elementary Schools in Seattle, where I facilitate weekly philosophy sessions during the school year. The imaginative and honest philosophical thinking of these students fuels my work.

I am deeply fortunate to have extraordinary colleagues and to work within a uniquely supportive university. I thank my colleagues at the Center for Philosophy for Children—Sara Goering, David Shapiro, Karen Emmerman, and Kate Goldyn—for sharing their gifts with me and for their dedication and fun-loving ways, and acknowledge also the many graduate students, undergraduates, and volunteers who make the depth of our work in the schools possible. The University of Washington's Department of Philosophy and College of Arts and Sciences has been behind the work of our center since its beginning twenty years ago, and I thank in particular our department chair Michael Rosenthal, former chair Ken Clatterbaugh, Dean Judy Howard, and department administrator Bev Wessel. I have also had the privilege to serve as the founding president of the organization PLATO (Philosophy Learning and Teaching Organization) and in that capacity to work with many committed and talented people around the country and world. I want to thank especially Roberta Israeloff, who has been my cherished partner in working to advance the cause of philosophy in schools, and all of the teachers who contributed lesson plans to this volume.

Finally, I thank my family—my husband Ron and our sons Will, David, and Jackson—for their enthusiasm for my work, their patience when I was deep in writing and oblivious to what was going on around me, their willingness to engage with me in philosophical conversations even when doing so wasn't of immediate interest, and their love.

Jana Mohr Lone

I have been fortunate to have the opportunity to practice philosophy with children and adolescents for the past twelve years of my life. These experiences have inspired me personally and professionally, shaping my identity as an educator and driving my commitment to precollege philosophy, education reform, and publicly engaged philosophy more generally. I thank the many students and teachers—from Memphis, Tennessee; Chapel Hill, North Carolina; Salisbury, Maryland; State College, Pennsylvania; and Belize, Central America—who opened their classrooms to me, warmly accepted a philosopher in their midst, and taught me a great deal about the value and potential of philosophical education. In many ways, this book is a reflection of these experiences and, in turn, an effort to provide support for continuing philosophical practice in schools.

I have benefited immensely from my colleagues over the years, many of whom influenced and shaped the ideas and commitments in this book. First, I thank Francis Kane for introducing me to philosophy when I was a child and, many years later, serving as my mentor both during and well beyond my tenure as an undergraduate philosophy student at Salisbury University. I thank Jana Mohr Lone and Roberta Israeloff for their tireless dedication to precollege philosophy, both through their leadership in PLATO (Philosophy Learning and Teaching Organization) and their willingness to provide advice and support to me and many others. I thank Deborah Tollefsen and my former graduate student colleagues at the University of Memphis Department of Philosophy. Together we built the *Philosophical Horizons* program; my years working with students and teachers in Memphis city schools and developing this program were some of the most formative of my life and I continue to draw upon them to this day. I also thank Nancy Tuana, Sarah Clark Miller, and my colleagues at the Rock Ethics Institute, for their feedback on chapters in this book, for their professional guidance, and for their support of my current precollege philosophy projects.

I thank my partner, Cori Wong, for her encouragement and enthusiasm as I completed this project. Your willingness to discuss my ideas and questions has been immensely helpful and your own dedication to publicly engaged philosophy is a source of inspiration for me.

I thank my parents, Dean and Roseanne Burroughs, and my siblings, Kevin, Melanie, and Timothy. My parents raised me to think and question, to be joyful, and to be committed to making a positive difference in the world, all while demonstrating unwavering love and commitment to our family. For this and much more, I am very grateful.

Michael D. Burroughs

Preface

In the past decade, there has been tremendous growth in precollege philosophy in the United States. More and more philosophers, graduate and undergraduate students, precollege teachers, and other educators have begun engaging in philosophical inquiry with precollege students or have become interested in the field. Increasing numbers of newly created university and college classes are focusing on precollege philosophy, for children and teenagers, involving faculty, graduate students, and undergraduates learning about methods for, and then leading philosophy sessions with, precollege students in local schools.

Our aim has been to write a book that would be a valuable resource in such classes, as well as useful for other philosophers and philosophy students, precollege classroom teachers, administrators and educators, policymakers, and precollege practitioners of all kinds. There is a relatively large body of literature, amassed over the past forty-odd years, on the value of philosophy and its significance for adults and children, as well as a wide range of helpful resources for introducing philosophy to children in a variety of ways (many of which we list in the bibliography and appendix).

This book offers additional practical resources for use in classrooms, as well as consideration of broader educational, social, and political topics currently underrepresented in the literature. Writing it required us to think deeply about the educational value of precollege philosophy, the philosophies of education that inform this philosophical practice, and the relevance of precollege philosophy for pressing issues in contemporary education (such as education reform, child development, and prejudice and privilege in classrooms).

We begin in chapters 1 and 2 with a discussion of what we take to be the primary motivations for practicing philosophy with young people. Broadly, these motivations are based on the belief that philosophy, at its core, is a practice that is fundamental to the human condition. Philosophy should not be reserved for students and faculty in higher education; asking, examining, and responding to essential questions—whether of the moral, political, existential, epistemological, or metaphysical variety—is a common practice that can be educational and beneficial from a young age. When philosophy is introduced in schools, young people are generally invested in its questions and the associated activities of dialogue and reflection that foster collaborative exploration.

If philosophical questions are to be raised respectfully, productively, and in a fashion that is conducive to student learning, it is important that educators and students facilitate the requisite learning conditions. To this end, we discuss in chapters 3–5 the philosophies of education and pedagogical approaches that we believe best support philosophical practice, including the importance of philosophical sensitivity and the elements of a learner-centered "community of philosophical inquiry." We go on to provide in chapters 6–8 many detailed philosophy lesson plans that can be used to practice philosophy with young people in elementary, middle, and high school classrooms. Covering a wide range of philosophical topics and including numerous classroom activities and discussion prompts, we intend that these plans will be useful for the precollege teacher, the experienced practitioner of precollege philosophy, and the novice educator alike.

In the book's final section we turn our consideration to pressing issues that, we contend, merit greater attention in the precollege philosophy literature. These issues include prejudice, power dynamics, social inequalities, and respect for children, as well as some of the broader policy issues surrounding efforts to bring philosophy into schools. If we want to provide an inclusive and respectful educational space for children, one that genuinely values the voices of every student, we must develop strategies to recognize and diminish the impact of social inequalities in the classroom community. We discuss topics ranging from prejudice toward children to the impact of social power and disadvantage in philosophy sessions, and outline some relevant considerations for precollege philosophers to take into account in their classroom practices. Although this discussion is not in any way exhaustive, by devoting significant attention to these subjects we hope to catalyze further thinking about the pedagogical, social, and political structures and strategies that can influence the success of philosophy in precollege classrooms.

Finally, the perspectives of children are always foremost in our minds. Through our shared decades of practice in precollege classrooms, we have learned from and been inspired and challenged by young people. In writing this book, we hope to foster opportunities for more adults and children to engage in philosophical encounters in an educational climate that nurtures respect for children, appreciation of their philosophical capacities, and dedication to supporting young people's efforts to think for themselves.

Part I

WHY INTRODUCE PHILOSOPHY TO YOUNG PEOPLE?

Chapter 1

Philosophy beyond the University

The title of our book contains two terms central to the practice of philosophy: *questioning* and *dialogue*. At its core, philosophy is the practice of asking questions that are fundamental to the human condition. As Thomas Nagel puts it, "The center of philosophy lies in certain questions which the reflective human mind finds naturally puzzling" (Nagel, 1987, 4). These questions—ranging from what we can know about our world, others, and ourselves, to the nature of right and wrong, and existence (among many other questions)—form the "raw material" of philosophy (Nagel, 1987, 4). At one time or another we all ask philosophical questions of some kind; we wonder about the meaning of our lives (and the end of life), consider our own values, and reflect on the rightness and wrongness of our actions. When we consider these topics—whether as children or adults—we are engaging in philosophical thinking. In most cases, these questions will not have definite answers; they make us aware of uncertainty and the philosophical possibilities inherent in life. As Bertrand Russell notes in *The Problems of Philosophy* (1997),

> Philosophy, though unable to tell us with certainty what is the true answer to the doubts which it raises, is able to suggest many possibilities which enlarge our thoughts and free them from the tyranny of custom. Thus, while diminishing our feeling of certainty as to what things are, it greatly increases our knowledge as to what they may be; it removes the somewhat arrogant dogmatism of those who have never traveled into the region of liberating doubt, and it keeps alive our sense of wonder by showing familiar things in an unfamiliar aspect. (Russell, 1997)

Although uncertainty can be uncomfortable, it also provides us with an opportunity to critically examine our beliefs and choices, to question, and gain knowledge by earnestly grappling with complex questions. Philosophy, in part, is defined by experiences of uncertainty as a basic part of the human condition and the questions that both inform and emerge from these experiences.

Philosophical questioning can be a solo activity: we can and do engage in philosophy on our own. But we can also ask philosophical questions and develop responses to these questions in dialogue with others. As philosophers, we can benefit greatly from questioning and talking with a community that recognizes and values philosophical dimensions of human life. For one, philosophical questions are challenging and we can gain insights and important forms of support from examining them with others. Historical philosophers ranging from Plato to Immanuel Kant present dialogue as a central means for gaining philosophical knowledge. Aristotle, too, points to the centrality of practicing philosophy in a community, noting that it is an activity best shared with one's friends (*Nicomachean Ethics*, 1172a–5). Moreover, as practiced in educational contexts (the focus of much of this book), philosophy often takes the form of classroom dialogue. Children and adolescents can engage in facilitated discussions of philosophical questions in a classroom setting and, in this way, be introduced to the practice and subject matter of philosophy more generally. For this reason we focus on dialogue and the formation of "communities of philosophical inquiry" (exploration of philosophical questions and concepts as catalyzed by the philosophical insights and interests of students) as central to philosophical practice with young people.

Despite the far-reaching presence of philosophy in human experience (whether in philosophical questioning or dialogue with others), the introduction and study of philosophy is not prioritized in most schools. In this chapter we will address some challenges faced by precollege philosophy, including prevalent conceptions of philosophy as a discipline reserved for adults and higher education. In response to these challenges we develop an initial account of philosophy as a broader *practice* of engaging in philosophical questioning and dialogue that can be introduced to children in schools. In doing so, we frame subsequent chapters that examine and provide resources and justifications for practicing philosophy with young people.

THE DISCIPLINE OF PHILOSOPHY AND ITS DISCONTENTS

In the United States (and numerous other countries), the study of philosophy—and, with it, access to an intellectual community devoted to philosophical contemplation and discussion—is largely absent in schools. Philosophy is generally understood as reserved for those attending and working in institutions of higher learning—students attending university (undergraduate and graduate programs) and professional philosophers (professors, lecturers, etc.). Thus, in educational contexts, the term "philosophy" functions, by and large, as a synonym for the academic discipline that is introduced in institutions of higher learning. One is a "philosopher" only insofar as s/he participates in this discipline, whether as a student or as a professional.

In some ways, associating the *practice* of philosophy with the *discipline* of philosophy as located in institutions of higher learning makes good sense. The presence of philosophy departments (and, more broadly, humanities programs) in colleges and universities contributes much to the core mission of higher education. By studying in academic philosophy programs, undergraduate and graduate students develop important skill sets (such as analytic thinking, critical literacy, and logical argumentation) and engage with questions, concepts, and ideas that contribute to our understanding of the world and ourselves.

However, at least in the United States, the association between the practice and discipline of philosophy has become rigid; to practice philosophy *just is* to study philosophy at a college or university (or having completed this study, to perform the work of the "professional philosopher").[1] A problematic consequence of this fixed association (or rather, this *identification*) is the isolation of philosophy as a field of study for a select few practitioners. The "philosopher" is a rare class of human beings, only to be found in institutions of higher learning. The characteristic activities of this class include studying philosophical texts, writing and publishing written work, teaching, and engaging with other academic philosophers (at conferences, in seminars, etc.). But many individuals will never attend university or take a philosophy course, let alone attend a professional philosophy conference. If the practice of philosophy is restricted, whether conceptually or in practice, to its limited manifestations in higher education, then the vast majority of persons do not engage in the practice of philosophy.

The divide between "philosophers" and the broader "nonphilosophical" population is further deepened by a number of practices and norms internal to the discipline. In recent years, several commentators—including a number of professional philosophers—have criticized these practices and norms. For one, these commentators take issue with the privileged place of esoteric practices in the discipline of philosophy; they point to the philosopher's propensity to conduct public presentations and author publications in jargon impenetrable to most individuals, including many other professional philosophers, as well as a lack of publicly engaged work that adequately responds to pressing social, political, and ethical concerns in the "real world."[2] By prioritizing these practices and by failing to support publicly engaged work, professional philosophy and philosophy departments continue to recede into the background of public concern and understanding.[3]

According to Robert C. Solomon, the failure of the discipline to take seriously and seek out multiple forms of philosophical practice, including philosophy's broader purpose in human life, "bespeaks a profound impoverishment" in contemporary philosophy (Solomon, 2001, 101). Solomon writes,

> The problem . . . is the way contemporary philosophy has rendered itself so "thin," cutting itself off from context, history, and culture. The philosophical games based on a dubious notion of "logical possibility" and the continuing insistence on necessary and sufficient conditions. . . . It is easy enough to appreciate why young philosophers continue to be enticed to join in such games, but few people outside academic philosophy departments find anything of interest or significance in them. Moreover, the compulsive nature of the games distracts us from confronting the problems that so-called real people face in their lives. (Solomon, 2001, 102)

Insofar as it emphasizes "philosophical games" of limited interest, contemporary philosophy excludes engagement with the broader public, leaving few, if any, possibilities for public engagement with the work of the professional philosopher.

This sense of exclusion from the discipline of philosophy is not limited to the broader public; many individuals working within the academy also experience alienation from prevailing forms of disciplinary work. In "How Is This Paper Philosophy?" (2012), Kristie Dotson discusses the alienation experienced by many philosophers in the face of prevailing disciplinary norms, leading some of these individuals to leave the academy. Dotson references a *culture of justification* in contemporary philosophy, an intellectual and social environment in which one's beliefs, ideas, or practices are evaluated in relation to "presumed commonly-held, univocally relevant justifying norms" (Dotson, 2012, 6). Within this disciplinary culture one is pressured, whether implicitly or explicitly, to make one's projects "congruent" with these (presumed univocal) justifying norms. Dotson's critique of this culture and its associated exclusionary practices hinges, in large part, on revealing the "sense of incongruence" with these norms that is experienced by diverse practitioners of philosophy.[4]

Taken in all, the conception of philosophy in question—one which is both isolated *from* the broader public and isolating *to* numerous individuals working within the academic discipline—has contributed to the discipline's state of "crisis" (McIntyre, 2011; Solomon, 2001, 103). Pointing to reductions in students, reductions in funding and employment opportunities, and recent closures of philosophy departments across the United States, Lee McIntyre contends that the discipline of philosophy has placed itself in a "corner of irrelevance":

> Outside the university, not many people may think that it is important to protect the rights of a few tenured professors to speak into an echo chamber. If we are not serving our students, the larger society, or making connections with other disciplines—if we are not prepared to defend philosophy, use it in the larger world, and show others why it is so important—we shouldn't be surprised if philosophy begins to disappear even within the one place where we thought it would be protected: the university. (McIntyre, 2011)

We reference these critiques of contemporary philosophical practice for three reasons, all of which relate to transforming and expanding our understanding of what it means to do philosophy.

First, as professional philosophers ourselves, we want to highlight problems that are often acknowledged, yet rarely adequately addressed. The conception of philosophy as an exclusionary or esoteric practice open only to a select few individuals is not new. Nor are we the first to discuss or critique this element of contemporary philosophy. But in the current economic and educational climate of our nation and the world, the negative consequences of this prevailing conception are growing—entire philosophy departments have been shut down and many more continue to struggle in the face of decreased funding and fading relevance within their institutions.[5] The result has been the steadily increasing retreat of philosophy, both within the university and from the public realm. Given these conditions, we believe it is important to address these conditions anew and to consider possibilities for changes in contemporary philosophy.

Second, we contend that at least one possibility for positive change in contemporary philosophy includes expanding conceptions of the "philosopher" and legitimate philosophical practice. Informed by our philosophical work both in universities and precollege institutions, we argue for extending philosophical practice and resources beyond the university to schools. Professional philosophers and the discipline as a whole can benefit from this expansion. Introducing philosophy in schools cultivates a new population of philosophers who may become interested in pursuing philosophy as a course of study or profession.[6] Involving young people in philosophical conversation has the potential to raise philosophy's visibility and widen its reach. Bringing philosophy into schools can help lift it from the margins of societal discourse and raise awareness of what a philosophical approach can offer to our collective thinking about ethics, social and political problems, etc. The broader introduction of philosophy in precollege education directly challenges conceptions of philosophy as an esoteric practice reserved for the few, opening up opportunities for philosophical engagement and instruction to persons of different ages, socioeconomic backgrounds, and areas of philosophical concern. Instead of a subject confined to the academy, philosophy should be understood as a common human endeavor.

Finally, this much-needed expansion of philosophy to schools, bringing with it the distinct skill sets and experiential benefits associated with precollege philosophy, has the potential to contribute to precollege education. Philosophy's emphasis on questioning and independent thinking, on uncertainty rather than certainty, can enliven classrooms and engage students by involving them in thinking about important questions that matter to them. Philosophy encourages students to question the assumptions that underlie our thinking and behavior. Further, philosophy supports the development of strong critical thinking and analytic reasoning skills in young students.[7] Moreover, introducing philosophy in schools facilitates an appreciation by students of the wide variety of perspectives from which the world can be viewed. By definition, a question of philosophy does not have one *settled* answer. The experience of becoming aware that there are many ways to see the same problem or concept—all of them unique and potentially valuable—is a powerful one for young people.

EXPANDING ACCESS TO THE PRACTICE OF PHILOSOPHY

Let us suppose that there is support from professional philosophers and educators for expanding access to philosophy and, further, that this expansion would include the introduction of philosophy in precollege classrooms.[8] Introducing philosophy in schools requires practicing philosophy with nontraditional students of philosophy—children and adolescents. This raises a number of important questions. First, are young students capable of practicing philosophy? Perhaps philosophical instruction has, by and large, been limited to postsecondary education for good reason, namely, because children (especially young children) are incapable of participating in robust philosophical discussion or analysis. If so, there is little reason to continue efforts to introduce philosophy in schools. Second, if children are capable of practicing philosophy, what form(s) does this practice take in primary and secondary education? That is, how would the classroom teacher or professional philosopher go about doing philosophy with children? Along with considerations of children's basic philosophical abilities or the child's proposed status as "philosopher," we must also consider practical elements and styles of philosophical pedagogy in precollege classrooms.

Both in theory and practice, philosophy has generally been reserved for adults. As conceptualized in much of the traditional Western philosophical canon, children are appetitive beings; they are, among other things, lacking in self-control, animalistic, irrational, and, as such, unfit for the rigors of philosophical thought and instruction. Given their lack of developed reason and self-control (and, in general, their metaphysical and political status as *incomplete* persons), children must be led to adulthood through controlled socio-educational measures. This characterization of children and the ends of education is located, with some variation, in the work of central figures in the Western philosophical canon, including Plato, Aristotle, John Locke, Immanuel Kant, and Jean-Jacques Rousseau. Plato in particular offers us paradigmatic examples of this conception of children and education:

> Children must not be left without teachers, nor slaves without masters, any more than flocks and herds must be allowed to live without attendants. Of all wild things, the child is the most unmanageable . . . the most unruly animal there is. That's why he had to be curbed by a great many bridles so to speak. (Plato *Laws*, 252 [808d–e])

> When young people get their first taste of argument, they misuse it as if it were playing a game, always using for disputation. They imitate those who have refuted them by refuting others themselves, and, like puppies, enjoy dragging and tearing with argument anyone within reach. . . . And as a result of this, they themselves and the whole of philosophy as well are discredited in the eyes of others. (Plato *Republic*, 235 [539b–c])

These passages are significant in that they gesture toward a broader view of childhood as a deficient stage of being, as a time in which the human being lacks the qualities needed for philosophical practice (as well as a lack of important forms of agency more generally). Such notions of childhood have contributed to shaping models of the legitimate "philosopher," which, if nothing else, is taken to be an adult (male). The conception of philosophy as unfit for children derives, in part, from historical yet continuing conceptions of the intellectual and metaphysical deficiencies of childhood.[9] This conception, taken in tandem with an image of the "philosopher" as adult, owes much to theories of childhood developed throughout the Western philosophical canon.

Responding to this conception of childhood and its various manifestations in full is beyond the scope of this chapter. Suffice it to say that many philosophers and educators (and others) find deeply problematic these conceptions of childhood as a deficient, incomplete stage of being. For the purposes of this chapter, it is important that we focus instead on the ability of children to practice philosophy. Along with establishing children's philosophical capacities, it is important also to consider the spectrum of legitimate philosophical practice. The activities of professional philosophers—including presentations at professional conferences, writing for publication in academic journals, and engaging with students and colleagues in the university classroom—are specialized modes of philosophical practice; they do not define philosophical practice. Those of us working with young philosophers in precollege classrooms understand the practice of philosophy as deriving from fundamental dispositions that most children possess. That is, children, from a young age, often raise philosophical questions, are interested in considering these questions with others, and, given a suitable educational environment, are capable of taking part in philosophical dialogue with adults and peers. We believe that philosophy has an important place in schools because philosophical practice, at its most fundamental level, is common to and practiced by children.

In a sense, professional or university-level manifestations of philosophy derive from the basic philosophical interest that can be seen in children. This point is captured well by the late Gareth Matthews, a professional philosopher and one of the pioneering figures of precollege philosophy:

I first became interested in the philosophical thought of young children by worrying about how to teach introductory courses in philosophy to college students. Many students seemed to resist the idea that doing philosophy could be natural. In response to their resistance I hit on the strategy of showing them that as children many of them had already done philosophy. It occurred to me that my task as a college philosophy teacher was to reintroduce my students to an activity that they had once enjoyed and found natural, but that they had later been socialized to abandon. (Matthews, 1980, vii)

The practice of philosophy begins with persons asking and seeking answers to fundamental questions pertaining to meaning, knowledge, truth, and values that, in some form and at some time, most of us entertain. For many children, asking these kinds of questions constitutes part of their exploration of the world around them. Children do not engage in philosophical questioning with the goal of production (of a publication, presentation, etc.) or only as they enter a designated space (the philosophy conference, university classroom, etc.). Rather, philosophical questions are present to children in an intimate way; their philosophical questioning is at once highly practical (in the sense that these questions are asked earnestly in an attempt to develop a better understanding of the world, others, and themselves) and, at the same time, profoundly playful. Children take up philosophical questions and state (or "try on") various positions in relation to the world and others. Through this process, and the educational relationships of recognition that sustain it, children adopt various modes of engagement with the world. We contend that the important place of philosophical thinking and questioning in the lives and development of children provides a powerful reason for philosophical practice to be cultivated from an early age.[10]

PHILOSOPHICAL PRACTICE

When practicing philosophy with children in precollege classrooms we find an abundance of willing collaborators. This is because we are not bringing philosophy *to* children. The child is not a *tabula rasa* upon which we write philosophical insights, questions, and arguments. Instead, we are exploring philosophy *with* children who are already possessed of philosophical concerns and an interest in philosophical questioning and discussion. Our aim in this work takes the form of providing fertile conditions for children's philosophical questioning while helping to cultivate their critical thinking and philosophical sensitivity.

In order to better illustrate the conception of a "fundamental" philosophical practice toward which we have been gesturing here, it might be helpful to consider this issue in light of some of the philosophical topics traditionally taught in institutions of higher learning. The academic discipline of philosophy is divided into subdisciplines or areas of philosophy such as *epistemology* or *ethics* (to name only two). Professional philosophers and students conduct research on the problems of these subdisciplines. The traditional problems of epistemology center on knowledge and the justification of knowledge claims and include questions such as: What is knowledge? When is one justified in claiming that s/he knows something? What are the limits of human knowledge? Traditional questions in ethics center on possibilities for human flourishing (the most optimal ways to live one's life), duties to oneself and others, and rules for conduct in society (as well as many other questions).

Although commonly associated with the pursuit of professional philosophy, epistemological and ethical questions are not the sole province of the professional philosopher or university philosophy class. For those of us who work in precollege classrooms, it is apparent that these questions are particularly important for children. With a little prompting, children ask epistemological questions about *how* we know something is the case and *why* a given state of affairs holds in the world. Children are also distinctly concerned with ethical questions concerning right and wrong, fairness, and equality. One need only engage children in a discussion about friendship (to cite one example) to see that they care a great deal about ethical questions. Children have clear commitments in regard to issues such as what makes for a *good* friend, what one owes to one's friends, and the importance of friendship (and other formative relationships such as the family) for living a good life.

None of this is to say that we should make no distinction between the activities of professional philosophers and children. Both parties practice philosophy for very different reasons, and the former—given their development, education, and training—are capable of engaging in philosophical questioning in a particularly rigorous and systematic fashion. We can draw a distinction between professional philosophers and philosophical children, but this distinction should not center on a conception of philosophy as the sole province of (adult) professional philosophers. To be sure, children do not generally write philosophical treatises or present work at conferences, but they certainly *do* engage in the practice of philosophy for the same reasons that serve as the motivation for most philosophical work. Further, they engage in this practice with a direct interest in the questions themselves, without being restricted by the traditional norms of academic philosophy. Indeed, professional philosophers would do well to emulate children's openness and playful embrace of philosophical questioning that transcends rigid disciplinary boundaries.

Our discussion of expanding what constitutes a valuable or legitimate philosophical practice can be usefully framed alongside Kristie Dotson's (2012) claim that philosophy must become more inclusive to diverse practitioners and alternative modes of philosophical engagement. Dotson argues for a shift in philosophy from a *culture of justification* to a *culture of praxis*. As opposed to a culture of justification—in which there is an assumed monolithic set of governing norms that determines the value of *all* philosophical practice—a move to a culture of praxis involves an expanded conception of what it is to do philosophy. In a culture of praxis, "what creates philosophical communities is a concern for contributions made according to one's interests and community involvement, rather than a shared set of justifying norms" (Dotson, 2012, 19). That is, no longer do we assume that all philosophical practices should be evaluated by a uniform set of governing norms; instead, we assess whether an approach makes a contribution in line with one's own (and/or one's community's) interests. This shift in culture allows for and supports diverse approaches to philosophy by acknowledging that different issues and philosophical problems will emerge as relevant among different communities (Dotson, 2012, 6, 17). For our purposes, one of Dotson's key insights is the move toward a system of validation that would support the existence of multiple philosophical communities and the recognition of multiple forms of philosophical practice. Our focus here has been to delineate one such additional (and we contend, valuable) community: children and adolescents.

PHILOSOPHICAL PRACTICE IN SCHOOLS

Whether working in the kindergarten classroom or with middle- and high-school students, practitioners of precollege philosophy generally focus on creating a community of philosophical inquiry *with* their students. A community of philosophical inquiry is an educational space that prioritizes dialogue and student engagement as catalyzed by the philosophical insights and interests of the (child or adolescent) participants.[11] Practitioners of precollege philosophy are also committed to learner-centered education at all grade levels, an education that both respects and seeks to develop the philosophical sensitivity of young philosophers.[12] But when acting on these theoretical and practical motivations, precollege philosophers must be responsive to the age and developmental level of participating students.

Although young children (such as children in kindergarten and the primary grades) possess philosophical interests and concerns that can be used as the basis for class discussion, they are still in the process of acquiring important social-emotional and reasoning skills. Therefore, conducting a learner-centered education with these students requires attentiveness to the distinctive interests, capacities, and worldview of developing learners. This involves the facilitator often taking a robust role in helping young students to form the initial structure of the community of philosophical inquiry (from setting up the classroom as a "discussion space" and helping form discussion rules, to demonstrating "posing a question," "listening to a friend," or "giving a reason," etc.). By doing so, the facilitator creates the conditions for young children to be successful in their attempts to interact and engage in dialogue with their peers. In addition, to foster this dialogue and maintain a learner-centered focus that best utilizes the philosophical sensitivity of young children, the facilitator will need to use age-appropriate discussion prompts, including (but not limited to) children's literature, artwork, children's songs, and child-friendly games. Using these discussion prompts allows the facilitator to engage children's attention and develop discussion around concrete, accessible questions. Throughout their work with young children, facilitators maintain a commitment to learner-centered, dialogical education within a community of philosophical inquiry while always making this process (and its related skill sets) accessible to young philosophers.[13]

As noted above, children are quite capable of engaging in philosophical discussion and possess philosophical concerns of their own. In many cases, these concerns emerge in discussions of important philosophical concepts, such as *knowledge*, *truth*, *justice*, *community*, and *personhood* (and many others). Each of these concepts has a rich history in the philosophical canon and, thus, the discipline possesses many resources that can be helpful to the philosopher (or facilitator) working with children. For example, when working with older middle- and high-school students a facilitator can draw upon a text from the Western philosophical canon—such as Plato's *Republic*, W. E. B. Du Bois' *The Souls of Black Folk*, or Simone de Beauvoir's *The Second Sex*—to help illustrate a philosophical problem or concept. Or facilitators might consult philosophical literature to increase their own knowledge and understanding prior to introducing particular philosophical problems or concepts to students.

However, direct engagement with the traditional philosophical canon is not a necessary condition for participation in precollege philosophy. Children already have questions and concerns about, for example, personhood and community, and the facilitator can harness these questions and concerns for the purposes of philosophical discussion. Therefore, the facilitator can view philosophical literature (and the canon more generally) as a resource to supplement dialogue in a community of philosophical inquiry (particularly among older children). But philosophical discussion and the development of a community of philosophical inquiry are quite possible with students—whatever their age or grade level—apart from direct contact with the philosophical canon.

As with younger students, facilitators working with older children and adolescents in middle- and high-school settings must continue to focus on the construction of a community of philosophical inquiry and the development of important philosophical skill sets. Philosophical pedagogy is not present in most schools and, thus, will be foreign to many students, regardless of grade level. But certain elements of the practice of precollege philosophy will change as participating students age and gain additional academic and social skills. For one, although children's literature and visual art can work quite well as discussion prompts for all ages, in communities of philosophical inquiry composed of older students facilitators can also begin to introduce philosophical text-based discussions (with the length and complexity of the text shifting in relation to the age, interests, and abilities of students). The facilitator can continue to use the structure of dialogue and learner-centered engagement to help students develop important philosophical (and academic) skill sets. Approached as equal participants in a community of philosophical inquiry, students take on greater ownership of the dialogue.

INQUIRING WITH CHILDREN

In this chapter we have considered both reasons for and elements of expanding access to philosophy beyond the university. Although this expansion can take different forms, we have focused on practicing philosophy with students in schools. The benefits of this expansion are many—for the discipline of philosophy, for students in schools, and for those philosophers who participate in precollege instruction of philosophy. In closing this chapter, we will discuss an additional motivation for practicing philosophy with children not yet considered.

As adults, participating in precollege philosophy allows us to experience a different relationship with children, one grounded in collaboration, caring, and intellectual partnership. Discussing the adult's relationship to the child in a context of philosophical engagement, Matthews writes,

> Philosophical thinking has been left out of the account of childhood that developmental psychologists have given us . . . [and] leaving it out encourages undeserved condescension toward children. If the most daunting intellectual challenges that Sam and Nick face are to learn the twelve-times table and the passive form of the verb "to be," condescension

toward these children as thinkers has some warrant in fact. But if Sam and Nick can raise for us in vivid and compelling form the puzzles of how the universe could have begun, then there are at least some contexts in which they should be considered our partners in a joint effort to understand it all. (Matthews, 1994, 12–13)

In educational contexts, the adult (teacher) is often the expert. As the expert, the teacher's job is to provide information for the children who, in turn, are in school to learn from the teacher. When caring, qualified, and expert in their fields, it is indeed important for children to be prepared to learn from their teachers; ideally, teachers have much to share with children that is pertinent to children's development and education. However, this form of relationship—with the child always in the position of learner—can crystallize in contemporary educational practice such that we fail to see that children, too, can teach adults and their peers. We overlook this possibility and its inherent educational value once we uncritically accept a conception of adult-child engagement based on a common top-down, corrective approach to children and educational practice.

Children in general face skepticism from adults (and often from other children) about their abilities to contribute to knowledge and understanding. Children's reflective and analytic capacities are typically underestimated, and their abilities to make sense of their own experiences can be undermined by adult dismissal. Matthews wrote eloquently about the ways adults frequently fail to perceive what he calls the "moments of pure reflection in children's thinking," speculating that

> perhaps it is because so much emphasis has been placed on the development of children's abilities, especially their cognitive abilities, that we automatically assume their thinking is primitive and in need of being developed toward an adult norm. What we take to be primitive, however, may actually be more openly reflective than the adult norm we set as the goal of education. By filtering the child's remarks through our developmental assumptions we avoid having to take seriously the philosophy in those remarks; in that way we also avoid taking the child and the child's point of view with either the seriousness or the playfulness they deserve. (Matthews, 1992, 52–53)

We sometimes assume that children's thinking is less mature or nuanced than that of adults, and that therefore what they say can offer little or nothing to what we already know. But childhood and adolescence are more than stages of "adults in training;" young people see the world in particular ways, and those perspectives can enrich the way all of us understand the world. In addition, children, like all other people, have distinct life experiences that, if acknowledged and understood, can inform a better understanding of our lives. In this sense, every stage of life has value and should not be reduced to mere preparation for the stages that precede or follow it. The insights of childhood are often lost when we reach adulthood, and can only be accessed when we listen to children.

For example, friendship has a unique and important role in the lives of children and adolescents. Learning to make friends and figuring out what friendship involves is a significant part of the work of young people, and they spend a considerable portion of their waking experience with their friends, in a way most adults no longer do. This gives children access to ideas and perceptions about friendship that can be enriching for adults. For instance, in a discussion about friendship, a fifth-grade elementary-school student remarked, "My friends are so much like me. I wonder if I've become more like them, or them more like me, because we're friends, or if we became friends because we were alike in the first place."[14] Her insight about the way we are attracted to people like us and her speculations about the way friends can influence each other led the class to think deeply about what it is that leads to friendship and whether a strong friendship between two very different people is possible.

Engaging with children in philosophical questioning and discussion provides us with a different form of interaction and collaboration than is normally found in precollege classrooms (and in adult-child interactions more generally). Philosophical questioning is unique in that it is not practiced solely for the purpose of finding answers, as is the case with most other forms of questioning. In addition to any answers that might be discovered, philosophical questions are important insofar as they help to generate additional possibilities and forms of thought that might have been previously unconsidered by those engaged in the questioning at hand. Unlike many questions in disciplines such as mathematics or chemistry, philosophical questions do not have one "right" answer. The philosophy teacher or facilitator (unlike, say, the math or chemistry teacher) is not in a position to be an expert in the sense of the person possessing the answer (or set of answers) that children must learn and reproduce.

For this reason, philosophical questioning and dialogue can unsettle the traditional teacher-student dyad and restructure educational practice in the classroom. When practiced well, philosophy can initiate open dialogue between adults and children, teachers and students. Philosophical interactions thus create the possibility for a different form of relationship between adults and children—one of recognition and respect as fellow philosophers navigating questions that are equally important and, at times, equally perplexing, to all involved. Precollege philosophy provides us with an opportunity to regard children as active, thinking persons, as opposed to passive learners. And regarding children in this way gives them the opportunity, in a very real sense, to regard *themselves* differently, as philosophers and thinkers valued in their own right.

NOTES

1. This association is much less rigid in other fields, such as mathematics, history, and literature. For example, although there are important distinctions between precollege and university mathematics (such as curricular and pedagogical distinctions), children are introduced to this field from a young age and need not wait until they are of age to attend university to explore mathematical problems and concepts in an organized educational setting.

2. In *Democracy and Education* (2011) John Dewey comments on the tension between philosophy as a basic social practice versus its relative isolation as a practice reserved for a chosen few: "The fact that philosophic problems arise because of widespread and widely felt difficulties in social practice is disguised because philosophers become a specialized class which uses a technical language, unlike the vocabulary in which direct difficulties are stated" (179).

3. This is not to say that professional philosophers do not perform work that is relevant to social, political, and ethical concerns. There are numerous examples of professional philosophers who recognize the need for philosophy to engage with pressing sociopolitical and ethical

issues. For example, see Sally Haslanger's *Resisting Reality: Social Construction and Social Critique* (2012) or Patricia Hill-Collins' *Another Kind of Public Education: Race, Schools, the Media, and Democratic Possibilities* (2009). These philosophers are noteworthy, in part, because they and their work take us beyond traditional areas of philosophical investigation and engage with pressing issues of public concern.

4. Many philosophers do not accept, for example, that authentic or rigorous philosophical arguments begin by assuming a "view from nowhere," or that one's status as an intelligent philosopher hinges on how aggressively critical s/he can be toward the work of others. Nonetheless, philosophers who resist these disciplinary norms can find it difficult for their work to gain "positive philosophical status" (Dotson, 2012, 13). The result, Dotson claims, is a philosophical environment that isolates and excludes diverse practitioners both within and beyond the discipline.

5. For recent examples, see Justin Weinberg's (2015), "A Philosophy Department's Impressive Fight for Survival," retrieved from http://dailynous.com/2015/04/06/a-philosophy-departments-impressive-fight-for-survival/, and Jonathan Wolff's (2010), "Why is Middlesex University philosophy department closing?" retrieved from http://www.theguardian.com/education/2010/may/17/philosophy-closure-middlesex-university.

6. It is also possible that expanding philosophy to schools would create additional employment opportunities for professional philosophers. This employment model for professional philosophers is common to many European nations. For discussion of precollege philosophy in Europe, see the United Nations Educational, Scientific, and Cultural Organization [UNESCO] (2011).

7. For an example of empirical research on precollege philosophy instruction and the development of critical thinking and reasoning in young students, see Trickey and Topping (2004, 2007). Also see chapters 3 and 11 in this book for additional examples of research on precollege philosophy and educational outcomes.

8. In fact, this expansion is already occurring and has been in the United States since at least the 1970s. Much of this progress is due to the work of Gareth Matthews, Matthew Lipman, Ann Sharp, and other pioneers in the field, as well as to the work of PLATO (Philosophy Learning and Teaching Organization) and several university centers around the country dedicated to precollege philosophy. Credit should also go to the many philosophy graduate students, professional philosophers, and other educators across the nation who teach philosophy in schools.

9. See Jenks (2005) and Wall (2010) for discussion and numerous historical examples of the "deficient model" of childhood.

10. This point is explored more fully in the next several chapters.

11. See chapter 5 for an in-depth examination of the community of philosophical inquiry.

12. See chapter 3 for discussion of the philosophy of education and learner-centered motivations that inform much of precollege philosophy.

13. For specific examples and illustrations of precollege philosophy (including numerous lesson plans), see part III ("In the Classroom").

14. Class at Whittier Elementary School, Seattle, Washington, spring 2014.

Chapter 2

Wonder, Questioning, and Reflection

The important thing is not to stop questioning. Curiosity has its own reason for existing.

— Albert Einstein

We have examined some of the reasons underlying the claim that engaging in philosophical practice with children and adolescents is important and beneficial. While our focus is on philosophy in schools, philosophy doesn't initially enter the lives of most young children through the classroom. Children begin speculating about philosophical topics early in their lives, asking their own questions about the world and exercising their capacities for expressing and exploring those questions. This chapter explores the central elements of children's first engagement with philosophy, as well as some of the principal features of philosophical practice more generally. We look here at what we take to be three primary philosophical activities: wondering, questioning, and reflecting.

WONDER

What does it mean to be normal?
Why am I here?
Does everything have a right to live?
What makes someone love you?
Can you think and feel at the same time?
Are numbers real?
Would life have meaning without death?

These questions are examples of the philosophical questions young people ask, illuminating their sense of the strangeness of the world and the possible limits of human understanding. They are grounded in wonder.

Plato refers to wonder as the origin of philosophy (*Theaetetus*, 155d3). Wonder is "a response to the novelty of experience" (Cobb, 1993, 28). Involving a sense of the mysteries that pervade the human condition, wonder leads to a desire to question and reflect about the deeper meaning of ordinary concepts and experiences. Fundamentally, wonder arises in childhood from an awareness of the novelty of being alive in the world, and eventually can lead to pondering such subjects as the meaning of being alive, the complexity of identity, the nature of friendship and love, how to live good lives, and whether we can know anything at all (among other topics).

Our ability to reflect about our lives and to use language to make sense of intricate and often inscrutable concepts makes wondering a basic human activity; integral to our identity is the possession of a conscious awareness of the perplexities of the human condition. Indeed, we would argue that an essential feature of leading a full and rich life is the ongoing development of our wondering selves, which sustains our appreciation for the partialness of our knowledge and the endless puzzles of existence.

Paul Martin Opdal draws a distinction between wonder and curiosity that is useful in thinking about wonder and its relationship to philosophy (Opdal, 2001, 331–44).[1] Opdal defines curiosity as an interest in finding something out, involving the kinds of questions that can be satisfied using accepted frameworks of knowledge (e.g., "What time is it?" "Why do we have time zones?"). Curiosity leads us to investigate further, and is a force behind, for example, science and technology. By contrast, Opdal contends, wonder is "the state of mind that signals that we have reached the limits of our present understanding, and that things may be different from how they look" (Opdal, 2001, 332) (e.g., "What is time?"). Wonder is evoked by a sense of the sheer ineffability of the world and the boundaries to our understanding of it. It emerges when we are struck by the oddness of what we encounter, and develop what Opdal calls "an uneasiness toward the given" (Opdal, 2001, 331).

Lipman puts it this way:

> When we find the world wonderful, it is because we seem to be confronted not by soluble problems, but by utter mysteries. . . . Children wonder not only about themselves, but about the world. Where did it come from? How did it get to be the way it is? To what extent are we responsible for it? And if not we, then who?
>
> Children look at their fingernails, and wonder where they came from. How does something like a fingernail grow out from one's body? But then, everything about their body seems fascinating to them.
>
> Likewise, a snail is fascinating to them—or a mud puddle—or the dark spots on the face of the moon. (Lipman, 1980, 32)

Of course, wonder is not only manifested through philosophical exploration, but can be displayed in many other ways; for example, through art, poetry, music, and religion or spirituality. Yet because wonder can lead to questions about the most basic frameworks of human experience, it often finds expression in philosophical inquiry. As philosopher Raymond Tallis observes, philosophy "invites us to be surprised and puzzled by the things that lie closest to hand, to find mystery in The Land of Near Beyond, a realm we normally rush past on the way to more distant goals" (Tallis, 2012, 14). The most ordinary of experiences give rise to philosophical perplexity, as we discover things about which to wonder and question in our everyday lives.

Although wonder has a central place in philosophical speculation, it is neither necessary nor sufficient for philosophy. On the one hand, wonder is not the only path to philosophy. An interest in reasoned analysis of unsettled concepts and questions can take place without any feelings of wonder, although for children (and many adults) the experience of wonder is often the catalyst for philosophical reflection. On the other hand, although it frequently motivates musing about philosophical questions, wonder does not, by itself, constitute philosophical practice, which involves the critical examination of arguments and ideas.[2]

For most children, however, philosophy begins in wonder. Opdal points out that children's capacities for wonder naturally transform into philosophical reflection. Children start to think about philosophical questions, Opdal observes, "because they find the grappling with basic facts fascinating in itself and because it gives order and unity to their world" (Opdal, 2001, 334). During early childhood, most children are wide open to the philosophical mysteries that pervade human life, often thinking about such issues as whether God exists, why the world has the colors it does, the nature of time, whether dreams are real, why we die, and the meaning of life. Wonder, then, usually constitutes children's gateway to philosophical questioning.

QUESTIONING

When wonder is articulated, it is often through questions. Almost as soon as they can formulate them, children start asking what we call "big questions," demonstrating a capacity to explore the most basic elements of life and society. Young children's "why" questions are not simply requests for explanations about how ordinary things work; they also are often manifestations of genuine wonder about the nature of human existence and perplexity about the nature of such concepts as friendship, love, identity, knowledge, beauty, and reality. For example, when a child asks, "What is time?" this is a different question than "How does a clock work?" Children apprehend that life is full of puzzling features, and they frequently ask questions about aspects of the world that adults often take for granted ("Why do we have numbers?").

Responding to children's expressions of wonder, then, involves taking their questions seriously. Unfortunately, this doesn't happen often enough. Children are typically underestimated, and in no area is this more likely to be true than in their capacities for genuine and sustained reflection about complex topics. A few philosophers are beginning to look at the epistemic injustices done to children when we fail to listen to and hear children's voices (see, e.g., Murris, 2013).[3]

When we fail to listen to children's questions, provide answers that close off further questioning, or react to a child's serious observation with something like, "Oh, what a cute comment," we miss an opportunity to engage with children's wondering about the world. Many adults seem to forget how much serious thinking they did as children, and we frequently miss or patronize children's attempts to communicate such thinking. If we look back, however, we begin to remember that it was in childhood that we began considering some of the deeper questions of our lives.

Wondering, unselfconscious, eager to learn—children's questions are an emblematic expression of the human desire for understanding. When such questioning takes a philosophical turn, this is an especially fruitful moment for encouraging a critical and inquiring approach to the world. Philosophy is a particularly powerful discipline for

sustaining the questioning mind of childhood, because the questions philosophy asks
are perennially unsettled. We can think about them our entire lives, and this ongoing
engagement with essential questions serves to hone our abilities to pay attention to the
deeper issues that lie beneath the surface of ordinary events.

Precollege philosophy pioneer Matthew Lipman writes, "The question puts doubt in
our minds and doubt is the beginning of inquiry" (Lipman, 2009, 32). Questions are
central to inquiry generally, and to philosophical inquiry in particular, because philosophical problems and possibilities for dialogue about them emerge from questions.
Rabbi Abraham Joshua Heschel suggests that philosophy can be defined as "the art of
asking the right questions" (Heschel, 1955, 4). As Bertrand Russell states,

> Philosophy is to be studied, not for the sake of any definite answers to its questions
> since no definite answers can, as a rule, be known to be true, but rather for the sake of
> the questions themselves; because these questions enlarge our conception of what is
> possible, enrich our intellectual imagination and diminish the dogmatic assurance which
> closes the mind against speculation; but above all because, through the greatness of the
> universe which philosophy contemplates, the mind also is rendered great, and becomes
> capable of that union with the universe which constitutes its highest good. (Russell,
> 1997, 156)

For philosophers, questions — and the relationships between various questions — are
the bedrock of the discipline. In order to articulate a philosophical problem, analyze
an argument, or understand an alternative view, we have to be able to formulate clear
and relevant questions.

Likewise, the ability to construct good questions is indispensable for navigating
one's way through contemporary life. Developing confidence and skill in questioning
allows children to evaluate critically the constant flood of information that bombards
them, gather what they need to make good decisions, and convey what gaps remain in
their understanding of particular topics or situations. The more accomplished a child
becomes at framing good questions, the more able he or she will be to think clearly
and competently for himself or herself.[4]

Before school begins, almost all very young children are alive with questions; they
seem to instinctively apprehend that this is the way to investigate and understand the
world. Often, adults try to provide answers to children's questions, and sometimes
they dismiss them. Most children under the age of seven or so are undeterred by adult
dismissals, and persist in questioning. At some point, however, elementary-school students absorb the message that questions are not particularly welcome in school. They
learn that having a question means that there is something they should have already
grasped but have not. Asking questions publicly broadcasts what they don't know, and
this has the potential to be somewhat shameful, or at least embarrassing. And so they
go silent. Walk into a sixth-grade classroom, and it's obvious that students pose questions with a tentativeness generally absent in kindergarten. Current research supports
this assessment, noting steep declines in questioning as children reach school age and
progress through school (Berger, 2014, 44).

The art of questioning has not historically been considered an important feature
of precollege education. On the whole, precollege classrooms traditionally have

discouraged questioning. As educator John Holt points out, schools tend to be "answer-centered" rather than "problem-centered":

> The problem-centered person sees a problem as a statement about a situation, from which something has been left out. In other words, there is in this situation a relationship or consequence that has not been stated and that must be found. . . . The answer to any problem, school problem, is in the problem, only momentarily hidden from view.
>
> But most children in school are answer-centered rather than problem-centered. They see a problem as a kind of announcement that, far off in mysterious Answerland, there is an answer, which they are supposed to go out and find. Some children begin right away to try to pry this answer out of the mind of the teacher. (Holt, 1982, 152–53)

When a teacher asks a question in a traditional classroom, typically the teacher is not attempting to initiate a dialogue about the question or to demonstrate the value of questioning, but rather is asking a question to which the teacher expects a particular answer (Wilen, 1991). Very little time is given to posing open-ended questions that require reflection, and teachers are actually discouraged from asking them. Linda Darling-Hammond writes,

> In addition to highly prescriptive curriculum and testing policies . . . the prescriptive teacher evaluation policies that exist in many states actually impede teachers from teaching responsively and effectively. One such policy, adopted in several states, requires that teachers be rated as "ineffective" for engaging in practices that take into account the needs and interests of their students. Despite research which suggests the importance of linking classroom work to students' personal experiences, the evaluation instrument codes as "ineffective" any teacher questions that "call for personal opinion or that are answered from personal experience." The coding manual notes that "these questions may sometimes serve useful or even necessary purposes; however, they should be tallied here in the ineffective column since they do not move the classwork along academically." (Darling-Hammond, 1993, 758)

Indeed, the current climate, with an ever-intensifying focus on standardized tests and other structural pressures on teachers, makes it more and more difficult for teachers to make the time to explore open-ended questions. Instead, teachers often ask questions that anticipate immediate student response, with the teacher looking for a specific answer.

In most traditional precollege classrooms, student questions are on the periphery at best. The far majority of the questions posed are asked by teachers.[5] Students spend significant portions of their schooling trying to ascertain the right answers to questions asked by teachers (whether aloud in class or in tests). The vast majority of questions asked by teachers are low-level cognitive questions requiring students to focus on the memorization and recall of factual information, rather than questions generating deeper student understanding (Wilen, 1991).

Studies have shown that teachers ask up to two questions every minute, and that less than 20 percent of these questions require higher-level thinking, despite research showing the educational value of questions that stimulate higher-level thinking (Mercer and Littleton, 2007). Most classroom questions are answered in less than a second, and in fact, teachers typically wait less than one second after asking a question before calling on a student to answer, waiting even less time before speaking after a student has answered (Appalachia Educational Laboratory, 1994).

In general, student questions are much less welcome (and much less prevalent) than teacher questions in most classrooms. Sometimes teachers view student questions as unnecessarily taking up class time with matters not on the lesson plan, especially amid the heightened emphasis on standardized test preparation, or as having the potential to undermine their authority, particularly in content-driven, teacher-centered traditional classrooms.

Too often, students' experiences in schools consist of memorizing just what is needed to demonstrate the skills needed for a particular grade, and never really learning very much in any deep way. But, as education professor Guy Claxton notes, "Good learning starts with questions, not answers" (Claxton, 1990, 27). What do we remember from our own schooling? It is usually those moments when we were personally engaged, when the topic at hand mattered to us. When questions begin with the learner, there is an opportunity for real learning to take place.

Lipman observes that it is when our knowledge is revealed to be "ambiguous, equivocal, and mysterious," that students are most inspired to think about the world (Lipman, 2003, 14). Questions are the keys to articulating that ambiguity and mystery. A teacher can encourage questioning by first appearing "as a questioner" (Lipman, 1980, 103).

Acting as a questioner and facilitator *with* one's students requires a marked departure from the epistemological conditions of teacher-centered pedagogy in which *just* the teacher *is* the source of truth and knowledge. By acknowledging her own fallibility as a knower and asking students to assist her and each other in the dual process of learning and knowing, the teacher provides a space for philosophical inquiry to take root. Importantly, this form of modeling also introduces students to a dynamic (as opposed to static) view of knowledge. Knowledge is no longer exclusive possession of the teacher, but is created and negotiated by the class as they come to grapple with significant questions and concepts.

In our experience, an important feature of philosophical inquiry with young students is asking them what questions they are wondering about and having these questions form the foundation for whatever philosophical exploration takes place. Philosophy classes with young students typically begin with some introduction to a philosophical question or questions, which could be a story, an activity, a puzzle, or just the posing of a question.

The students are then asked to articulate the questions the prompt led them to wonder about. The bulk of the session is spent discussing the questions of interest to the students, so that it is their questions that determine what topics will be explored and the entire content of the inquiry. This can be a new, and empowering, experience for many children. When the classroom discussion begins with the children's questions, and the lesson that follows is based on what interests and puzzles the students, the philosophy session belongs to them.

Young children quickly figure out which kinds of questions lead to more interesting discussions. It's always inspiring to watch a group of, for example, eight-year-old students considering carefully which question will inspire the best discussion, paying little attention to whether the question was their own or came from one of their friends.

One of the benefits of focusing on the children's own questions is that they learn to evaluate questions: they develop skills at identifying the features of good questions and knowing which kinds of questions are likely to be most effective depending on the goal (receipt of necessary information, a good discussion, awareness that they don't understand something, etc.).

One important way of characterizing questions is to distinguish between *lower-order* or *closed-ended* questions, which require students to remember and recite, and *higher-order* or *open-ended questions*, which invite them to think openly and creatively. As a general rule, lower-order or factual-recall questions tend to be closed, with a single right answer, and are likely to begin with what, who, when, or where. Higher-order questions are more likely to start with how, why, or which, and tend to be open—inviting a range of possible responses.[6]

Research suggests that teachers ask far too many closed-ended questions and not nearly enough open-ended questions (Appalachia Educational Laboratory, 1994; Mercer and Littleton, 2007; Wilen, 1991). This keeps the lesson plan moving forward, and maintains the illusion of control over the learning process. But a classroom in which closed-ended questions are dominant often fails to address student needs for meaningful content and critical thinking. One rich resource for helping students learn how to ask their own questions, and to understand the difference between closed-ended and open-ended questions, is the Right Question Institute, based in Cambridge, Massachusetts. The organization has developed an effective approach to cultivating questioning along with materials to help teachers to implement the approach (see Rothstein and Santana, 2011).

Encouraging students to explore the questions that interest them has the potential to change classrooms from places that, as John Holt puts it, "run on right answers," into spaces where uncertainty and inquiry are welcome (Holt, 1982, 40). Arthur Applebee argues that high-school curricula should be structured based on "conversations that matter" (Applebee, 20; see also Simon, 2001, 220–31). We think this is true for elementary and middle schools as well. When schools welcome uncertainty and questioning, genuine learning on the part of students is supported.

We believe that the deepest and most authentic kind of learning occurs when students participate in thinking about a subject (and are not just passive recipients of what is being taught), and a new clarity emerges for them personally. In particular, inquiring about philosophical questions engages students in thinking for themselves about questions for which there are no final and settled answers that the students are expected to "get right."

When student questions and perspectives take center stage, the classroom becomes a place filled with meaning and relevance, where the subject matter being explored is connected to students' life experiences and the topics considered are seen as valuable and relevant to students. Katherine Simon remarks,

> Human beings are occupied with questions of meaning. We want to know if life has a purpose; we want to connect the meaning of our individual lives to those of other people and maybe even to the universe as a whole. We want to make sense of the pain we endure and to understand the sources of wonder and joy. (Simon 2003, 2–3)

Philosophical questions abound in all of the subjects traditionally taught in precollege classrooms, and facilitating inquiry about such questions can result in a shift, especially after some weeks of such discussions, to deeper engagement in the curriculum generally. One by-product of this shift is that students begin focusing their attention on each other, rather than always on the adult leading the class. They become genuinely interested in what each other has to say. In philosophy classrooms, students routinely wait quietly while classmates struggle to express complex ideas. The students have become the producers (and not just consumers) of knowledge, and begin to see the ways in which dialogue about their questions can lead to deeper understanding.

Looking for meaningful engagement, students discover a space in which it is their concerns, worries, questions, and ideas, that matter. Robert Coles writes about children's abiding interest "in reflecting about human nature, about the reasons people behave as they do, about the mysteries of the universe as evinced in the earth, the sun, the moon, the stars" (Coles, 1990, 332). Yet so much of primary and secondary education emphasizes knowing the answers—as if we had utter clarity about most aspects of life—instead of asking the questions. Encouraging children's interest in questioning and thinking about some of life's most fundamental questions gives them the opportunity to wonder with their peers about the things that matter to them, and doing so helps learning become personally meaningful to them.

REFLECTION

We have described the importance of both wonder and questioning for children's introduction to philosophy (as well as the practice of philosophy more generally). Closely related to the creation of a classroom environment in which wonder and questioning are welcome is space for reflection. As in the case of questioning, ensuring that children have time to reflect is not generally a priority in schools (or in society generally). But reflection is essential for students to analyze and understand their own beliefs, to assess what they know and don't know, and to examine carefully the knowledge claims presented to them (by, among others, their teachers and fellow students). Encouraging children to take moments away from active engagement in the world to reflect about the meaning of what they're doing and thinking—to become accustomed to carving out quiet time to think—is especially important in our accelerated culture.

Dewey emphasizes the importance of reflective thinking, defining it as an "active, persistent, and careful consideration of any belief or supposed form of knowledge in the light of the grounds that support it and the further conclusions to which it tends" (Dewey, 1933, 9).[7] Reflective thinking involves stepping back and examining how we think and what we know, considering such questions as the following: What assumptions have I made? How did I approach this problem initially, and how successful was this strategy? Have I changed my mind in the course of the discussion or learning session? What surprised me? Such thinking helps students to think in both conceptual and abstract terms, to search for the assumptions that are being made in the views put forward, and to understand better their own views and the reasons they maintain them. Students given time to reflect are more likely to develop the habit of thinking about their experiences and learning and constructing meaning from them.

In general, reflection has become less a part of most of our daily lives than perhaps ever before, and children are absorbing the model we set and the culture they encounter. Taking time for reflection can help students develop tools for understanding the information they are constantly receiving, for examining critically its sources, and for discerning what is important and what is not. Reflection involves thinking deeply about a subject or event, and is invaluable in young people learning to trust their own judgments about what matters. Reflection is intentional—daydreaming or remembering earlier experiences alone doesn't constitute reflection—and requires directed thought about a particular topic. Distinct from other kinds of thinking activities—for instance, problem-solving, imagining, questioning, planning, deciding, organizing information—reflection involves consideration of the nature of an experience and its potential meaning.[8]

Making time for students to gather their thoughts and questions sends an important message: student thoughts matter. Creating space for reflection in a classroom can make a significant difference in the quality of student participation in the classroom. For many students who tend to be quieter and less comfortable expressing their ideas and questions by speaking in a large group, a commitment to quiet reflection time affirms a mode of learning that is not dependent on speech. Students given more time to think in a safe, quiet space recount that they then feel more a part of the classroom community.[9] When there is a pause to allow quiet reflection, both ideas and student voices emerge that might go otherwise unexpressed. Students who are less likely to engage in discussion seem, after a period of silence, to be more at ease sharing their thoughts, which can open the door for their greater participation in discussions generally.[10]

Taking time for reflection can be as simple as asking the class to take a minute to think about the reading or discussion that has just occurred. For example, after reading aloud a story to elementary-school students, let them know the class will take a few minutes of reflection time to think about the story and the questions it has raised for the students. The classroom becomes quiet as the students seek to elicit and organize the meaning of the story for themselves. Likewise, at the end of a lesson, students can be asked to reflect about what has just happened. What new understanding have they gained, if any, and what in particular triggered it? Do they have questions they didn't have earlier? We have observed that the simple act of taking a few minutes of quiet so that everyone has time to think can change the tenor of the classroom environment.

Moreover, the large essential questions that are being examined in philosophy sessions—Who am I? Why am I here? What is justice? Why do some people have easier lives than others?—demand time to explore. Making clear that an essential element of philosophical practice involves reflection sets the tone for the thoughtful deliberation required by the rich and unsettled territory of philosophical practice. This is not an experience that can be hurried along.[11] Philosophy requires commitment and concentration. A philosophical approach to questions and ideas does not lead to easy resolution; moreover, once you become engaged in philosophical thinking, the list of other questions and considerations that arise can go on virtually endlessly. When involved in a philosophical dialogue, it's easy to lose track of time, becoming completely immersed in the subject at hand.

Philosophical thinking flourishes when we carve out time for the kind of deep reflection it demands. One of the many pleasures of philosophical inquiry is that this activity pushes us to slow down, pay attention, and think as deeply and imaginatively as possible. We have to take time to analyze whether a view we have is justified, whether there might be other ways to think about it, and the way in which even seemingly minor differences in how something is stated can produce significant changes in meaning and implications. Making time for this kind of reflection is often not a priority in our lives, and young people don't learn how important it is to spend time thinking about their own thinking and the larger, abstract questions that are implicated in the most ordinary moments of their lives—unless we show them the way.

FROM WONDER TO INQUIRY

Young people hunger for dialogue about "big questions." Attuned to the mysteries imbedded in the most ordinary of life experiences, most children wonder about such essential concepts as reality, identity, goodness, justice, and fairness. They are drawn to what Matthews calls "the naïvely profound questions of philosophy" (Matthews, 1992, 3). The questions of even very young children reflect this orientation.

Cultivating children's philosophical capacities enhances the reasoning and creative thinking skills that they need to make sense of the world *for themselves*. Early wondering about the world can lead to reflective deliberation about meaningful and important questions. Philosophy's emphasis on questioning, and the critical and creative thinking that's essential to it, facilitates children's abilities to acquire the tools they need to become self-directed learners and independent thinkers. One of the primary tasks of becoming an adult is making sense of the world and one's place in it. When we encourage children to wonder and question, we help them develop proficiency in reasoning and thinking, as well as develop an ongoing awareness of the profound mysteriousness of life.

In part II, we turn to an analysis of learner-centered and dialogical practices in the precollege classroom, as well as an exploration of the kinds of capacities needed for engagement in philosophical practice (what we call "philosophical sensitivity") and the classroom environment best suited to this practice (involving the development of a "community of philosophical inquiry").

NOTES

1. But c.f. Ball, Phillip, *Curiosity: How Science Became Interested in Everything* (2013).

2. In chapter 4 we discuss some of the basic skills necessary for philosophical practice, including philosophical sensitivity and its associated facility for recognizing philosophical dimensions of experience.

3. We explore epistemic injustice against children in greater depth in chapters 9 and 10.

4. Educator Tony Wagner recounts his several hundred conversations with business, nonprofit, philanthropic, and education leaders about the core skills necessary for success in today's workplaces, and he notes that the ability to ask good questions was mentioned most frequently. Tony Wagner, *The Global Achievement Gap* (2008), 1–17.

5. And when students are encouraged to ask questions, it is often certain children—those who do well in school, who are native English speakers, who are white, who are male, etc.—whose voices are privileged. For more discussion of the relationship between privilege and class participation see chapter 10.

6. An example of a closed-ended question: What year did the Civil War begin? And an open-ended question: Why did the Civil War begin?

7. A full exposition and analysis of Dewey's work on reflective thinking is outside the scope of this chapter. For a thoughtful discussion of this work by a teacher-educator, see Carol Rodgers, "Defining Reflection: Another Look at John Dewey and Reflective Thinking," *Teachers College Record* 104.4 (2002): 842–66.

8. For additional discussion of the nature and value of reflection in educational contexts, see Gardner (1998) and Boud, Keogh, and Walker Torp and Sage (1985).

9. See, for example, Watkins, 2004.

10. We examine in chapter 10 various strategies for engaging more reticent students in discussion.

11. Our colleague at University of Hawaii, Thomas Jackson, often remarks that when doing philosophy it is important to remember not to be in a rush. At its core, this is about providing students with the time necessary to think deeply about their own views and take in and evaluate the perspectives of others.

Part II

MAKING SPACE FOR QUESTIONING AND DIALOGUE

Chapter 3

Learner-Centered Education and the Dialogical Model

In part I, we discussed some of the central motivations for introducing philosophy to young people. We examined the place of precollege philosophy in expanding access to philosophy beyond the university, as well as the importance of providing a space for questioning, dialogue, and reflection in schools. Following these initial discussions—broadly, addressing *why* precollege philosophy is a valuable component of K-12 education of childrens and adolescents—we now turn to an exploration of pedagogical approaches that are central to practicing philosophy with young students.

In the United States, precollege philosophy is defined, in part, by its commitment to *learner-centered* (as opposed to *teacher-centered*) pedagogy.[1] However, it is not always clear what, exactly, is meant by learner-centered teaching and how it is practiced in the classroom context. Our focus in this chapter is to consider some of the important elements of learner-centered teaching, distinguish it from teacher-centered pedagogy, and discuss significant areas of connection between philosophical dialogue and learner-centered pedagogy in precollege classrooms.

ORIGINS OF LEARNER- AND TEACHER-CENTERED PEDAGOGY

An early (and now canonical) form of the distinction between learner- and teacher-centered pedagogy emerges in Dewey's distinction between *traditional* and *progressive* education. As presented by Dewey in texts such as *Experience and Education* (1938) and *Democracy and Education* (2011), the distinction between traditional and progressive education is fundamental to educational theory and marks an opposition between two contrasting conceptions—education as "development from within" or "formation from without" (Dewey, 1938, 17). The latter approach—characterized by Dewey as traditional education—originates *outside* the students, with the teacher introducing them to "bodies of information and . . . skills that have been worked out in the past" (Dewey, 1938, 17).

In traditional pedagogy, the teacher is *the* educational authority and mediator between cultural knowledge and student. Aided by a variety of pedagogical tools (lectures, textbooks, top-down class discussions, etc.), the traditional teacher acts as the primary arbiter of learning and decides upon relevant areas of knowledge for her students to master as well as the means by which they will be mastered.[2] In short, traditional education positions the teacher as the primary (if not exclusive) source of knowledge and educational direction in the classroom. Whereas the teacher is active and the focus of class attention, the students—if performing their roles well—are passive, maintaining an attitude of "docility, receptivity, and obedience" (Dewey, 1938, 18). The students are passive agents in the classroom who are limited to listening and learning from the teacher and, when prompted, documenting their learning through preselected assignments.

In this framework, the teacher selects preestablished subjects, skills, and areas of knowledge—from particular historical narratives and works of literature to mathematics and scientific knowledge—that must be introduced to students so that they can master them and, eventually, take their places as full (adult) members of society.

Paradoxically, then, while engaging with cultural artifacts and preestablished knowledge, the primary goal of traditional education is future-directed. Traditional education is not concerned with the present interests and capacities of students, but rather, with preparing students for "future responsibilities and . . . success in life" (Dewey, 1938, 18). To this end, all curricula focus on the development of capacities and acquisition of knowledge that, once acquired, will allow students to take their places in society and carry on the traditions of their predecessors.

Dewey introduces progressive education—and, with it, an early formulation of learner-centered pedagogy—by contrasting its aims and methods with those of traditional education:

> To imposition from above is opposed expression and cultivation of individuality; to external discipline is opposed free activity; to learning from texts and teachers, learning through experience; to acquisition of isolated skills and techniques by drill, is opposed acquisition of them as means of attaining ends which make direct vital appeal; to preparation for a more or less remote future is opposed making the most of the opportunities of present life; to static aims and materials is opposed acquaintance with a changing world. (Dewey, 1938, 19–20)

There are a number of significant contrasts with traditional education here, but in making our way toward a discussion of learner-centered pedagogy for precollege philosophy classrooms we will focus on two central points. First, whereas traditional education imposes lessons on the student "from above" or from "outside," in progressive education, interests, curiosities, and experiences "within" the student act as starting points for the learning process.

Education is no longer solely defined by student mastery of preselected bodies of information; learning through personal experience and social interaction in the classroom now become central elements of education. Established knowledge and traditions do maintain an important place in progressive education, but the mode of student and teacher engagement with these cultural artifacts changes. As Dewey notes, educators must recognize that students (like other persons) are immersed in present concerns and learn from the past most successfully when a "vital connection" is maintained between the past and their current experiences (Dewey, 2011, 44). By including the "vital energy" and "powers and purposes" of the students in the educational process, the progressive educator can make central areas of knowledge and skill (whether literature, history, arithmetic, or any other subject area) more accessible to students (Dewey, 1938, 45).

Second, the progressive change in subject matter and form of instruction requires another, related, departure from traditional education. In traditional pedagogy the teacher is the focal point of the class; students can learn from the teacher, but the process of learning—the methods and material used—are all determined in advance by the teacher. In "On Learner-Centered Teaching," Jonathan Zophy provides a clear image of the teacher-centered classroom:

> Desks and chairs are in neat rows facing the teacher, who is at the front of the room often partly hidden from view behind a lectern. Students sit "attentively" taking notes ready to answer questions posed by the teacher at the end of the lecture or during discussion sections. It is nearly a universal truth that students rarely take notes on what is said by other students. That is so in part because the very set up of the classroom presupposes that the only things worth knowing are the things the instructor and maybe the textbook have said are worth knowing. The design of the traditional classroom makes the teacher the focus of attention. If there are discussions, they will in most cases be led by the instructor and they will seldom amount to more than questions raised by the teacher and answers given by the students. (Zophy, 1982, 185–86)[3]

Conversely, a learner-centered approach to pedagogy destabilizes the traditional teacher-student dyad by making students "partners in the teaching-learning process" (Zophy, 1982, 190). The role of teachers shifts such that they are no longer the sole determinants of the learning process, but instead, facilitators and guides working with students to develop their interests and help them to make connections with important areas of knowledge. This shift of focus provides space for students to become "active participants in learning" and "co-constructors of knowledge" (Meece, 2003, 111).

In her canonical work on the subject, Maryellen Weimer describes learner-centered teaching as follows:

> We make the distinction between learner-centered and teacher-centered instruction as a way of indicating that the spotlight has moved from teacher to student. When instruction is learner-centered, the action focuses on what students (not teachers) are doing. . . . This learner-centered orientation accepts, cultivates, and builds on the ultimate responsibility students have for learning. Teachers cannot do it for students. They may set the stage, so to speak, and help out during rehearsals, but then it is up to students to perform, and when they do learn, it is the student, not the teacher, who should receive accolades. (Weimer 2002, xvi)

With the move to learner-centered pedagogy, traditional classroom roles and responsibilities undergo a significant change, as do the methods and forms of instruction. The learner-centered teacher collaborates with students, utilizing their interests, concerns, and motivations as key starting and structuring points in the learning process. In turn, the students now take on increased responsibility; they are active agents in the educational encounter and must contribute to (rather than merely accept) this process in order for it to be successful.

DIALOGICAL EDUCATION

A primary component of learner-centered pedagogy involves dialogical methods of teaching. In *Pedagogy of the Oppressed* (1993), Paulo Freire introduces a central conception of dialogical teaching, marking a distinction between the "banking concept of education" and "problem-posing" (or "dialogical") education.[4] The banking concept of education resembles teacher-centered pedagogy—the teacher is active and the student is passive—and carries a related conception of knowledge as a "static" possession of the teacher that is passed on to the student through "narration" (Freire, 1993, 71–72). Insofar as it relies on this dual conception of pedagogy and knowledge, education suffers from "narration sickness":

> Narration (with the teacher as narrator) leads the students to memorize mechanically the narrated content. Worse yet, it turns them into "containers," into "receptacles" to be filled by the teacher. The more completely she fills the receptacles, the better the teacher she is. The more meekly the receptacles permit themselves to be filled, the better students they are. Education thus becomes an act of depositing, in which the students are the depositories and the teacher is the depositor. Instead of communicating, the teacher issues communiqués and makes deposits which the students patiently receive, memorize, and repeat. (Freire, 1993, 72)

This "sickness" (as Freire characterizes it) can be cured, in part, by rethinking the educational roles of teachers and students, as well as the conception of knowledge in "banking" pedagogy. The "teacher-student contradiction" must be resolved such that the teacher no longer acts as the exclusive distributor of knowledge and the student as an "empty mind" for her "deposits" (Freire 1993, 79, 75). Instead, the roles of the teacher and student are redrawn through the practice of dialogue.[5] Central to this change in roles is a commitment to learning through dialogical interaction in the classroom (or educational context more generally), as well as a shift in the conception of knowledge.

Learning through dialogical interaction requires that knowledge no longer be seen as a static, preestablished product that can simply be given to students by the teacher. Rather, learning and gaining knowledge is an ongoing process that occurs *between* class members (teacher and students) in dialogue, uniting "the teacher and the students in the joint act of knowing and re-knowing the object of study" (Freire, 1987, 14). The result, Freire contends, is a radical departure from traditional (banking) roles in the classroom. In dialogical education,

> from the outset, her [the educator's] efforts must coincide with those of the students to engage in critical thinking and the quest for mutual humanization. His [the educator's] efforts must be imbued with a profound trust in people and their creative power.

To achieve this, they must be partners of the students in their relations with them. (Freire, 1993, 75)

Freire's defense of dialogical education gains support from both canonical and contemporary educational research on dialogue and social learning.[6] Dialogical teaching provides the opportunity for students to become "active meaning makers" and "participants in the production of their own knowledge," as opposed to passive recipients of learning (Reznitskaya, 2012, 448; Skidmore, 2006, 506).

Moreover, research has shown that when students are engaged as autonomous and active learners, they learn material more effectively and perform better on educational outcomes than their passive peers (McCombs and Whisler, 1997; Benware and Deci, 1984). Thus, incorporating dialogue and, likewise, rethinking the traditional roles of teacher and student in order for dialogical education to take place can contribute to fostering the intellectual growth, increased comprehension, and academic success of students.

DIALOGUE IN THE PRECOLLEGE PHILOSOPHY CLASSROOM

In many ways, the aims of learner-centered and dialogical pedagogy are united in precollege philosophy. Dialogue is a key component of precollege philosophy sessions, and treatment of students as "coinvestigators" and "students-teachers" is fundamental to our practice. In planning a lesson or discussion, the precollege philosophy teacher incorporates student questions, concerns, and interests, and relies on these elements as starting and structuring points for class discussion. Thus, the focal point of the class shifts from the teacher alone to both teacher and peers in open discussion. In opposition to teacher-centered (or "banking") pedagogy, precollege philosophy calls for students to contribute to dialogue and the development of knowledge, thereby taking responsibility for their own learning and gaining confidence as active epistemic agents in the classroom.

Dialogical teaching and the pedagogical relationships that sustain it remain relatively rare in schools. Given the still-dominant practice of teacher-centered pedagogy in contemporary education, student engagement is often consigned to *conversation* (Gardner, 1996). In classroom conversations, students are asked to speak and are prompted to state opinions or feelings on matters raised by the teacher. While this form of instruction does move beyond strict forms of teacher-centered pedagogy, it is often limited to one-off exchanges of information, thoughts, or feelings, primarily between individual students and the teacher. That is, conversation lacks a sustained collective inquiry and mutual exploration of questions and concepts among the students, which are fundamental to dialogue.

In dialogue, the sharing of thoughts or feelings (the end of classroom conversation) acts as a starting point, a beginning to an ongoing discernment and exploration of concepts, ideas, and questions through inquiry. Students and teacher sustain this process as they seek out truth and meaning relating to the subject under consideration. As Haynes notes,

[Dialogue] is so much more than just sharing ideas and airing opinions. There is a dynamic orientation and draw implicit in dialogue. It is concerned with collaboratively solving problems, resolving dilemmas, developing new ways of thinking and understanding: rigorous searches for "truth." (Haynes, 2008, 143)

The aims of dialogue in precollege philosophy are inextricably tied to a style of pedagogy in which students and teacher engage in open discussion on a chosen prompt (text, question, idea, etc.), raise claims, arguments, and counterarguments, and seek to construct knowledge as a group. Dialogue flourishes when students and teacher engage in a "cooperative inquiry" such that they can challenge each other, question, appeal to reason, and revise positions as needed (Fisher, 2007, 618). Although useful for some educational purposes, other pedagogical strategies—conversation, monologue, and recitation, for example—lack these aims as well as the reciprocal sharing of ideas and questions that is essential to dialogical communication.

In addition to discussion of the nature of dialogue and dialogical teaching in precollege philosophy, it is important to describe classroom conditions that foster these practices.[7] First, as discussed at length in chapter 2, whether working with kindergarten, elementary-, middle-, or high-school students, there is a need for teachers to demonstrate the fundamental value of questioning and critical reflection. This need is all the more pressing given the answer-centric state of most precollege classrooms. Second, in order to establish a space for dialogue it is essential to build relationships of care and mutual respect in the classroom.

As in the case of questioning, teachers play an important role here, modeling caring and respectful behavior toward students. Many educators are instructive in this regard—from Robert Coles' respect for students involved in school desegregation efforts in the American South to Vivian Paley's creation of caring and collaborative classrooms with kindergarten students.[8] Along with many others, these educators provide examples of caring and respectful interactions with students and highlight the centrality of these interactions for creating successful dialogical relationships with children.

This is not to say that children, as a group, enter classrooms devoid of care and respect for others and must be taught these dispositions by the teacher. On the contrary, those of us practicing philosophy with children have learned a great deal from them about caring for a friend or respecting the accomplishments (no matter how great or small) of a classmate. Rather, by demonstrating care and respect in word and deed—through the supportive comment, the encouraging glance, and listening and authentically responding to young philosophers—teachers establish an environment in which students can feel more comfortable sharing their beliefs and ideas.[9]

The importance of creating caring and respectful classroom conditions has gained increasing support from educational research. In their discussion of learner-centered education from the child's perspective, Daniels and Perry (2003) cite a multitude of studies that confirm what many teachers already understand quite well:

Feeling secure that their personal needs for relatedness and competence will be understood by teachers frees children for the pursuit of learning. On the other hand, if children do not trust that their teachers know them well enough to provide appropriate care and opportunities for demonstrating competence (i.e., learning new things), they may begin to disengage from learning in school.[10] (Daniels and Perry, 2003, 104)

Offering these forms of support for students is particularly (though by no means exclusively) important in precollege philosophy classrooms, especially during initial class sessions. Open dialogue can require a certain vulnerability in class members (students and teacher). When we share ideas, questions, and arguments with others, we are, at the same time, making a request; we are asking to be heard, to be taken seriously as a knower and collaborator.[11]

To be overly critical or flippant in the face of these offerings (questions, ideas, arguments, etc.) can be taken as rejection and have a detrimental impact on a student's self-confidence, sense of inclusion, and willingness to engage in dialogue. But by explicitly discussing the place of care and respect in the classroom during early philosophy sessions, the teacher, along with students, can help to create a classroom in which vulnerability and openness are sources of opportunity and shared learning. In turn, the supportive actions of class members within dialogue reinforce these values. As we make note of insightful questions, offer assistance as a student attempts to clarify a position, and highlight areas of growth during the course of discussion, we demonstrate the centrality of care and respect to successful philosophical dialogue. In doing so, we acknowledge children as unique persons with their own interests and concerns, capable of contributing to dialogue and of teaching the teacher, thus allowing mutual respect and new forms of teacher-student learning to become possible.

In addition to collaborating with students to develop an open, caring, and respectful classroom, it is helpful to introduce discussion practices that support and foster dialogue. As with open questioning, many students will lack experience with classroom dialogue and, so, will benefit from guidance from the philosophy teacher and experienced classmates. During initial class meetings the group can select guidelines or rules that will help structure productive philosophy discussions.[12]

To be clear, this is not a matter of the teacher authoring and declaring rules to children; rather, the process of drafting guidelines should be shared democratically among all class members. These guidelines can develop from group consideration of forms of interaction that will best support discussion and communication (e.g., listening, speaking, and being heard by others). By facilitating an opening discussion on "good discussions," the teacher can open a space for class members to consider and nominate conditions of a successful dialogue. Students can then discuss what they take to be the most important rules to support dialogue, whether it is "listening when a classmate speaks," "being respectful of all class members," or "asking a question when you don't understand a comment" (or something else entirely). At the conclusion of this discussion (or multiple discussions), the class will have an established set of rules to encourage and support productive dialogue.

Alongside discussion guidelines, the creation of classroom dialogue will benefit from a well-selected prompt.[13] The prompt serves as an accessible point of entry into philosophical concepts and questions and is useful for motivating subsequent discussion. Simply put, we want to select discussion prompts that are intriguing for students and that invite them to take part in discussion with class members. The choice of prompt will shift based on a range of factors, such as the ages, experiences, and interests of class members. For example, when working with young children, numerous works of children's literature—from *The Giving Tree* and *Frederick* to *I Like to Be Little*, and *The Rainbow Fish*—can work as excellent resources to begin philosophical discussion. In these and many other works of children's literature, we find rich philosophical themes (from friendship and community to justice and identity) presented in a format that is inviting for young philosophers (imaginative design, stories, and interesting characters).[14]

Alternatively, one might begin a discussion session through the mediums of art, music, or movement. If prompted with a direct question, it is possible that young philosophers will be tentative with verbal articulations of philosophical concepts and ideas, especially during early sessions. But by taking a different approach and asking students, for example, to write or draw their ideal school or community, their best friends, or their favorite dream, they can tell us and each other a great deal about their philosophical commitments and beliefs.

These artistic statements can then serve as fruitful foundations for philosophical dialogue as students describe their art or writing, and why they chose to create it (as opposed to other potential pieces). Discussions with older students can also begin with a wide variety of prompts, from short passages from philosophical texts and films, to an inviting question posed by a student. As sessions continue and group relationships and interests take shape, the teacher can keep track of particular areas of student concern and base future discussion prompts on questions, comments, and ideas that have been contributed by students. In this way, classroom dialogue takes on a learner-centered focus from the start and is enriched by the contributions of both students and teacher.

The use of discussion guidelines and prompts brings with it consideration of the role of the teacher in philosophical dialogue.[15] We have already discussed the centrality of learner-centered pedagogy for precollege philosophy; in our work with children we dismiss top-down practices of indoctrination and domination. Fortunately, the questions of philosophy are particularly well-suited to help teachers avoid these practices.

Although philosophical questions—for example, conceptual questions on the nature and conditions of knowledge, the good life, and existence—have *better* or *worse* answers (i.e., answers that have or lack reasoned support), they generally do not have *absolute* answers. The precollege philosophy teacher should engage with students in formulating and exploring questions as, in truth, this (as opposed to delivering final answers) is central to the practice of philosophy as a discipline.

While engaging with students in this way, the teacher will play a central role in listening to student feedback and discerning the questions and ideas that are of greatest interest to the class. As a facilitator, the teacher will also help students develop accessible and manageable starting points for discussion and, further, will introduce facilitation techniques to assist the process of the dialogue as it progresses. The facilitator can ask clarification questions, restate student comments for clarification, and provide general "scaffolding" to assist the development and progression of dialogue.[16] Describing the teacher-as-facilitator, Haynes writes,

> Teachers play a vital role in empowering children by creating meta-discourse. This can be
> achieved through the injection of comments and questions that draw children's attention

to features of their thinking and to the bigger picture of ongoing inquiry. . . . Practice at listening to and joining the meta-discourse that the teacher creates helps children to make connections between apparently disparate parts of the enquiry. It also encourages them to practice reviewing and helps the skill of summarizing. It signals that winning or losing an argument is not highly valued for itself by emphasizing that there is value to be gained by exploring the process of argument, engaging in thinking and introducing new ideas. (Haynes, 2008, 77)

Thus, to adopt learner-centered dialogical practices in the classroom does not mean that the teacher ceases to be an active participant in the learning process. As Dewey argues in his discussion of progressive education, an essential "business of the educator" always remains; namely, by drawing on their backgrounds and training, educators can identify productive educational experiences that support student growth (Dewey, 1938, 38). Likewise, philosophy facilitators—in selecting prompts to spark philosophical discussion and the skilled use of facilitation techniques—can rely on their experience and skill to help structure high-quality educational experiences for young philosophers. Of course, every class and every student is unique, with distinct interests, concerns, and abilities. In order to be successful, discussion facilitation will always require robust collaboration with and contributions from students. Within this collaboration both "students-teachers" and "teacher-student" will play central roles in guiding productive discussions and educational experiences more generally.

Through learner-centered practices such as dialogue and active listening, we can engage students as meaning makers, co-constructors of knowledge, and active participants in the learning process. Further, by encouraging open questioning and demonstrating care and respect in the classroom, we begin to move beyond the teacher-student binary, rethinking traditional classroom roles and creating a space for students to teach the teacher and each other. In the next chapter, we turn to the skills and capacities needed for facilitating precollege philosophy discussions, involving what we call "philosophical sensitivity."

NOTES

1. For prominent discussions of learner-centered teaching in educational theory, see Weimer (2002), Peters (1966), and McCombs and Whisler (1997).

2. The use of these pedagogical tools—lectures, textbooks, and class discussions—does not necessarily denote a teacher-centered approach to learning. For example, the use of a textbook can be more or less learner- or teacher-centered, depending on whether it is used as another support for the epistemic authority of the teacher or, conversely, as a starting point for classroom dialogue and collaborative work with students.

3. Zophy focuses on the teacher-centered classroom in a college setting. However, the key features of this characterization—for example, the teacher as center of student attention, the traditional organization of classroom space, and the passivity of students—can also be found in teacher-centered precollege classrooms.

4. In *Pedagogy of the Oppressed*, Freire develops a conception of critical pedagogy, inspired by his experiences teaching illiterate populations in Latin America. Freire approaches education as a potential site of collaboration with colonized and subjugated populations where

learning takes place through critical dialogue on, among other things, the political structures that support economic, social, and educational oppression. For Freire, the dialogical method is not merely an educational tool, then, but also a means of political change and a practice that can empower the oppressed. Alongside the explicit political ends of dialogical education in Freire's work, dialogue can play an important educational role in any classroom setting. This is because, as Freire contends, the practice of dialogue leads to a shift in the "epistemological position" of student and teacher, allowing both to be active participants in the learning process (Shor and Freire, 1987).

5. Describing this shift in epistemological positions, Freire writes,

The teacher-of-the-students and the students-of-the-teacher cease to exist and a new term emerges: teacher-student with students-teachers. The teacher is no longer merely the-one-who-teaches, but one who is himself taught in dialogue with the students, who in turn while being taught also teach. They become jointly responsible for a process in which all grow. . . . Here, no one teaches another, nor is anyone self-taught. People teach each other, mediated by the world, by the cognizable objects which in banking education are 'owned' by the teacher. (Freire, 1993, 80)

6. Jean Piaget (1928) and Lev Vygotsky (1962) both illuminate the social-cultural dimensions of knowledge production, highlighting the centrality of collaboration and social interaction for learning in childhood. Contemporary education scholars have built on these longstanding (if still neglected) insights, emphasizing the centrality of social and dialogical learning for student motivation and comprehension (Alexander, 2006; Nystrand, 1997; Murphy et al., 2009). Current research supports a shift from traditional "monologic" forms of teaching (often referred to as "recitation") to increased "dialogic" interactions between teachers and students in precollege classrooms (Reznitskaya, 2012, 446; Mercer and Littleton, 2007; Skidmore, 2006, 504).

7. For additional accounts of dialogical teaching and the classroom conditions that support this practice, see Alexander, 2006; Fisher, 2007; and Lipman, 1980, 2003. For a more critical view of dialogue, see Burbules, 2000.

8. See Coles, 1990, 2003, and Paley, 2009.

9. For further discussion of the centrality of caring in education, see Noddings, 2013. For recent discussion of and educational research on active listening, see Clark and Moss, 2011, and Delfos, 2001.

10. Numerous social-emotional education researchers also document the importance of caring and supportive classroom environments for student learning and development. See Denham and Weissberg, 2004, and Cohen, 2006.

11. See chapter 5 for a fuller discussion of vulnerability and the important role of intellectual safety in precollege philosophy classrooms.

12. See, for example, the activity associated with the book *Stuart Little* described in chapter 6.

13. We provide a brief introduction to philosophy discussion prompts in this section. For detailed examples of prompts for young people of all ages, see part III of this book. We explore the facilitation of philosophical inquiry more fully in chapter 5 and offer further discussion about philosophy prompts in chapter 10.

14. See Wartenberg, 2009, 2013; Haynes and Murris, 2012; Lone, 2012.

15. We discuss the role of the precollege philosophy teacher more thoroughly in chapter 5.

16. For a helpful discussion of some techniques for facilitating philosophy discussions see Lipman, 1980, 2003 and Haynes, 2008.

Chapter 4

Philosophical Sensitivity

The problem about philosophy, and about life, is how to relate large impressive illuminating general conceptions to the mundane ("messing about") details of ordinary personal private existence. (Murdoch, 1992, 146)

PHILOSOPHICAL SENSITIVITY: AN INITIAL ACCOUNT[1]

At some levels, teaching philosophy involves certain certification requirements. In general, teaching philosophy in a college or university requires a PhD or enrollment in the institution's doctoral program, and in community colleges this necessitates a master's degree in philosophy. No such requirements exist at this time for secondary and primary school philosophy teachers in the United States, and whether any certification structure should be established for precollege philosophy teachers is an open question. A full treatment of what teachers at various levels need in order to teach philosophy competently is beyond the scope of this chapter. Instead, what we are interested in exploring here is a foundational facility for engaging in philosophical practice at all levels, or "philosophical sensitivity."

Although much has been written about the nature of philosophy and how to define the discipline,[2] there has been scant examination of the capacity to appreciate philosophical questions and make philosophical judgments, how this capacity can be cultivated, and why developing it is important. It is not clear, in other words, what one needs in order to engage in philosophical inquiry and do it well, whether you are seven or seventy years of age. We attempt here to describe in relatively broad terms the basic facilities necessary for philosophical practice, which we define as a general capacity to engage in questioning and reflection about the unsettled questions underlying the human condition and the world in which we live.[3]

Philosophical sensitivity involves awareness of the philosophical dimension of daily life, a feeling for the perplexities that lie behind much of what we say, do, and think. We foster it by nurturing our capacity to identify and consider fundamental questions about the human condition, and to continue our investigations no matter what answers we find. Philosophical sensitivity starts with the inclinations most children have to

reflect about the fundamental mysteries underlying experience and behavior, with
wondering about the world. It continues with the expression of that wonder through
questioning and a developing awareness of the philosophical dimension of experience.

Our conception of philosophical sensitivity understands it as a kind of perceptual
capacity, in the Aristotelian sense of a faculty that can be developed over time and
with education and training. For Aristotle, it is the development of our facility for
moral perception that eventually can lead to the intuitive recognition of the central
aspects of complex ethical problems.[4] This perceptual capacity, fostered through experience and education, cultivates in us a more nuanced ability to observe with ease the
morally important features of our experiences.[5]

The more deeply we've developed this moral awareness, the more easily we recognize the ethically salient features of our experiences. Aristotle's theory gives us an
illuminating framework for understanding how it is—experientially—that we recognize the important elements of moral problems, which provides a useful paradigm for
developing an account of how it is we become aware of the significant *philosophical*
features of the world.

Like Aristotle's conception of moral perception, philosophical sensitivity is a perceptual capacity involving awareness of the abstract, general questions that permeate
human existence. As discussed in chapter 2, this capacity often develops in response
to feelings of wonder, beginning with an interest in the unresolved questions that
haunt virtually every aspect of our lives. Thinking about such questions heightens our
awareness that the way things appear to us doesn't necessarily correlate with the way
things are, and generally leads to recognizing other, related questions.

When cultivated, such sensitivity reveals a world rife with philosophical possibility,
and we begin to pick up on the philosophical content of even the most ordinary situations or issues. This involves selecting out certain facets of experience and assigning
them particular connections to one another, and in this way, giving philosophical
shape to what is perceived. The development and exercise of philosophical sensitivity
occurs over time and requires work; it is cultivated through education, experience, and
interest. We will take up the cultivation of this capacity later in this chapter.

A WAY OF SEEING

Philosophical sensitivity reflects one's individual concerns and perspective: a philosophically sensitive person perceives the world in a way that is shaped by his or her
unique qualities. Philosophical sensitivity is not necessarily connected to one's moral
character in the way that moral perception is, but it nevertheless resembles moral perception in that it is manifested in particular ways, depending on a person's own skills
and point of view. Our distinctive vantage points lead to each of us noticing in the
philosophical universe the issues our individual perspectives generate.

Philosophical sensitivity, then, spans a broad array of perspectives; that is, it is
not necessarily the case that two philosophically sensitive people will see the same
issues in a particular situation, which may yield multiple philosophical possibilities
for individuals who have developed this sensitivity differently as a result of their distinct histories. However, they will all possess the same general capacity to recognize

philosophical assumptions and considerations behind what we say and do, and be open to inquiry about their own philosophical insights and beliefs. That is, seeing the world through a philosophically sensitive lens gives a particular shape to what we perceive, though the particulars of the shape will vary for each individual.

Although philosophical sensitivity entails reflection about general and often abstract questions, typically it is in the particular features of our lives that these questions are raised. The capacity to identify abstract questions in the most ordinary aspects of everyday experience is central to philosophical sensitivity. This involves a keen attentiveness to the specific details of situations and the way these details shape philosophical content. For example, in a discussion about current events, a philosophically sensitive person will notice the assumptions being made and the larger concepts (fairness, justice, equality, etc.) that are being contested, although different philosophically attuned individuals might pick up on different aspects of that particular philosophical landscape.

There are other sensitivities that constitute nonmoral perceptual capacities analogous to philosophical sensitivity, the discussion of which will be helpful in understanding this conception more fully. To take two examples, one can develop particular sensitivities to the natural world ("naturalist sensitivity") and to the aesthetic dimension of life ("aesthetic sensitivity"). Like philosophical sensitivity, these are ways of seeing that bring to light particular facts of the world that are not easily seen without cultivation of certain capacities.

Naturalist sensitivity involves an awareness of the multilayered distinctions among living things and the ability to see relationships, details, and changes in the natural world that many of us miss. For example, a naturalist will notice subtle differences among plants, rocks, insects, and flowers that will elude those of us not so habituated. He or she will "see" a complex web of interconnected organisms, not easily observable by people who have not cultivated this capacity. As a person develops this sensitivity, he or she is able to see more easily and clearly such intricate aspects of the natural world.

Likewise, someone who possesses aesthetic sensitivity is attuned to the aesthetic dimension of life. He or she apprehends features of music, visual art, dance, or other artistic media that those of us not so trained don't perceive. Listening to music, for example, a musician will pick out particular characteristics that the rest of us miss. Similarly, the training and experience of an art critic allows him or her to recognize a painting's attributes and the connections between its elements and the composition as a whole that will not be apparent to others.

These kinds of perceptual capacities (philosophical, naturalist, aesthetic) are constituted by an ability to apprehend features of experience that are not obvious without training. They are distinctive ways of seeing the world. As we acquire philosophical sensitivity, we become aware of the philosophical dimensions of what people say and do in ways others fail to observe, noticing the differences in philosophical orientation at the core of much speech and behavior.

For example, the discussion above of a naturalist sensitivity makes reference to "the natural world," a phrase that is intended to reference plants, animals, and various features of nature. But what does the word "natural" really mean? People tend to use this term to refer to parts of the world not created by human beings. But don't human beings count as "natural?" What about food or flowers grown by human beings: do they count as natural? And so on.

Aristotle points out that as we attain virtue, we become more virtuous—that is, virtue builds on itself (*Nicomachean Ethics*, 1104a27–1104b4). In the same way, someone developing naturalist or aesthetic sensitivity expands that sensitivity as he or she observes the natural world or listens to and plays music (or looks at and creates visual art, and so forth). Likewise, the more philosophically aware we become, the broader the scope of what we notice and can explore. Nurtured over time, this capacity strengthens our facilities for discerning the background questions that lie just beneath the surface of ordinary moments.

Just as Aristotle's moral perception involves learning to identify the important moral aspects of a particular state of affairs, the development of philosophical sensitivity results in an ability to distinguish more and more effortlessly the philosophical aspects of particular situations, so that this capacity becomes almost second nature. Like naturalists, artists and musicians, and art and music critics, we are then able to help others to notice the philosophical aspects of given situations.

THE PHILOSOPHICAL SELF

Aristotle maintains that "all human beings by nature reach out for understanding" (*Metaphysics*, 980a21). Most young children are moved to sort out and try to comprehend the strangeness of the world. As discussed in chapter 2, almost as soon as they can formulate them, children start asking questions about human existence and the nature of reality. This is the beginning of the "philosophical self": the part of us that recognizes as deeply puzzling many of the basic facets of our own existence.[6] "Why are we here?" "Are colors real?" "What is the meaning of life?" "What is essential to identity?" "How did it all begin?" "How do we know we're not dreaming?" Ask philosophers why they became philosophers, and most will point to a time in their youth when they began thinking deeply about these kinds of questions.

The philosophical self is fascinated by the puzzles at the heart of everyday life and the deeper meaning of the ordinary concepts we use, and is manifest in the propensity to ask searching questions about them. One of the strengths children bring to this enterprise is the free play of imagination. They are willing to entertain a wide range of questions and possibilities, some of which adults would rule out immediately as implausible. But part of philosophical exploration *is* openness to ideas that might run contrary to our ingrained thinking, and children generally exemplify such openness.

Perhaps it is the importance of pretending in childhood—the constant trying out of identities, whether it be superheroes, real-life adult roles such as teachers, firefighters, professional athletes, etc., or characters from books and films—that accounts, at least in part, for the ease with which children play with philosophical ideas.[7] For children, the examination of philosophical ideas is both a serious activity and a playful one, merging wonder, imagination, questioning, and reflection.

We traditionally recognize as important the development of children's physical selves, intellectual selves, moral selves, and social and emotional selves, but there is little attention paid to the cultivation of the philosophical self. Consequently, this part of most children remains undeveloped. Children absorb the message that the concrete details of life are more important than intellectual abstractions and that there is no time for philosophical thinking, that these kinds of questions are trivial (or too difficult) and will get us nowhere, or that religion can answer them all for us. This is a loss. The opportunity to engage in speculative reflection at young ages encourages children to acquire a habit of questioning their own beliefs and ideas and also fosters independent thinking.

Development of the philosophical self entails cultivating our capacity for philosophical sensitivity. While everyone has the makings of a philosophical self—in the same way we all have an artistic self—not all of us end up with the same proficiency for philosophical thinking. This varies, depending on individual levels of interest in exploring the philosophical dimension of experience, the opportunity to engage in philosophical encounters with others, and the training and education we have received. In most cases, we tend to have a greater proclivity for developing the capacities for which we seem to have some innate talent or skill, and those drawn to a philosophical approach to life will be more likely to develop a facility for engaging in philosophical inquiry.

In some ways, philosophical sensitivity is related to educator Howard Gardner's conception of existential intelligence, which he defines as exhibiting "the proclivity to pose and ponder questions about life, death, and ultimate realities" (Gardner, 1999, 60–64).[8] Gardner defines existential intelligence as

> the capacity to locate oneself with respect to the furthest reaches of the cosmos—the infinite and the infinitesimal—and the related capacity to locate oneself with respect to such existential features of the human condition as the significance of life, the meaning of death, the ultimate fate of the physical and the psychological worlds, and such profound experiences as love of another person or total immersion in a work of art. (Gardner, 1999, 60)

Philosophical sensitivity entails an awareness of what Gardner calls existential questions (related to life, death, and reality) as well as other philosophical issues such as morality, knowledge, art and beauty, justice and freedom, and so on. These questions emerge from reflection about human existence and the world in which we live. Although many of them are not likely to be resolved in any final way, they nonetheless play an essential role in reflection about the meaning of the human condition.

LITERATURE AND PHILOSOPHY: ILLUSTRATING PHILOSOPHICAL SENSITIVITY

Literature provides an accessible and familiar avenue for illustrating the expression of philosophical sensitivity. In reading literature, philosophical sensitivity is manifested in an ability to draw out the questions of philosophy that are intimated by the particulars of various texts. Much literature is replete with philosophical concerns, and children's literature in particular is generally rich with philosophical suggestiveness. Once you become aware of the philosophical questions and puzzles that underlie a great deal of children's literature, you are able to more easily recognize them when you read children's books. In a similar way, as you begin to identify the perplexities inherent in everyday experience, they begin to be evident everywhere. This can be exemplified by looking at literary texts.

In a marvelous passage about reading in Proust's *In Search of Lost Time*, Marcel, the narrator, describes sitting outside:

> When I saw an external object, my awareness that I was seeing it would remain between me and it, lining it with a thin spiritual border that prevented me from ever directly touching its substance; it would volatize in some way before I could make contact with it, just as an incandescent body brought near a wet object never touches its moisture because it is always preceded by a zone of evaporation. In a sort of screen dappled with different states of mind which my consciousness would simultaneously unfold while I read, and which ranged from the aspirations hidden deepest within me to the completely exterior vision of the horizon which I had, at the bottom of the garden, before my eyes, what was first in me, innermost, the constantly moving handle that controlled the rest, was my belief in the philosophical richness and the beauty of the book I was reading, and my desire to appropriate them for myself, whatever that book might be. A real human being, however profoundly we sympathize with him, is in large part perceived by our senses, that is to say, remains opaque to us, presents a dead weight which our sensibility cannot lift. If a calamity should strike him, it is only in a small part of the total notion we have of him that we will be able to be moved by this; even more, it is only in a part of the total notion he has of himself that he will be able to be moved himself. The novelist's happy discovery was to have the idea of replacing these parts, impenetrable to the soul, by an equal quantity of immaterial parts, that is to say, parts which our soul can assimilate. What does it matter thenceforth if the actions, and the emotions, of this new order of creatures seem to us true, since we have made them ours. (Proust, 2002, 86)

Here, the narrator Marcel is demonstrating philosophical sensitivity. Sitting in a garden and reading a novel, he looks around and, as he perceives the objects around him, he contemplates the way in which his perception of them distorts what the objects really are. He wonders about the relationship between appearance and reality. Considering the book he is reading, and the act of reading it, he analyzes the distinction between how we understand other people through novels and the way we understand the people we know in the world. He notes that we are only marginally able to understand the other human beings in our lives as, again, our perceptions of other people distort who they really are, and he follows that by thinking about how limited our abilities are to understand even ourselves. He then speculates about fiction and the way in which novels can help us to understand behavior and emotion in ways that our relationships with real people cannot.

Marcel's approach to what he sees is philosophical. Drawing from concrete experiences (sitting outside, reading a book), he generalizes to more fundamental and abstract issues about existence, perception, knowledge, understanding of other minds, and aesthetics. What is the relationship between the way the world appears to us and the way the world really is? What is the relationship between our understanding of other people and the people they are? What is the purpose of reading literature? These questions seek to examine our ordinary understanding of the world and to penetrate the assumptions that underlie that understanding. Much of literature abounds with philosophical questions like the ones Proust explores.

WHAT MAKES A QUESTION A PHILOSOPHICAL QUESTION?

If philosophical sensitivity is understood, in part, as the ability to recognize and explore philosophical questions, it is important that we consider what makes a question a philosophical one. Unsurprisingly, philosophers disagree about this topic. It's difficult to define the boundaries of philosophical questions—no finite list of philosophical questions exists. What characterizes philosophical inquiry is not the content of a particular question, but the approach with which the question is explored. For example, someone might ask whether something is just; a philosophical approach might be to respond, "What is justice?" Philosophical inquiry tends to focus on general, abstract questions that are not likely to lead to answers that are settled and incontestable. So, a question that can be settled by reference to empirical facts (What are you cooking for dinner?) is less likely to lead to a philosophical discussion.

It can be helpful to instruct philosophy students to keep asking questions of increasingly greater abstraction about the subject under examination (e.g., friendship: "Why is she your friend?" "What makes someone a friend?" "What is friendship?"); this can often lead you to an interesting philosophical discussion. For example, a student might ask a question about the fairness of the law that children under age 18 are not permitted to vote. Philosophical sensitivity leads one to notice that many philosophical threads underlie this question: "What is fairness?" "What does fairness require?" "Is it always unfair to discriminate against particular groups?" "What is a child?" "What kinds of capacities are necessary to make good choices?" And so forth. Asking these more general questions, in turn, can help to tease out the issues underlying the initial questions posed and reveal background assumptions, contributing to a deeper analysis of the problem or topic being explored.

There are, of course, paradigmatic examples of philosophical questions, as well as questions that are not likely to lead to philosophical exploration (see, e.g., Lipman, 1980, 31–40). One way to identify at least roughly when something, at least on the surface, is *not* a question of philosophy is to ask if it's possible to settle it by reference to empirical facts. If so, it's not a philosophical question, no matter how difficult it may be to answer. For example, the question, "How many grains of sand were on Rethymno Beach in Crete in 1645?" is not a philosophical question, though there may never be a settled answer. By contrast, questions like "How can we know anything?" or "What makes an action the right thing to do?" are emblematic philosophical questions.[9]

Many philosophical problems implicate several disciplines. For example, hybrid questions such as "What is the mind?" or "What does it mean to be alive?" involve both philosophy and science, with no clear way to delineate the borders for what is philosophical and what is empirical. There is often continuity between philosophical and empirical questions that makes the latter challenging to identify in many instances. Moreover, many philosophical questions cannot be explored meaningfully without reference to empirical facts (e.g., an exploration of whether the death penalty is morally permissible requires some knowledge of its practical consequences).

As we discussed in section I, philosophical problems are those that are unlikely to be answered in any final way. This does not mean, of course, that they are questions without answers. Teachers and students will sometimes initially think that philosophy involves "questions that have no answers," or "there are no right answers" in philosophy, and suppose that philosophy discussions simply involve students stating their opinions, with every possible answer to a philosophical problem being equally good. However, there is a distinction between a question being *unanswerable* and a question that is *contestable*. An unanswerable question is one that has no answers — "What does a married bachelor look like?" Philosophical questions are unsettled but not unanswerable. There are answers to philosophical problems, but they are neither final nor incontestable (once they become so, the problem ceases to be philosophical).

Moreover, the fact that philosophical questions are contestable does not mean that possible answers to these questions cannot be evaluated. Some answers *are* better than others, depending on the reasoning given to support them. The more we think and talk about an issue, the clearer it becomes which resolutions are less persuasive and which are more promising and might be tentatively acceptable or at least in the right direction.

Philosophical inquiry, then, is not at all just a matter of students stating their opinions, with every opinion being equally worthy. Contributions to a philosophical discussion are evaluated based on the quality of their reasoning, and counterarguments and objections presented. Although we are unlikely to reach a complete and definitive resolution, as we discuss and analyze a philosophical problem, we make progress by ruling out some answers as insufficiently supportable and accepting some others as provisionally correct.

Although some questions are more likely to lead to a philosophical inquiry than others, philosophical questions can be asked about almost every facet of life; they are not restricted to any particular subject matter. Fundamentally, there are no limits to the questions that can inspire philosophical exploration. In many ways, it is our responses to questions, and not the questions themselves, that determine whether a philosophical exchange will ensue.

A philosophical discussion can be inspired by the simplest of questions — those that might not, at superficial hearing, seem philosophically promising. In fact, it's important not to judge immediately the philosophical potential of the questions children ask. In our experience, children can raise issues adults initially assume are not philosophically interesting, but when this assumption is checked and we remain open to what the child is really asking, the question being asked might be quite profound. Fundamental to philosophical sensitivity is the ability to recognize and distinguish the deeper issues that underlie many questions and comments, and to see philosophical potential when it might not be obvious.

HOW DO TEACHERS AND OTHER ADULTS CULTIVATE PHILOSOPHICAL SENSITIVITY?

For Aristotle, essential for developing our moral perceptual capacities is habituation through both practice and example: experience is required to grasp the moral significance of particular situations and greater skill at doing so is generated as a result. Practice and training are also necessary to cultivate our facilities for apprehending the philosophical dimension of experience, and the more we consider the deeper questions raised by everyday life, the more skilled we become at doing so.

Practice and training can occur in multiple ways: for example, engaging in structured philosophical discussions, reading philosophy, listening to philosophical lectures, and observing others facilitate philosophy discussions. Essential to this process are models (in the form of philosophers, both historical and contemporary, and other philosophy teachers) and some basic conceptual tools.

Developing philosophical sensitivity does not mean learning a set of rules for when a philosophical question arises and how to address it. In another parallel with Aristotle's conception of moral perception, no decision procedure governs how to identify and grapple with philosophical questions (see, e.g., McDowell, 1998, 23, and Nussbaum, 1990, 54–105). There is no blueprint for when and how to spot philosophical problems and no list of all possible philosophical questions. Instead, philosophical sensitivity, like moral perception for Aristotle, involves the development of a way of seeing.

Like the habituation of moral perception, cultivating philosophical sensitivity involves training our perceptual capacities. We gradually come to understand the world differently as our education and experience in philosophical questioning and reflection enable us to notice and draw out aspects of our experiences that would otherwise elude us.

Although most of us wondered about philosophical questions early in our lives, in the United States, people are generally not introduced to philosophy in any formal way unless they take a philosophy class in college. Precollege teachers interested in teaching philosophy in their classrooms, therefore, often have had very little exposure to philosophy. Even those who have had some exposure typically have had little experience thinking seriously about philosophical questions themselves, as opposed to studying the arguments of historical or contemporary philosophers. Although many teachers have an interest in and some talent for philosophical sensitivity, most have not had the training, education, or experience necessary to have cultivated this capacity.

Perhaps the best way for teachers and other adults to begin developing philosophical sensitivity is to gain experience participating in a community of philosophical inquiry (CPI), in which philosophical topics are explored in a collaborative group.[10] Intensive exposure over a weekend, for example, to the kinds of materials, discussions, and conceptual methods that precollege philosophy can involve is a valuable experience for aspiring philosophy teachers. After such an experience, teachers can begin trying out philosophy sessions in their classrooms, and, in ideal situations, participate in ongoing local philosophy classes or groups.[11]

Another way to cultivate philosophical sensitivity is, of course, to read and think about philosophy or take philosophy classes at a nearby university or college.[12] There are also many accessible adult philosophical works, magazines and periodicals, and other online resources (see appendix).[13] Observation of others leading philosophy sessions and engaging in identifying philosophical questions and thinking about philosophical issues is an important element of the development of philosophical sensitivity. Of course, in the United States no widespread examples of such sessions at the precollege level exist for teachers to observe. However, if there is a nearby university, teachers can seek out small, introductory college philosophy classes to observe. There is also a substantial amount of philosophy resources available online (see appendix).

Similar to the development of responsiveness to and appreciation of great literature, music, or visual art, nurturing philosophical sensitivity takes time and commitment. It starts with an interest in the puzzles that are endemic in human life. Experience, education, and practice with philosophical inquiry and discussion can then help us to cultivate an enhanced appreciation for the philosophical dimension of the natural and human worlds and the skills essential to inspire others to develop this awareness.

WHY IS PHILOSOPHICAL SENSITIVITY IMPORTANT?

We believe that it is crucial to encourage young people to hold onto their sense of wonder and to help them develop the confidence to ask questions, try out new ideas, and trust their own judgments. Cultivating philosophical sensitivity is instrumental in preserving an awareness of the world's mystery and the philosophical dimensions of human experience. Our skill at encouraging young people to pay attention to these aspects of life supports their development of the analytic and imaginative skills necessary to construct an intentional, rich, and authentic understanding of the world.

Moreover, encouraging young people to think philosophically in classroom communities helps them to appreciate the wide variety of perspectives from which the world can be viewed. Because, by definition, a philosophical problem does not have one settled answer, philosophical engagement with others illuminates the vast range of perspectives possible for approaching essential questions. The experience of becoming aware that there are many ways to see the same thing—all of them unique and valuable—is a powerful one. Philosophy teaches us that any view must be taken seriously, no matter how outlandish it seems, if there are good reasons offered for it. Especially in this time in human history, when greater and greater presumed certainty about knowledge, identity, moral beliefs, and the conditions for a good life lead people to extreme acts of violence and oppression, it's imperative that our students grasp that there are a multitude of ways to understand the world.

In our view, the most powerful method for introducing philosophy in classrooms involves the construction of a CPI. The next chapter will discuss the nature of this classroom community, its potential for enriching precollege education, and offer a range of ideas for developing and sustaining a CPI in schools.

NOTES

1. This chapter has been adapted from an article by Jana Mohr Lone (2013).
2. See, for example, Russell, 153–61; Edmonds and Warburton, chapter 1; Sellars, 1.
3. Some of the ideas explored here have also been discussed in *The Philosophical Child* (Lone, 2012) and in the essay "Teaching Pre-College Philosophy: The Cultivation of Philosophical Sensitivity" (Lone, in Lone and Israeloff, 2012).
4. This conception of "moral perception" does not refer specifically to sensory perception, but to the conscious awareness of particular aspects of a moral situation. Likewise, what we

mean by "philosophical sensitivity" also involves sentience—awareness of the puzzles underlying human experience.

5. As Aristotle writes, "We should attend to the undemonstrated sayings and beliefs of experienced and older people, or practically wise ones, no less than to the demonstrations; in that, because they have an eye formed from experience, they see correctly" (*Nicomachean Ethics*, 1143a35–b5). We learn both from listening to those more experienced than ourselves and from our own experiences to develop our capacities to see the important features of moral situations.

6. Although we refer to the part of us that seeks to comprehend the larger questions of human life and the world as "the philosophical self," we do not intend by using this phrase to posit the existence of multiple selves; by the philosophical self we simply mean the philosophical aspect of the self, in much the same way we might refer to the "artistic self." Our "philosophical selves" make use of particular abilities and talents, or what Howard Gardner would call "intelligences" (Gardner, 1993). (See more about the relationship between philosophical sensitivity and Gardner's work later in this chapter.) The philosophical self is not itself a capacity, but an aspect of ourselves manifested by philosophical sensitivity. To the extent we cultivate philosophical sensitivity, we keep alive the philosophical self—just as our efforts to develop our aesthetic sensitivity maintain what we might call the artistic self.

7. For examples and discussion of the significance of children trying out various identities, see Schapiro, 1999, 732–34; Gopnik, 27–31; Cobb, especially 53–61; see also Friquegnon, 15–16.

8. Gardner characterizes the human intellect as multifaceted and greatly varied across cultures and individuals. He contends that individuals draw on "multiple intelligences," a range of autonomous intellectual competences that underlie a wide range of human activities—from the ability to work effectively with numbers and language to musical and kinesthetic ability (Gardner, 1993, especially 77, 105, 135, 217). Although the theory has been met with a mixed critical reception, it has proven useful for many educators and inspired a wide range of educational programming in K-12 schools. While Gardner has noted that it can be challenging to distinguish between intelligences and other human capacities or skills (Gardner, 2006b), to date he has endorsed eight relatively distinct intelligences. Although existential intelligence is not yet accepted by Gardner as an autonomous intelligence because he believes there is still insufficient evidence that this intelligence draws on a unique brain center or has officially a distinct evolutionary history, existential intelligence continues to be regarded as a prime candidate for one of the multiple intelligences (In fact, Gardner has said informally that he currently considers there to be eight and a half intelligences) (Gardner, 1999; 2006a, 41). Many scholars now consider existential intelligence to be a distinct intelligence (see, for example, Armstrong, 2009; see also Allan and Shearer, 2012).

9. Thanks to Mitchell Green at the University of Connecticut for suggesting many of the examples in this paragraph.

10. See chapter 5 for an in-depth treatment of the CPI.

11. Helpful here would be the construction of a national teacher workshop format, along with the presence of a core group of facilitators in various regions who are trained both to lead such workshops and to support ongoing communities of philosophical inquiry among teachers. Involvement in a community of people who are developing their philosophical skills is a powerful and effective way for teachers to start to cultivate philosophical sensitivity. The national organization PLATO (Philosophy Learning and Teaching Organization) has been working on this effort, and several regional precollege philosophy centers, like the University of Washington Center for Philosophy for Children, run regular workshops for teachers.

12. While extensive exposure to philosophy texts can be valuable, it seems to us that such intensive study is not essential for precollege philosophy teachers, at least not for those

introducing philosophy prior to high school. Teachers with sufficient experience participating in communities of philosophical inquiry or similarly structured philosophy programs can, with strong skills in facilitating student discussions and a high-quality curriculum, successfully facilitate philosophy discussions among younger students.

13. Discussing the philosophical topics raised by picture books and other books for younger readers can be a rich way for teachers, parents, and other adults working with children to develop philosophical sensitivity. For a longer discussion of this topic, as well as a bibliography of philosophically suggestive children's books, see Lone, 2012. Using picture books to inspire philosophical inquiry was pioneered by Gareth Matthews in the United States (see Matthews, 1980, 1992, 1994), by Karin Murris in South Africa, and by Joanna Haynes in England (see, e.g., Murris, 1992, and Haynes and Murris, 2012). Works recently published about this method include books by Thomas Wartenberg (2009 and 2013) and the edited volume *Philosophy in Children's Literature* (2012). A number of picture books are discussed in the lesson plans in part III of this book.

Chapter 5

The Community of Philosophical Inquiry

Most precollege philosophy teachers, and especially those teaching elementary and middle-school students, approach classroom philosophy sessions as arenas for discussions about the ideas and questions of philosophy, as opposed to being primarily focused on what historical and contemporary philosophers have to say about these ideas and questions. That is, we engage young people in the practice of philosophy, rather than (or as a substantial part of) studying it. Instead of (or along with) reading Plato, Descartes, or Simone de Beauvoir (among many other philosophers) and analyzing their arguments, for example, young people explore the sorts of questions that intrigued these philosophers in structured, collaborative classroom discussions.

In previous chapters we considered the importance of encouraging student wonder, questioning, and reflection, examined some of the elements of learner-centered education and classroom dialogue, and discussed the ways in which these pedagogical commitments are fundamental to precollege philosophy. A powerful model for this educational approach is known as the CPI. In this chapter, we discuss the community of inquiry generally as a classroom structure that supports collaborative discussion and exploration in any subject, and then turn to an examination of the CPI and the importance of this approach in precollege philosophy classes.[1]

LIPMAN AND THE COMMUNITY OF INQUIRY

A community of inquiry is defined as "a group of individuals who collaboratively engage in purposeful critical discourse and reflection to construct personal meaning and confirm mutual understanding" (Garrison, 2011, 15). Participants in a community of inquiry work to examine a problematic concept or situation, following the inquiry where it leads, consistent with logic and critical reasoning.

Lipman's detailed conception of the community of inquiry, along with his practical strategies for its development in a precollege classroom, constitutes what was perhaps his most significant contribution to the field of precollege philosophy. Promoting what he calls a "reflective paradigm" of education, Lipman, following Dewey, sees education *as* inquiry (rather than viewing education as involving the teaching of the end products of inquiry). In other words, genuine education involves students learning to think critically and well about subjects in which they are invested. Therefore, Lipman contends, the appropriate model for classroom learning in general is the community of inquiry.

A key feature of a community of inquiry is that it is a shared experience, one in which the possibility exists for all the members of the classroom community, students and teacher(s), to learn from one another. As Lipman puts it, "Students who thought that all learning had to be learning by oneself come to discover that they can also use and profit from the experience of others" (Lipman, 2003, 240). The energy and excitement that can ensue when students become aware both that other students can contribute to their learning and that they can contribute to the learning of others can be transformative.

The community of inquiry, as Lipman conceives it, includes the following characteristics:

1. The enterprise is based on mutual respect.
2. Students build on one another's ideas and follow the argument where it leads.
3. Students challenge each other to supply reasons for their opinions.
4. Students assist one another in drawing out inferences from what has been said.
5. Students endeavor to identify one another's assumptions. (Lipman, 2003, 13–16)

Essential to the process is the emergence of the more problematic or puzzling aspects of situations and concepts in the curriculum, rather than an emphasis on the "facts" students are expected to memorize and learn. The members of the community of inquiry come together in a spirit of intellectual freedom to explore these issues.

THE COMMUNITY OF PHILOSOPHICAL INQUIRY

A community of inquiry can, of course, be used to explore any subject matter in the classroom.[2] The special features of a community of *philosophical* inquiry ("CPI") involve the content (i.e., philosophical topics). The CPI maintains all of the features of a general community of inquiry, but here the substance of the inquiry is philosophical, involving larger abstract questions, which underlie and overlap among all subjects. As discussed in the previous chapter, the identification of a philosophical topic is not an uncontroversial matter. Philosophical topics examine meanings, attempt to clarify concepts, and generally engage questions that are not likely to be answered in any final way. This does not mean that philosophical topics involve questions without answers, but, as discussed in chapter 4, the answers continue to be contestable, rather than final and settled.

There has been a great deal written about the formation of a CPI (see, e.g., Lipman, 1980, especially pages 82–101; Haynes, 2002, 21–30; and McCall, especially pages 80–92). We will discuss what we take to be four of its central features.

First, the members of a CPI are engaged in a structured, collaborative inquiry aimed at building meaning and acquiring understanding through the examination of philosophical questions or concepts of interest to the participants. The focus of a CPI is on following the logical force of the argument, with the questions and ideas on the table determined by the individual perspectives of the group members.

Ultimately this enterprise is not about *teaching* young people philosophy, but about *doing* philosophy with them by structuring an environment that allows them to talk with each other about the philosophical issues that puzzle them. As facilitators, we help to ensure the philosophical integrity of the session—ensuring that the discussion is primarily philosophical and that students are encouraged to articulate their views, to seek understanding, to discern their assumptions and the underlying logic of their beliefs, to build on each other's reasoning, and to pay attention to the differing perspectives of the class members, all within the context of the topics and questions that matter to them.

Second, a CPI entails a consensus of "epistemological modesty": an acknowledgment that all members of the group, including the facilitator, are fallible, and therefore hold views that could end up being mistaken. We engage in philosophical inquiry with young people not to bestow our philosophical insights on them, but to facilitate their ability to think for themselves about some of the fundamental aspects of human existence, to develop an awareness of the wide variety of perspectives with which people apprehend the world, and to develop strong analytic reasoning and critical thinking skills. Teachers in a CPI demonstrate a reticence about advocating their own philosophical views, and model a comfort with uncertainty, with the fact that there are no final and agreed-upon answers to most of the questions being explored by the CPI.

Third, participants in a CPI generally refrain from using much technical philosophical language or direct references to the work of professional philosophers to construct their arguments. This helps to ensure that the group focuses on exploring the questions themselves and not the past or current history of the subject as analyzed by particular philosophers. Moreover, and particularly in settings where some of the participants possess strong backgrounds in academic philosophy, this can serve to "level the playing field" between students who have more familiarity with philosophical inquiry and students with less experience.

Fourth, and fundamentally important to the successful development of a CPI, is the establishment of an environment of intellectual safety, one in which any question or comment is acceptable, so long as it does not belittle or devalue others in the group, and which allows trust and a corresponding willingness to present one's thoughts to participants (Jackson, 2001, 459–65). Such an environment lays the groundwork for the kind of open sharing of thoughts and ideas, some more fully formed than others, without fear of being attacked or denigrated, which is essential in a rich and productive learning community. The teacher's role is pivotal in establishing this environment:

> The [facilitator] is open and caring, demonstrates respect, and embraces the uniqueness of students and their perspectives and does so in a classroom format in which all are invited to participate actively, engage in personal self disclosure while trusting the confidentiality of such openness, and where the [facilitator] maintains a sense of control and direction to facilitate learning. (Schrader, 2004, 98)

The teacher both models openness and respect for others' ideas and constructs a structured space that invites the students to engage thoughtfully and with an appreciation for multiple perspectives.

While an intellectually safe learning community involves trust, respect, and an atmosphere conducive to taking intellectual risks, it does not promise comfort. Communities of inquiry are dedicated to the open and rigorous exploration of difficult and contestable issues and the intellectual growth that results, the process of which can often provoke feelings of perplexity and uncertainty (what the Greeks called *aporia*).

This can be an uncomfortable experience: having one's assumptions or views disputed, being introduced to a perspective very different from one's own, coming to see that one's beliefs are internally contradictory or that a particular view one held turns out to be mistaken, having to defend a position about which one feels strongly, etc. Taking these possibilities into account, Ashby Butnor writes,

> In some sense, one must be ready for anything—for changing one's mind, becoming aware of one's own implicit assumptions, being attracted to or disturbed by new perspectives, struggling through a difficult idea, or impressing even oneself with an articulate expression of insight. (Butnor, 2012, 29)

Feeling intellectually safe, therefore, is not to feel complacent or unchallenged—it is to feel supported in one's struggles to make sense of the world.

Working authentically to understand our experiences, with openness to the perspectives of others, necessitates vulnerability. We are vulnerable when we express our ideas with the possibility of them being called into question, when we respond to another's views and risk a critical reaction. In his work *Ethics in Light of Childhood*, John Wall suggests that vulnerability involves "an openness and relationality to the world" (Wall, 2010, 39). In other words, by engaging with others, we open ourselves to being changed by them. We respond to each other's ideas and questions in a philosophy session and the encounter then shapes our thinking and the development of our perspective.

We make ourselves vulnerable when we honestly express what we think and believe. In order to protect and encourage such vulnerability, an environment of trust and support is essential.[3] The facilitator works to create and sustain such an environment by paying careful attention to the classroom's interpersonal and social power dynamics, by demonstrating respect for diverse learning styles, openness to multiple points of view and respect for student questions and contributions, and by modeling an intellectual playfulness and epistemological modesty that encourages consideration of a wide range of ideas and possibilities.[4]

As discussed in chapter 3, one practical tool to begin to fashion an intellectually safe atmosphere is to help the students set the rules for the community of inquiry at the beginning of the year. Student-created rules, in our experience, invariably turn out to include some form of the following: listen when other students are speaking; respect other people's ideas; when you disagree with someone, focus on the idea and not the person. The rules can be posted so that they are always visible during philosophy sessions, and you can remind the students of them from time to time. We've found that the students become particularly invested in the rules when they have created them.

THE STRUCTURE OF A PHILOSOPHY SESSION

In general, CPI sessions comprise five main parts: (1) a prompt,[5] (2) time for reflection, (3) emergence of the questions the prompt has raised for the students, (4) the discussion, and (5) some form of closure for the session. Typically, the facilitator of the session will introduce some prompt—a text, film, piece of music, or some activity to inspire philosophical wondering. With kindergarten and primary school students, stories, art, music, activities, and movement are accessible prompts for introducing philosophical practice. For upper elementary and middle school students, more complex texts can be introduced, and writing can become a more central aspect of philosophy sessions. By the time students reach high school, philosophical texts themselves can provide motivation for the inquiry that follows.

After the prompt is introduced, it's useful to provide some reflection time for students to consider the questions and ideas the prompt might have raised for them. Giving students an opportunity to draw or write at this point makes room for reflective thinking and can bring in students who might be less comfortable speaking in a larger group. You can also have students share their questions in pairs or small groups. This both encourages the participation of more students, and imparts a slower cadence to the session that is conducive to serious and sustained thinking.

Next, and in some ways most important, is the emergence of the questions students have about the prompt. You can ask, "What questions did this [prompt] make you wonder about?" The students voice whatever is puzzling or interesting to them in the form of questions, which can be written on the board. For example, after listening to Hans Christian Andersen's story "The Ugly Duckling," which can inspire thinking about aesthetics at all ages, students might ask questions such as: Was the "ugly duckling" really ugly? If so, what made him ugly? Did he stop being ugly at the end of the story? What does ugly mean? How do we decide what is ugly and what is beautiful? At some point (when the space on the board runs out or at some other arbitrary moment), all of the questions for that session will be on the board.

Often, a considerable part of a precollege philosophy class will be spent having the students think about their questions and then listing their questions and choosing which question(s) to discuss. It can be easy, sometimes, especially in the goal-driven society in which we live, to see this part of the session as a precursor to the real work, the philosophy discussion itself. Indeed, when first beginning philosophy sessions in precollege classrooms, teachers and other facilitators can become impatient about the time it takes to get all the students' questions on the board and decide what to discuss.

In fact, though, the time spent helping students to formulate their own questions and ensuring that the discussion starts with those questions is just as valuable as the time spent actually talking about them. For one thing, as we discussed in greater length in chapter 2, learning to articulate questions in a clear way, so that your question accurately describes whatever it is that's puzzling you, is an important skill that can only be developed with experience. Moreover, devoting time to listing and analyzing student questions lets the students know that asking questions is itself a valuable practice, quite apart from the discussion of them (let alone answering them).[6] Especially because teachers generally introduce most of the questions asked in a classroom, time spent encouraging student questions is invaluable.

The list of student questions becomes the source of possible agenda items for the philosophical discussion that follows.[7] Lipman emphasizes the importance of ensuring that the question or questions for discussion are then chosen by the students, and not by the teacher, noting,

> This is a pivotal moment. If the teacher selects the questions, the students are likely to interpret that as a vestige of the old authoritarianism. Fortunately, a number of alternatives compatible with democracy are available. The order of questions to be discussed can be determined by voting, by lot, or by asking someone who didn't submit a question to make the necessary choice. In any event, this recognition of the elevated status of the question (and the reduced status of the answer) will help the students remember that questioning is the leading edge of inquiry; it opens the door to dialogue, to self-criticism, and to self-correction. (Lipman, 2009, 14)

When the students choose the question, it's an empowering experience for them. This signals to them that there really is something different going on here: the teacher's agenda isn't determining the content of the inquiry—they are. Especially in the early stages of the formation of a CPI, student selection of the questions that will form the basis for their discussions demonstrates appreciation of young people's agency and ownership of their own classroom experience. *It's their questions that matter.*

PHILOSOPHICAL INTEGRITY

Is there a potential conflict between having students determine the content of the philosophy session and the goal of philosophical depth and integrity? Catherine McCall in Scotland, for example, has developed a somewhat different approach to the development of a CPI, in which the primary focus is on the philosophical dialogue itself and not on the students' questions or ideas for shaping the discussion (McCall, 2009, 105).

McCall's method requires that the teacher, rather than the students, choose the question that will be explored, with the primary criterion being which question has the greatest philosophical potential (McCall, 2009, 90).[8] McCall contends that Lipman's approach, following that of Dewey, places the formation of a democratic community, and not the philosophical depth of the discussion, at the center of precollege philosophy sessions.

In our view, the formation of the CPI is at the core of precollege philosophy sessions. The heart of the transformative potential of philosophical inquiry is student engagement in a dialogue grounded in the questions that most appeal to the group and the collaborative attempt to construct meaning and cultivate deep understanding. Lipman's statement that "questioning is the leading edge of inquiry" reflects the primacy of the question. The students' responsibility for choosing the question to begin their discussion enhances the democratic nature of the community and is consistent with the objective that the inquiry be centered around issues that perplex *the students.*[9]

Moreover, we do not believe that assigning responsibility to the students to choose the question has the effect of diminishing the philosophical content of the dialogue that follows. In our experience, students generally do choose one of the top two or three most philosophically rich questions, and this is especially true as the CPI matures. In fact, students learn, as the CPI progresses, to make better and better deci-sions about which question is the most philosophically promising, an important skill that would not be cultivated if the teacher always chose the question to be discussed.

With practice, students learn how to discern which question might be the most fruit-ful and why. Consistent with this, the teacher can encourage the students to voice their views about which question is likely to be the most philosophically promising, and work to bolster their skills at making good choices in this regard, rather than impos-ing on them his or her own view about which questions hold the most philosophical potential. Precollege philosophy teachers regularly observe the growing philosophical sophistication and richness of the questions asked by students over the course of a school year.[10]

Futher, it is not always the case that the philosophy teacher is the best judge of which question has the most promise for inspiring a philosophically interesting discus-sion. Adults can be mistaken about the significance of the questions asked by students. We have had the experience of listening to young people pose questions that at first hearing seemed relatively trivial, only to discover as the discussion ensued that the questions asked were in fact quite profound.

In any event, and especially early on, the teacher can probe the philosophical poten-tial of the question the class has chosen (e.g., in one third-grade philosophy class, the question chosen was "Why were the boy's friends animals?" and in the initial discus-sion about the question, it became clear that that the underlying question was "Can we be friends with animals?"[11]). If the question chosen by the students ultimately turns out not to be a very fruitful one, it is the teacher's task to help the students move toward one of the other, more philosophically interesting, questions previously raised by the students.

Empowering students to choose the subject of the inquiry also contributes to their ability to engage in authentic discussions, in which the students are *actually* having a discussion; that is, they are speaking and listening to each other about topics in which they are personally invested.[12] Students can become accustomed to classroom discourse that is predominantly directed toward the teacher, and which involves issues about which the students do not care very much.

Classroom communication, in many ways, takes place in an isolated sphere, sepa-rate from the everyday world in which students talk to one another about issues that matter to them. An authentic discussion in the classroom must involve communication between students about issues that mean something to them. Entrusting students with the task of deciding which question most merits exploration enables the conditions necessary for the CPI to engender such exchanges.

We want to foster students' confidence and skill in asking questions. Understanding the ways in which questions are at the core of a CPI session allows us to support young people as they cultivate the inclination to question.[13] Haynes writes,

When young children are starting out in philosophy, what they understand is that the community of enquiry is a place where they are encouraged to formulate questions about the things that puzzle them. They are helped in this process of turning a puzzled response into a question. They come to realize that we can make all kinds of use of our mystifica-tion. (Haynes, 2002, 95)

In order to encourage students to engage in "creative questioning," it's essential that we trust their judgment and their abilities to identify many of the philosophically puzzling aspects of human existence and engage in inquiry about them.

THE PHILOSOPHY DISCUSSION

Once the students have chosen the question that will be explored, a natural first step in the ensuing discussion is to ask the student who asked the opening question to describe what it is he or she is wondering about. From that point, there is no lesson blueprint in a CPI session that determines exactly what will happen. What comes next will depend on the students' interests, the way in which the discussion develops, and the particular participants. In philosophy sessions in which the students' philosophical questions shape the scope of the inquiry, the teacher's responsibility is to guide the students in the inquiry, but not to control the content of the discussion.

The questions that the students analyze are those that have been generated by the class; therefore, the teacher generally doesn't know, going into the session, what the topic(s) under consideration will be. To some extent, then, the teacher relinquishes control over the philosophical direction of the session; unperturbed by this, he or she is able to demonstrate a kind of flexibility about and responsiveness to content and trajectory of the discussion.

The teacher's role here is a robust one, but it is subtle. Although there is no step-by-step lesson plan detailing all aspects of the philosophy session, the teacher must pay close attention to the initiation and progress of the dialogue, looking for connections among what students say, asking for clarification and for reasons supporting particular statements, and in general staying attuned to the philosophical content of questions and ideas that might otherwise be lost.

This entails the teacher maintaining a delicate balance, supporting students' attainment of philosophical clarity and depth while refraining from imposing on the discussion his or her own preferences for subject matter and the direction of the discussion.[14] What is important is that the teacher is attentive to ensuring the philosophical integrity of the CPI; that is, that it principally engenders *philosophical* discussions.

What makes a discussion philosophical? A philosophical discussion involves the following three elements: (1) the exploration of abstract, unsettled questions; (2) arguments and counterarguments that are constructed to support particular ways of understanding or resolving these questions; (3) the objective of making progress in developing the meaning of the ideas explored or furthering the participants' understanding of a concept (see Haynes, 2002, 94–96; Lipman, 1980, 102–28).

To be able to inspire and help sustain a philosophical exchange, a teacher must possess philosophical sensitivity and pay close attention to the philosophical potential of students' comments and questions. This requires at least some familiarity with some of the most fundamental questions of philosophy (questions about knowledge, morality, language, reality, beauty, and art, etc.) and skills at seeing the philosophical content of students' questions and comments. For example, in a discussion about love, a fifth-grade student remarks, "Love is different in different relationships—whether it's a family, or friend, or like a boyfriend or girlfriend." "So what is love, then?" the teacher asks. "Do you have love in all those relationships? Is it possible to have a friendship without love? Or a family relationship without love?"[15] This exchange led to an inquiry into the nature of love itself.

The role of the philosophy teacher in the discussion includes tracking it when it moves in a philosophical direction. Of course, every minute of every philosophy session won't be philosophical (or interesting). There will be periods of time when the discussion makes a turn out of the philosophical (into science, say, or stories from personal experience), and periods of transition and messiness.

The point is not to prohibit personal or other nonphilosophical examples or stories, as they can be useful in the context of exploring particular issues of philosophy, but to limit them to those relevant to the inquiry. For example, the topic of dreams, while philosophically rich, has a high potential for veering off into student descriptions of interesting dreams they've had. The teacher can allow some of that to help orient the discussion, but can help to move the session into some of the deeper questions about dreaming—What is dreaming? Why do we dream? Would you choose to dream or not?

The aim is to ensure that the discussion is primarily philosophical, as opposed to an opinion-sharing, group-therapy, or other kind of enterprise. It is crucial, therefore, that philosophy teachers possess skill at recognizing when an exchange has philosophical potential and when it risks veering off into side issues irrelevant to the discussion. The facilitator must push for depth in reasoning, relevance, consistency, and quality thinking.[16] This involves a balance between eliciting the questions and topics that most interest the students, helping the students to stay focused on tracking a philosophical topic, and letting the discussion develop of its own accord. In our view, three features are essential to accomplish this balance successfully: openness, respect, and trust.

First, openness involves the teacher's willingness to operate, as we have discussed, without a rigid agenda for controlling the discussion's content,[17] allowing the substance of the session to grow organically as students take the inquiry in the direction to which their inclinations lead. We want students to cultivate a deeper understanding of complex topics and the multiple vantage points from which they can be approached and analyzed. In order to help them to do this, we have to really listen to what they're saying and try to reflect back their comments and ideas, rather than steering them in a particular direction. Our role is to protect the integrity of the process, but not to control where it leads. Because the topics addressed in philosophy discussions are unsettled, there is room for students to offer their questions and ideas without looking for the expected answer, allowing for free and imaginative intellectual experimentation.

Second, respect requires attentiveness to student perspectives and a space that allows all student voices to emerge. When students speak, it can be helpful to restate their ideas and comments for the group in a way that honors precisely what the student has said and not what the teacher thinks might best move the discussion forward. The facilitator's role here is to connect students' comments to one another and assist the students in maintaining the thread of the inquiry. It is useful here to refrain from responding to each student comment, getting mired in one-on-one exchanges with individual students.

Remember that it is more important that the students respond to one another. Whatever response you are considering, it is likely a student will express the idea if given the space to do so. Encouraging students to voice their diverse ways of seeing the world will help them to recognize access to a multiplicity of perspectives will enhance their own understanding.

Third, trust is essential if the CPI's philosophical exchanges are to be deep and authentic. Trust among the students, between the teacher and students, and generally in the process of developing a CPI flourishes when the teacher manifests sensitivity to both the dynamic of the group and the vantage points of each individual student. Here it is imperative that the teacher model and encourage the expression of diverse perspectives and take into account the varying comfort levels and communication styles of the students, while at the same time helping the students to shape a rigorous environment that allows for any view to be expressed and challenged.

PROGRESS IN A PHILOSOPHICAL DISCUSSION

A philosophical discussion should ultimately proceed in a forward movement. This doesn't mean that it won't loop back and forth, analyzing various conceptual issues and then returning to earlier questions, rather than developing in a straight line. However, there should be some forward movement—greater clarity about a particular concept, appreciation of the variety of perspectives, appreciation of the complexity of a topic, deeper awareness of the assumptions we make and the reasons we make them, and recognition of alternative ways of approaching a subject. This requires listening carefully to, and being able to recognize assumptions in, what is being said. It is also crucial to keep the thread of the inquiry and encourage students to connect with what others have said. The teacher, and ultimately the students, should articulate connections and distinctions among the views offered in the discussion.

Progress in a philosophical discussion does not mean that it ends in agreement. Many, if not most, philosophical discussions conclude with open issues and contrasting views. After all, philosophers have long explored philosophical topics and almost never reach final agreement on the resolution of a given question. It's important to be able to be content with disagreement and to develop a comfort with uncertainty. One of the benefits of engaging in a CPI is that students learn that disagreement can be healthy and even enlightening. Many of the topics addressed in philosophy sessions can be approached in multiple ways, and student perspectives will, at times, conflict. When such conflicts allow for new ways of looking at particular questions, and don't entail animosity or personal attacks, students come to appreciate that many questions can be answered in a wide variety of ways, depending on individual perspectives and experiences.

Sometimes teachers are concerned that students will be frustrated by the lack of final answers to philosophical questions. In our experience, however, young people are relatively untroubled by the lack of final resolution for the questions being considered. Asked about the lack of settled answers in philosophical discussions, a fourth-grade student comments,

> I think part of what I like about philosophy is that there aren't final answers. I sometimes come to an answer myself, but I know that it might change. Mostly I really like listening

to other people's ideas and knowing that there might be a new idea that would make me change my mind.[18]

Young people don't seem to expect final answers in the way that perhaps many adults do, and helping them to continue to cultivate a comfort with uncertainty is important in a world in which many of the issues they will face will be uncertain, and their resolutions provisional.

CLOSURE IN A PHILOSOPHY SESSION

The lack of a final resolution in the discussion makes it especially important to provide some closure for the class at the end of a philosophy session. This can take the form of recapping the discussion, describing where it started and the various paths it took, recounting some of the questions asked and responses given, reminding the students of some of the views that were tested and ultimately discarded or revised, and/or articulating the new questions that emerged. The teacher, especially in the early days of a community of inquiry, can take on this role, and/or students can be asked to contribute their insights about the discussion. This ends the session in an open-ended way while providing a meaningful context for what has taken place.[19]

The CPI constructs a space in which students can explore, with the help of a skilled facilitator, complex and essential questions that are of deep interest to the group. One of the delights of philosophical engagement in the classroom is the way in which philosophical questions can be found in every subject and virtually every classroom activity. We turn next, in part III, to a variety of lesson plans and ideas for inspiring philosophical inquiry with students, from their earliest years in school through high school.

NOTES

1. Parts of this chapter have been adapted from the following articles: "Philosophical Sensitivity," by Jana Mohr Lone, originally published in *Metaphilosophy*, vol. 44:1–2, 2013, and "Questions and the Community of Philosophical Inquiry," by Jana Mohr Lone, originally published in *Childhood and Philosophy*, vol. 7:13, 2011.

2. See, for example, Gregory, 2007, 282–84.

3. Critical to the construction of an intellectually safe classroom environment is an awareness of the power dynamics in a classroom, including the ways in which some students' voices can be privileged. For an extended treatment of this topic, see chapter 10.

4. We note here that specific strategies for constructing an intellectually safe CPI that accounts for student vulnerability will vary somewhat depending on students' ages. Younger children new to philosophy will at first require more scaffolding to support their successful engagement in philosophical practice and their emerging speaking and listening as well as interpersonal skills, while older students struggling with identity and other pivotal issues in adolescence will need different strategies.

5. Precollege philosophy educators utilize a wide and varied range of tools for inspiring philosophical discussion, including picture books, young adult literature, the Lipman

curriculum published by the Institute for the Advancement of Philosophy for Children, and other curricula created specifically for precollege philosophy sessions, as well as activities and games, films, music, visual art, etc. See part III, the appendix, and the bibliography for a variety of resources for K-12 philosophy sessions in classrooms.

6. Susan Gardner has written about the centrality of questioning in being able to understand the perspectives of others. Gardner, "Questioning to Hesitation, Rather than Hesitating to Question: A Pragmatic Hermeneutic Perspective on Educational Inquiry" (paper given at Mini-Conference on Philosophy for Children, American Philosophical Association Pacific Division meeting (San Diego, 2011).

7. Some precollege philosophy educators recommend organizing and categorizing the questions at this point. In his article "A Framework for Facilitating Classroom Dialogue," for example, Maughn Gregory recommends organizing the questions into some order that will structure the inquiry, including looking for relationships among the questions (Gregory, 2007, 282–84). Although we agree that it can be helpful to point out questions that seem very similar, or to clarify the meaning of particular questions, in general, spending too much time grouping and categorizing the questions is of less interest to students than choosing a question and moving into the discussion. See also Lipman, 1988, 157.

8. Likewise, in McCall's method, the facilitator always calls on students to contribute; in contrast, in a CPI, students can call on one another and use other methods for determining who will be next to speak. In our experience, having students call on one another, especially as the CPI is progressing, accelerates the formation of an environment in which the students talk to one another rather than directing their remarks to the teacher.

9. We do not intend to assert, however, that there is *never* a time at which it is appropriate for the teacher to choose the question(s) for discussion. Especially once the CPI has developed over some time, there may be texts or activities in which it makes sense for the teacher to introduce a specific question or to choose from a list of student questions in the interests of time or some other consideration. In the ordinary course of a CPI session, and especially at the beginning stages of a philosophy community, we believe that it should be the students who make this choice.

10. There is a significant relationship between young people having control over the questions shaping the discussion and the role of epistemological modesty in the CPI. Epistemological modesty involves an acknowledgment that our beliefs are fallible, that they might turn out to be erroneous. Assigning responsibility to the students for choosing the question enhances the CPI consensus of epistemological modesty in two ways. First, the teacher is not understood as infallible in his or her ability to discern the most philosophically fruitful question. Second, as Lipman remarks, "Each question has a global potential of putting a portion of the world in question, and this helps pave the way to fallibilism, the practice of assuming one's incorrectness in order to discover errors one didn't know one had made" (Lipman, 2009, 32). Giving the students the opportunity to "put the world in question," and then to determine which question to discuss, supports their learning that questions can illuminate the tentativeness of our claims to knowledge.

11. Class at John Muir Elementary School, Seattle, Washington, winter 2014.

12. In her work advocating the central place of inquiry and argument in the classroom, Deanna Kuhn has pointed out the importance of student participation in authentic conversations. In authentic conversations, discourse between students resembles ordinary conversation in the sense that there is an expectation that they are speaking and listening to one another, rather than student communication being directed only to the teacher. There is also a clear purpose for having a conversation that is understood by the participants (Kuhn, 2005, 122–25).

13. Lipman observes that

to question is to institutionalize and legitimize doubt, and to invite critical evaluation. It hints openly
of new options and fresh alternatives, in contrast to the stale dichotomy of true/false answers. One
must constantly be on the lookout for new ways of encouraging student questioning, not as a matter
of habit, but because many practices and institutions, while poorly justified and of dubious, question-
able merit, can be found out only by creative questioning. (Lipman, 2009, 32)

14. Of course, not every precollege philosophy class or session will be run as a CPI.
Especially in high school, it can often be valuable to provide an introduction to the history of
philosophy and to some of the more famous philosophical arguments made in various areas of
philosophy. However, for inspiring philosophical discussions *among* students, the creation of a
CPI is a powerful method, in part because of its emphasis on the content of the inquiry being
decided upon by the students.

15. Class at Whittier Elementary School, Seattle, Washington, spring 2013.

16. For a thoughtful discussion on the important role of the facilitator in helping students to
engage in coherent analysis and rigorous thinking, see Gardner, 1995, 38–49.

17. This does not mean, of course, that teachers leading philosophy sessions won't plan
ahead for potentially fruitful themes that might be explored or for interesting activities for
examining those themes. However, it does mean that we are not bound to a lesson plan agenda
that requires that students cover certain topics in the course of the philosophy discussion.

18. Class at Whittier Elementary School, Seattle, Washington, winter 2013.

19. Students can also be asked for some reflective thoughts or questions after the discussion.
Creative activities can be utilized, such as generating a group poem using a prompt based on
the discussion, or asking students to draw a representation of one of the topics discussed. Once
students are old enough, the use of philosophy journals, in which students can write a reflection
at the end of the discussion, adds an additional dimension to the experience.

Part III

IN THE CLASSROOM

Chapter 6

Philosophy in Elementary School

As we have noted, children often begin thinking about philosophical issues when they are very young, wondering about all kinds of fundamental life questions—What does it mean to be a person? Do animals think? Are dreams real? Parents and grandparents can address such questions by talking one-on-one with their children and grandchildren (see Lone, 2012, esp. pp. 7–39). For teachers, facilitating philosophical discussions with groups of very young students, in preschool and early kindergarten in particular, involves helping the children to develop some of the basic skills essential to group inquiry—being able to listen to others, following the thread of a conversation, learning to ask clear questions, and articulating reasons for why they think the way they do.

Sara Stanley offers a lesson plan that can be used daily in a preschool or kindergarten classroom to help young children develop their reasoning skills, and Leah Boonin has contributed a plan for using young children's own discussions to foster philosophical exchanges. Many of the other lesson plans in this chapter can also be used in classrooms with preschool children. As children get to primary school and up, their abilities to participate in classroom philosophical discussions expand, and we have found that elementary school is a fruitful time for students to be introduced to structured philosophical inquiry.

This chapter describes a range of ideas for inspiring philosophical inquiry in elementary-school classrooms. Most of these lesson plans are designed around picture books, which are powerful resources for inviting children to engage in philosophical questioning and reflection. A unique mixture of literature and visual art, these books generate the discovery of meaning through a combined visual and verbal experience. The whole of a picture book—not just its meaning or story, but its illustrations and book cover as well—fosters a creative approach to wondering about the questions the story provokes.

Picture books, accessible and comfortable for all ages, often raise essential questions about topics like fairness and justice, art and beauty, ethics, life and death and the nature of reality, social and political issues, and the nature of knowledge. Although this chapter is geared toward elementary-school–age students, all of the philosophy lessons discussed can also be used with middle-school and high-school students as well as with adult students. We have found that picture books inspire lively philosophical exchanges with older students as well as college undergraduates. Listening to stories being read aloud, an experience many of us had when we were children, is conducive to creating an open and relaxed atmosphere for thinking about deep and fundamental questions.

After reading to or with the students, ask them, "What are you wondering about after hearing this story? What questions did this make you think about?" With students of the third grade and up, create philosophy journals and invite the students to write their questions there. This gives students who are more reticent about speaking in larger groups an opportunity to express their ideas. Then ask students to volunteer their questions, and write them all on the board. Have the students vote on which question to discuss.

Many of the lesson plans that follow suggest questions to consider when reading particular picture books. These questions are not meant to be exhaustive—they are possibilities for questions that can inspire philosophical exchanges, based on questions that have come from students when discussing these books. The lists of possible discussion questions are meant to provide some ideas for teachers preparing to use these books to help generate classroom philosophical conversations, but these lists should not be used in place of asking the students what questions the stories raise for them so that, as much as possible, the discussions emerge from the students' questions. Although we do not think it is imperative that philosophy discussions always begin with asking students to consider what questions the prompt inspired for them (several of the lesson plans below are more directive), we recommend this approach as a general practice. The clear message to students when philosophy sessions depend on their responses to the prompt is that philosophy can be found everywhere, and everyone's questions matter.

LESSON PLAN
A QUESTION BOARD*

Topic: Reasoning
Time: Anywhere from 10–30 minutes

Objectives

- To help young children develop their reasoning skills
- To help young children make choices and learn to justify them

Materials Needed

1. A display board to display the choice cards
2. Two labels, also displayed on the board, that say: "Good because . . ." and "Bad because . . ."
3. A set of good or bad choice cards (see below)
4. A set of student name cards

Description

This activity is useful for young students who have not yet begun philosophical training. It can be used as a short, daily thinking exercise, a longer, inquiry-based activity, or as an exercise for parents to try with their children.

At the start of each session, put up a choice card (e.g., "Chocolate rain?") and the two labels ("Good because" and "Bad because") on the display board. It's helpful to place the display board close to where the children arrive, as this allows parents and caregivers to share the day's question with the children. You can also include on the board examples of questions to ask the children to help them develop their reasoning.

Name cards can be stuck to the board with Velcro or Blu Tak. Adding an illustration to the choice cards helps make the choices look more child-friendly.

To start, form a question for the children using the choice cards, beginning the question with "Would it be good or bad if." For example, "Would it be good or bad if there was chocolate rain?"

Children place their names on the appropriate good or bad idea label. (See below for the labels.) You should stand by the board and model asking for reasons and reasoning. If parents are there, encourage parents to share their ideas so that the children can see that everyone's opinions are welcomed. This modeling pays off as parents quickly begin to see that the purpose of the exercise is to find out why the children give the answers they give.

Questions to Ask

1. But what would be good about that choice?
2. What might happen if that was the case?
3. What wouldn't happen?
4. How would you feel about that?
5. What would you have to do if you chose that?
6. Do you think everybody would like that?

You can revisit the day's question at snack time, which would allow you to extend the thinking into longer, inquiry-based activities.

Conclusion

Over time, the daily question-board activity develops more than just the children's voices. It allows children to understand that their opinions matter. They learn to become critical reviewers of their own ideas and those of their peers.

Through presenting these questions, we are modeling important philosophical skills. The children are consolidating the process of inquiry, making choices, justifying their views, asking secondary questions, and sharing their ideas. This process enables the children to become the facilitators of their own ideas and eases the transition into the whole class community of philosophical inquiry.

CHOICE CARD IDEAS

Boys in pink dresses
Talking chickens
Chocolate rain
Girls playing football
Tiny elephants
No money
Flying cars
Giant babies
Magic wands for everyone
Children in charge

*This lesson plan was contributed by Sara Stanley, an early years lead teacher and educator for twenty years, who is now a philosophical play and storyworld educational consultant in both the United Kingdom and South Africa.

LESSON PLAN
CREATING OUR OWN PHILOSOPHICAL STORY*

Topic: Reasoning skills
Time: 1–10 minutes

Objectives

• Deepen and clarify children's thinking on topics that interest them
• Introduce children to the fun of playing with ideas

Materials Needed

Some way of recording the conversation with children (this could be a notepad, computer, or other electronic recording device)

Description

The most productive way to do philosophy with very young children is as informally as possible. Good discussions happen with young children when something that they find interesting is drawn out and supported by an attentive instructor. Listening to young students, instructors are sure to observe the beginnings of philosophical inquiry emerge. This activity can take place at any point that a teacher observes an interesting conversation taking place among the children.

Activity

- Note when some of the children are beginning to have a potentially philosophically interesting discussion (e.g., you observe two students—call them "Caroline" and "Brent"—arguing about the existence of fairies).
- Enter the discussion and formalize things a bit, asking for clarification and provoking the children to further discussion. (What reasons do you have for thinking they are/are not real? Are there other things that you think are real that you have never seen? Have you seen Mars? And so on.)
- Record the conversation (which in some schools requires advance parental permission).
- Ask the participating children their permission to tell other students about the discussion. You now have a philosophical story with the potential to be of great interest to the other students in the class because it was created by their peers.
- Ask the class, "Do you want to hear about something interesting that Caroline and Brent said about fairies?"
- Play the recording for the class and facilitate a short conversation about the topic, if they are responsive.

In this informal setting, the philosophy instructor must be alert and ready to foster philosophical inquiry as it develops. One might wonder how best to identify the ideas and questions worth tending. Don't worry too much about that. If a particular line of inquiry does not provoke interest, move on to another topic.

Conclusion

Some of the questions that very young children often want to explore include aesthetics questions (questions about what makes something art and what makes art good young—children are tickled and provoked by the story of Duchamp's urinal); metaphysical questions (such as those about fairies, unicorns, and monsters—teachers should be careful here to lead the children in deepening their thinking without pushing any particular conclusion); ethical questions (e.g., the meaning of fairness and kindness); philosophical questions about animals (e.g.: Can animals talk/think/feel/wear clothes? Do we have special obligations to them?); and ontological questions about everything (such as: Does wearing diapers make a baby a baby? Can you be a grown-up and not be a parent?).

Left to play on their own, children will come upon philosophical issues, which you can then help them explore; this helps them discover that their thoughts can be powerful, their ideas worth listening to, and that playing with ideas and words can be fun.

*This lesson plan was contributed by Leah Boonin, an early childhood educator from Boulder, Colorado, who holds a master's degree in philosophy and who writes about the intersection of preschool and philosophy in her blog *Preschool Philosophy: Thoughts on How We Ought to Be with Kids*.

LESSON PLAN
THE THREE QUESTIONS BY JON MUTH

Topics: Ethics; questioning
Time: 30 minutes to an hour, depending on ages of the children

Objectives

- To express the questions students think are most important in life
- To consider how we can know the right thing to do in difficult situations
- To explore the meaning of being a good person

Description

Jon Muth takes Leo Tolstoy's short story, *The Three Questions*, as the starting point for an account of a young boy's search for an understanding of the moral dimension of his life. Nikolai asks his friends to help him to find the answers to what he considers the three most important questions:

- When is the best time to do things?
- Who is the most important one?
- What is the right thing to do?

Nikolai's search for the answers leads him to seek the help of someone he believes is wiser than himself, who helps him to conclude that the meaning of life rests in the relationships we form and the way we treat others.

The story raises some interesting philosophical questions about the nature of thinking about philosophy in general and ethics in particular. In Nikolai, we meet a sympathetic person whose search becomes, in a sense, our own, and through his experience we begin to imagine the ways in which we might search for the answers to the questions of our lives. In this story, the experiences and beliefs of not only the character Nikolai, but also of the author Jon Muth and his source Leo Tolstoy, underlie the questions the story explores.

This book is a good one to use in the first philosophy session, as it invites the children to consider which questions they consider most important. You might start by asking them, after you have read the story aloud, "What do you think are the most important questions?" Put their questions on the board and ask students what makes these questions important. If you have time, the students could then choose one question to discuss, and/or you can use the list of questions to choose topics for discussion over several weeks.

Questions Raised

- What do you think of Nikolai's questions? Do you think they are the most important questions in life?
- What do you think are the three most important questions?
- Do you believe that what we think about these questions changes over time and with experience? Should it?

- Are the most important questions in life the same for everyone?
- How do we know the right thing to do when we are faced with a difficult decision?
- What does it mean to do the right or wrong thing?
- What does it mean to be a good person?
- How do you know if you are a good person?
- Give an example of an action that is wrong. Why do you think the action is wrong?
- Give an example of an action that is right. Why do you think the action is right?
- Is there a right way to act in all or most situations, and can we come to know what it is?

Activity: What are the most important questions?

This activity works particularly well for third-grade students and up.

- Ask students to write down a list of the questions that they think are the most important.
- Have students break up into groups of three, and ask them to share their questions with one another.
- Have each group choose one or two questions to share with the whole class. Each group should be prepared to explain why they think these questions are important.
- Have the class come back together, in a circle if possible, with the groups sitting together. Go around the circle and have each group state the question(s) with which they came up and the reasons they are important. Then spend five to ten minutes (depending on class size and time) talking about each question.
- You can end this activity with a reflective question about one of the topics that inspired the most engaged discussion, and/or you can ask the students to choose one of the questions discussed to probe more deeply in the next philosophy session (if helpful, you can find a stimulus for that session that provokes further thinking about the question chosen).

LESSON PLAN
STUART LITTLE, "THE SCHOOLROOM," BY E. B. WHITE

Topics: Social and political philosophy; questioning and developing the community
Time: 40 minutes to an hour, depending on ages of the children

Objectives

- To reflect on what things are most important in life and consider what rules best protect the "important things"
- To develop a set of rules governing classroom discussions

Description

Stuart Little, who, despite being the son of human parents, looks exactly like and is the same size as a field mouse, has taken a one-day job as a substitute teacher in this chapter of the novel. He tells the class that he would like to be "Chairman of the World," noting that the chairman has to know what's important. He asks the students what they think is important and then suggests that the world needs some rules to run properly. The students suggest rules like "No stealing," "No being mean," and "Don't kill anything except rats."

Note: It is fun to read this chapter with students as a kind of play, in which students are assigned characters and recite that character's lines.

The chapter is also a good one for use early in the year. The reading helps students to think about what the rules of the classroom in general, and of philosophy sessions in particular, should be. The reading fosters consideration of what the important things are and what kind of structure we need to support people's ability to obtain and keep these important things. You can follow the reading and discussion with the activity described below.

Questions Raised

- What are the important things?
- In a society, what rules do we need so that people can have these important things?

Activity*

- Pass out index cards to the students and ask them to envision a classroom in which they are bound by only one rule. What rule would that be? Each student then writes down this one rule on the index card.
- Once students have formulated their rules, collect the index cards and then, after mixing them up, pass them back. Each student should now have a rule that he or she didn't write.
- In groups of two, students then work to come to an agreement about which of their two rules they would choose to be bound by. Depending upon class size, you can repeat this process with groups of four and have those groups come to an agreement on one rule out of the two each group had decided upon earlier.
- Once the full list of rules has been winnowed down, write the remaining rules on the board.
- The students then discuss and eventually vote on the five rules that they will choose to be bound by for the remainder of the class. (Remind the students that they will always have the option of reconsidering the rules they choose; if good reasons can be given for changing them and if the class agrees that the changes are warranted, then the rules can be changed.)

*This activity was created by David Shapiro, education director of the University of Washington Center for Philosophy for Children and a full-time faculty member in philosophy at Cascadia College in Bothell, Washington.

LESSON PLAN
BIG QUESTIONS AND HOW WE ANSWER THEM

Topics: Logic and reasoning; questioning; epistemology
Time: 45 minutes to an hour

Objectives

- Learning how to articulate reasons for believing something to be true
- Learning how to evaluate whether reasons given for a belief are good ones

Description

- This activity begins by grouping students into groups of three or four. Each student is handed a blank index card and each group is handed an index card on which is written one of the following questions:
  - Do you have to see, hear, or touch something in order to believe it exists?
  - Are you responsible for the environment?
  - Are mistakes good or bad?
  - Should you always agree with your friends?
  - What is more important, to be happy or to do the right thing?
  - Are numbers real?
  - Is life fair?

Each group is given a different question.

- Next, the students are asked to answer the question given to their group by writing their individual answers on their blank index cards, without talking to anyone else. At this point they do not need to give reasons for their answers.
- Then, tell the students to listen to all of the instructions before they do anything.
  - If they think that the answer they wrote down is completely true, stand up.
  - If they think that their answer is mostly true, sit on the desk.
  - If they think that their answer is only slightly true, stay seated.
  - If they no longer think that their answer is true, sit on the floor.*
- After they've done this, ask the students who are sitting on the floor why they decided that their answers were no longer true. Facilitate a brief discussion about this.
- Then ask all the students to sit back down with their groups. Give each group another blank index card. Each student will then share with his or her group their answers to the question the group was given, and the group should decide on an answer with which they all agree. Then they should choose one student to be the group's scribe, and that student will write the group's answer on the group's index card, along with two to three reasons the group comes up with to support their answer.
- The next part of the activity works best if the students can come together in a circle, with each group sitting together.
- Start by asking one of the groups to read their question and answer, along with the reasons for their answer.
- Then instruct the other students:
  - If they are completely convinced by the group's reasoning, stand up.
  - If they are mostly convinced by the group's reasoning, sit on the desk.
  - If they are only slightly convinced by the group's reasoning, stay seated.
  - If they are not at all convinced by the group's reasoning, sit on the floor (or if the students are sitting on the floor at this point, have them kneel).

- Ask the students who are not at all convinced why this is so. Then facilitate a brief discussion with the whole group about the question and the reasons for answering it in various ways.
- Repeat this process with each group, spending time having a discussion about each of the questions. If there's time and the students are engaged in these discussions, this can take two philosophy sessions.
- Time permitting, it's nice to end with a reflection question to which the students can respond in writing, in philosophy journals or just on paper, such as: Did your view or your reasons change as you discussed the question with your group and then the whole class? Why or why not?

Conclusion

Students often struggle to come up with good reasons for their views, and working with a group to explain to the class why they think a given answer is a good one helps them think more deeply about what they believe and why. The whole-class discussions about each question are deepened by having the group of students who have already thought about the question lead off the conversation. This activity is reliably engaging for students and allows every student to be involved.

*This part of the activity is based on an activity created by Matthew Lipman and Ann Gazzard for *Getting Our Thoughts Together: Instructional Manual to Accompany Elfie*, 2003.

LESSON PLAN
WHY? BY LINDSAY CAMP AND TONY ROSS

Topics: Epistemology; questioning
Time: 30 minutes to an hour, depending on ages of the children

Objectives

- To consider the consequences both of asking questions and failing to ask questions
- To examine what makes a question a good question

Description

Lily, in response to virtually anything that happens, asks the question, "Why?" Her dad tries to respond to her questioning, but sometimes, when "a bit tired or too busy," he says only, "It just does, Lily. It just does." One day, a giant spaceship lands and the aliens that emerge from the ship announce that their mission is to destroy the planet. Terrified, no one responds, except Lily, who asks, of course, "Why?" After a series of "why" questions, the aliens realize that they don't know why, and they leave.

Does asking questions have the potential to make a difference in the world? How do we know when to ask a question and what makes a question a good question?

Discussions of this story often lead students to consider the nature of questioning, and to examine how and why learning to question can help us understand and perhaps even change the world.

Questions Raised

- Why ask why?
- What is the purpose of a question?
- Why do we ask questions? What makes a question a good one?
- Is curiosity a good thing?
- Why do you think Lily's father sometimes became annoyed with Lily when she asked "Why?"
- Could a question really save the world? Could it destroy it?
- Can asking "why?" be dangerous? Can failing to ask "why?" be dangerous?

LESSON PLAN
KEEP THE QUESTION GOING*

Topics: Logic and reasoning; questioning; epistemology
Time: 30 minutes to an hour, depending on ages of the children

Objectives

- To learn how to ask good questions
- To listen and respond to what other students say
- To consider the importance of questioning in philosophy

Description

This game involves students generating questions collaboratively. The exercise runs easily for about ten minutes and can go for a half hour or more with discussion. It is often a good exercise to use early in the year as it helps students listen to each other and gets them thinking about what makes a question a good one.

The activity begins as a simple "energizer"-type exercise, meant to get students listening to each other while keeping in mind the importance of questions in philosophical inquiry. It requires students to listen to each other and respond in a manner that constructs a coherent sentence — in this case, a question.

- Make sure that students are arranged in such a way that they can more or less see each other. A circle is ideal but, even if students are sitting in rows, it's helpful if they can all turn so that they can keep an eye on their classmates as the exercise proceeds.
- The first student offers a word that will serve as the start of a question, and each student around the room then offers a word to continue the formation of a question. The goal of the exercise is for students to see how long they can keep a question going, one word after another, each word added by a subsequent student.

- You can stipulate certain kinds of questions for each round: "factual questions," "historical questions," "philosophical questions," "scientific questions," or any category agreed beforehand with students.
- When a student thinks that the question has ended, he or she claps his or her hands, indicating that a new question is to begin. So, for instance, suppose the first student begins with the word, *How*, the next says *does*, the next *life*, the next *begin*. At this point, that last student might clap hands to indicate the question is finished. Or, if not, the following student could clap his or her hands to indicate the question is finished, or can choose to keep the question going, perhaps by adding the word *on*, to which a subsequent student might say *Earth*, and then clap.
- One guideline to communicate to students is that it's not permitted to just add the word *and* to the end of what the previous student has said. Students should be discouraged from creating never-ending chains such as "How did life begin on Earth and Mars and Pluto and . . .?"
- It's also important to emphasize that students should listen to each other and refrain from shouting out suggestions to their fellow students.

For kindergarten students, this activity can work well in smaller groups. Over time, a kindergarten class of twenty or twenty-five students will be able to formulate questions as a bigger group. With first- or second-grade students, after a few rounds of the activity, as the students become more adept at formulating clear questions, you might suggest that the next round aim at formulating some interesting and provocative questions that the class might like to explore together. At this point, the exercise becomes less about the length of the question and more about the quality of the question.

At the conclusion of the activity, lead a reflective discussion about it. Ask the students what questions the game raises for them, and have them choose which of their questions to discuss.

You might ask the students what they think makes a given question more interesting or more "philosophical" than another question. You might also say, for example: "Can we make any of these questions better by adding words, taking them away or changing them?"

*This game was created by David Shapiro, education director of the University of Washington Center for Philosophy for Children and a full-time faculty member in philosophy at Cascadia College in Bothell, Washington.

LESSON PLAN
WHAT'S YOUR REASON?*

Topics: Logic and reasoning; epistemology
Time: 40 minutes to an hour, depending on ages of the children

Objectives

- To learn how to articulate the reasons students have for their views
- To evaluate what constitutes good reasons for believing something

Description

This game involves students writing down claims supported by reasons and then guessing each other's claims after listening only to the reasons.

- Hand out four note cards (or note-card-sized pieces of paper) to each student. Ask them to write down, on each of the four cards, one claim they believe in, for a total of four. At least one of these should be a normative claim (involving something people should or should not do), and at least one of them should be a false claim. Asking students to include a claim that's false reinforces the idea that we also have reasons for believing things that something is not true.
- Once they've written down the claims, give them ten to fifteen minutes to write down, on the other side of the paper, three reasons they have for believing the claims to be true—or false as the case may be. (Writing down reasons for the false claim can be quite challenging for some students, who say things like, "How can I have reasons for it if it's not true?" This can lead to some interesting discussions about how we can—or if we can—have knowledge that something is false.) They can appeal to whatever outside sources of information they want to during this time.
- Now divide the students into two teams.
- After the teams have formed, collect their index cards, making sure to keep the cards from both teams separate.
- The exercise now proceeds sort of like a game of charades. The goal is for students to be able to guess what the claim is from the reason(s) cited for believing it.
- Starting with Team One, pick the first student in line or ask the entire team to collaborate. Start by reading one of the three reasons from one of the cards written by the other team.
- If the team or student can guess the claim from the first reason, that team gets three points. From the first and second reasons, two points, from all three reasons, one point.
- Sometimes disagreements arise about whether a reason offered for a claim is a good one. This is great—do encourage discussion about this!

*This game was created by David Shapiro, Education Director of the University of Washington Center for Philosophy for Children and a full-time faculty member in Philosophy at Cascadia College in Bothell, Washington.

LESSON PLAN
GOOD NEWS, BAD NEWS*

Topic: Logic and reasoning
Time: 40 minutes to an hour, depending on ages of the children

Objectives

- To start to learn how to follow a chain of consequences
- To consider how one event or idea logically follows from another
- To examine the possibility of connections between seemingly unrelated events

Description

To begin the exercise, tell the students this is an exercise to get them thinking about two sides of an issue by thinking about possible consequences—both good and bad. As an example, consider that old joke: A guy goes to the doctor for some tests. He comes back a week later and the doctor says, "Well, I have some good news and some bad news. The good news is, the tests came back and we determined that you only have 48 hours to live." The guy says, "That's the good news? What's the bad news?" The doctor says, "Well, we tried to get in touch with you all day yesterday."
After the groans that this inevitably solicits, another more tasteful example might be in order, something like, "The good news is, our hometown baseball team won yesterday. The bad news is, their star player was injured." With this basic illustration on the table, the class will be ready to move into the exercise.

- Pass out sheets of paper on which are preprinted alternating lines of "The good news is: _____," and "The bad news is: _____." The paper is filled; there are six or seven of each, alternating one after another. (You can simply have students write the phrases before each sentence on a piece of paper during the exercise, but experience has proven that the exercise works better when preprinted sheets are used.)
- Explain to students they will simply follow the line of consequences where they lead and that they might enjoy being surprised by the result. But stress the serious point behind the exercise—predicting consequences is an important preliminary to making any judgment.
- Students begin by writing ONE piece of good news at the top of their papers, as well as their names. Emphasize that students should complete only the first piece of good news! Often a student will already be in the process of filling out the entire sheet. Reiterate that students have been asked to merely fill out the first piece of good news; go no further!
- Tell the students that no names of anyone in the class can be mentioned, and that derogatory comments are not permitted.
- After all the students have completed writing their first piece of good news, they each hand their papers to the person next to them; that person reads the good news and writes a piece of bad news that follows from it. Again, emphasize, just the bad news! The second student then folds down his or her paper so only the last piece of bad news is visible. He or she then hands that paper to another student who reads the visible piece of bad news, writes an associated good news, then folds down the paper so only the good news just written is visible, and then hands it to another student, and so on and on until the paper is completely filled.
- Arrange the activity so students don't pass their papers to the same person every time. As each paper is completed—it ends with a piece of bad news—have students return it to a pile in the front of the room. When all the papers are turned in, hand each one back to the original writer of good news. Students read the papers and are asked to notice especially the first and last lines and the degree to which they could have predicted that last line from the first.

• Ask students to share their papers and express whether they think that all of the good and bad news items followed from the previous news. Why or why not?

*This game was created by David Shapiro, education director of the University of Washington Center for Philosophy for Children and a full-time faculty member in philosophy at Cascadia College in Bothell, Washington.

LESSON PLAN
HORTON HEARS A WHO BY DR. SEUSS

Topic: Epistemology
Time: 30 minutes to an hour, depending on ages of the children

Objectives

• To consider how we know what we think we know
• To examine under what circumstances we should believe what some people tell us

Description

Horton the Elephant, while splashing "in the cool of the pool," hears a small noise, like a very small yelp, but sees nothing but a "small speck of dust blowing past through the air." Horton speculates that a very small creature must be on top of the dust speck and be feeling afraid that the dust will blow into the pool. Concerned, "because a person's a person, no matter how small," Horton gently lifts the speck with his trunk, places it on a clover, and tries to protect it.

The other animals in the jungle make fun of Horton, conjecturing that he is "out of his head." Horton then hears the small voice on the clover confide that he is the Mayor of a town called Who-ville, and that Horton has saved all the Whos and their buildings. As the other animals chase him and ultimately threaten to imprison Horton and boil the dust speck, all the small Whos make enough noise to finally be heard by the other animals, who then recognize that there are indeed very small persons in the clover.

Questions Raised

• Did Horton know there was a person on the dust speck when he heard the sound?
• How did he know it?
• Why do you think the other animals didn't believe him?
• Would you have believed Horton?
• When should we believe what we see or hear?
• Do you have to see, hear, or touch something yourself in order to believe it's there?
• Can you think of something you know exists even though you can't see, hear, or touch it?
• What does it mean to say, "a person's a person, no matter how small?"

LESSON PLAN
HARRY POTTER AND THE SORCERER'S STONE, "THE MIRROR OF ERISED," BY J. K. ROWLING

Topic: Epistemology
Time: 40 minutes to an hour, depending on ages of the children

Objectives

- To examine the relationship between the way the world appears to us and our knowledge of the world
- To consider whether images and dreams can give us knowledge

Description

Most children are familiar with the *Harry Potter* stories. In this chapter of the first *Harry Potter* novel, Harry discovers the "Mirror of Erised," a mystical mirror that shows people the "deepest and most desperate desires" of their hearts.

When Harry looks into the mirror, he sees images of himself surrounded by a loving family, and he becomes entranced by the images he sees, wanting to return to the mirror again and again to stare into it. The school's headmaster, Dumbledore, finally tells him he is moving the mirror to a different place and asks him not to search for it, warning Harry, "The mirror will give us neither knowledge nor truth," and "it does not do to dwell on dreams and forget to live."

Questions Raised

- What do you think you would see looking into this mirror?
- Would the mirror be able to tell you something you don't already know?
- Can the mirror really tell you the deepest desire of your heart? If you don't already know what it is, can it really be your deepest desire?
- What does Dumbledore mean when he tells Harry that the mirror cannot give him knowledge or truth?
- Must knowledge about the world be knowledge about the way the world really is (and not just how it appears to us)?
- Can images like those in the mirror give us knowledge?
- Could you develop some self-understanding through looking at what you see in the mirror that you wouldn't otherwise have?

LESSON PLAN
SILENT DISCUSSION: *THE HOLE* BY ØYVIND TORSETER

Topic: Metaphysics
Time: 50 minutes to an hour, or can be broken up into two 40-minute segments, to conduct the activity and then debrief

Objectives

- To explore the puzzling identity of holes
- To consider what makes a discussion a good discussion

Description

In this story, a man is moving into a new home, and he notices a hole in the apartment. The hole seems to move around, appearing in a wall, on the floor, in a door, etc.

The man makes a phone call, saying, "I've found a hole . . . in my apartment . . . it keeps moving . . . take it with me . . . to you?" Attempting to capture the hole in a box, he heads out the door with the box and takes it to a lab for tests.

The book has a die-cut hole that runs through the entire book, and in every page the hole is part of the story.

This story is one that can be effectively discussed through a "silent discussion" activity.

Questions Raised

- Are holes part of the world?
- Are holes physical objects? What are they made of?
- If holes are made of nothing, how do we perceive them?
- What makes something a hole? Does it have a shape?
- Do holes really exist?
- If you fill a hole, is it no longer a hole?

Activity

This activity takes place in silence, with all communication done in writing. It can be used for many of the books and other lesson plans in this book, with all ages.

Write three or four questions on the board related to the prompt, before breaking the students up into groups of three. Provide each group with a white poster board and colored markers or pens. Explain to the students that this is a silent discussion and there will be time to speak in both the small groups and the large group later. Let them know that once you have finished reading the story, the rest of the activity will take place in silence, and that the poster board will be used to communicate their thoughts and ideas to one another. The questions on the board are starting prompts.

After the story is read aloud, the students can respond to the questions and/or come up with new questions, using the poster boards. The written conversation can stray to wherever the students take it. If someone in the group writes a question, another member of the group can address the question by writing on the poster board. Students can draw lines connecting a comment to a particular question. More than one student can write on the poster board at the same time.

Afterward, still in silence and at your prompting, the students can walk around the room and read the other poster boards, adding written comments to the other boards as they see fit. After this part of the activity, they will have the opportunity to debrief verbally with their original small group.

Step One: After giving the instructions, pass out a poster board to each group of three students and a marker or pen to each student. Then read the story aloud to the students. The students, working in their groups of three, can then comment on the questions to each other and/or ask new questions by writing on the poster board, and proceed to have a written and silent conversation about the story and the questions it raises. This part of the activity takes fifteen to twenty minutes.

Step Two: Still working in silence, the students leave their groups and walk around reading the other poster boards. Students bring their markers or pens with them and can write comments or further questions for thought on other poster boards. This part of the activity takes ten minutes or so.

Step Three: Silence is broken. The groups rejoin back at their own poster boards and can look at any comments written by others. Now they can have a free verbal conversation about the questions, their own comments, what they read on other poster boards, the comments their fellow-students wrote on their poster boards, and the activity itself. This part of the activity takes ten minutes or so.

Step Four: Class discussion—debrief the process with the large group.

- What did you learn from doing this activity?
- How comfortable were you staying silent?
- What makes a discussion a good one? Give two characteristics of a good discussion and two characteristics of a poor one.
- How does this activity contribute to or detract from having a good discussion?
- What ideas or thoughts written on the poster boards particularly struck you?
- What questions were particularly interesting to explore?

You can also spend some time exploring these substantive topics with the group.

LESSON PLAN
LET'S DO NOTHING BY TONY FUCILE

Topic: Metaphysics
Time: 30 minutes to an hour, depending on ages of the children

Objectives

- To examine the nature of nothing
- To explore what it means to "do nothing," and whether "nothing" exists

Description

Frankie and Sal, after concluding that they have "done it all," try to think of what's left to do. Then a brilliant idea emerges. Frankie exclaims, "Let's do nothing!" All throughout the day, Frankie and Sal try to do nothing. The trouble is that doing nothing is not easy. If you blink, you're not doing nothing. If you open your eyes, you're not doing nothing, but if you close them, you're not doing nothing. Finally, the boys conclude, "There is no way to do nothing."

Young children love to talk about the nature of nothing. The puzzle of defining "nothing," and trying to make sense of what we mean when we use the term "nothing" can help students to begin to grasp the idea of a paradox. Is nothing something? If so, how can it be nothing?

Questions Raised

- What do we mean when we say we are doing nothing?
- Is there a difference between doing nothing and not doing something?
- What would it mean to do nothing?
- Is it impossible to do nothing if you're alive?
- What exactly is nothing?
- Can "nothing" exist?

LESSON PLAN
THE BIG ORANGE SPLOT BY DANIEL MANUS PINKWATER

Topics: Ethics; social and political philosophy; metaphysics
Time: 30 minutes to an hour, depending on ages of the children

Objectives

- To consider the relationship between individual rights and obligations to the community
- To examine when conformity is acceptable and when it is not
- To explore the ways in which our homes reflect our identities

Description

Mr. Plumbean lives on a street where the houses are all the same, painted red with olive-colored roofs and windows with green trim. He and his neighbors all like this, characterizing their street as a "neat street." One day, a seagull drops a can of bright orange paint on Mr. Plumbean's house, leaving a big orange splotch on the house. Everyone on the street sympathizes with Mr. Plumbean, who will have to paint his house again, and that's what Mr. Plumbean plans to do.

But, instead, Mr. Plumbean looks at the house for a long time. Finally, in response to his neighbors' urging, Mr. Plumbean takes out some paint and paints his house. But instead of using the house's original colors, he paints it a rainbow of colors. Over the next couple of days, he adds to his house a clock tower, palm trees, a hammock, and an alligator.

Horrified, one by one the neighbors stop in to see Mr. Plumbean and talk with him about their dissatisfaction with what he's done to his home, reminding him that all the houses have to be the same for their street to continue to be a "neat street." But the neighbors, after visiting Mr. Plumbean, sitting under the palm trees, drinking lemonade, and talking, repaint their own houses to "fit their dreams."

The story inspires conversations about conformity and independence and our obligations to our communities. It is interesting to consider whether Mr. Plumbean was right to paint his house in a way different from his neighbors, when part of the community agreement was that they would keep their houses looking the same. Does Mr. Plumbean have the right to have his house look the way he wants it to look, even if it offends his neighbors? You can explore with students whether and how we should balance our individual desires with our obligations to our communities.

Questions Raised

- Why did Mr. Plumbean paint his house the way he did?
- Was he right to paint his house in a way different from his neighbors' homes, when part of the community agreement was that they would keep their houses looking the same?
- Did Mr. Plumbean have the right to paint his house however he liked?
- Would Mr. Plumbean be justified in his choice to paint his house in different colors if the neighbors had continued to want all the houses to look the same?
- What if he painted words expressing his hate for an ethnic group? Would that be okay? At what point does his right to make an independent choice give way to his obligations to his neighbors?
- Do you think Mr. Plumbean dreamed of a house that looked like the way he painted it or do you think he just dreamt of an extremely colorful house?
- Do you think that Mr. Plumbean's house truly looks like his dreams? Or did he just interpret his dreams and paint his house the way he thought it would have looked like in his dreams? Is there a difference? If so, what is it?
- Is there something that you identify with as strongly as Mr. Plumbean identifies with his house?
- Why do you think Mr. Plumbean felt so strongly about his house (after he painted it)?
- What made Mr. Plumbean's decision to paint his house to "fit his dreams" so compelling to his neighbors that after spending time with him they all changed their minds about how their street should appear?

LESSON PLAN
AN ANGEL FOR SOLOMON SINGER BY CYNTHIA RYLANT

Topics: Ethics; metaphysics
Time: 30 minutes to an hour, depending on ages of the children

Objectives

- To consider what makes something a home
- To examine the experience of homesickness
- To explore the relationship between memory and home
- To reflect about the relationship between poverty and home

Description

Solomon lives in a men's hotel in New York City, far from his boyhood home in Indiana. He is unhappy in New York City and doesn't feel at home there. He misses the landscape and people of Indiana. Then he discovers the Westway Café, "where all your dreams come true." The server—known as Angel—helps him see how he might find some of the beauty of Indiana right in the middle of the city. Solomon begins to feel connected to the city, learns a new way to see his surroundings, and to understand the meaning of home.

   The story raises questions about the nature of home and the experience of homelessness, and whether our feelings about what makes something (or someplace) a home can change over time. You can also ask students to draw a picture of a home after reading the story, and to share their drawings and describe what makes the subject of the drawing a home.

Questions Raised

- What is a home?
- Is a home defined more by location or by the people with whom we share a place?
- Is "home" place, or is it something else?
- Could you make a home out of a hotel room? If not, why not?
- What changes something from a house (or apartment) to a home?
- Can a home change? When we move, is our "home" still where we were born or raised or previously lived, or can it shift to our new location?
- Can a person have multiple homes?
- Is Solomon homesick?
- What does it mean to be "homesick?"
- Why do people get "homesick"?
- Are our memories of a place or a time sometimes not fully accurate?
- Can memories make a place a home?
- Do we idealize the past? Why would we do that?

LESSON PLAN
A SHELTER IN OUR CAR BY MONICA GUNNING

Topics: Ethics; social and political philosophy
Time: 30 minutes to an hour, depending on ages of the children

Objectives

- To examine the experience of homelessness
- To consider the relationship between a shelter and a home
- To consider the effects of poverty and social class
- To reflect about the meaning of love

Description

In *A Shelter in Our Car*, Monica Gunning depicts the experiences of eight-year-old Zettie and her mother, who have come to the United States after Zettie's father's death. They are temporarily homeless, due to the struggle Zettie's mother has been having to find reliable work. After they have spent some time in a shelter, which, Zettie comments, was noisy and crowded, Zettie's mother decides that it's better to use their car as a shelter.

The story begins with Zettie waking up in the car to sirens and flashing police lights. Zettie and her mother use the park's restroom to wash up in cold water in the morning, and they search for food and try to stay away from the police. Zettie endures being bullied at school by children who call her "Junk Car Zettie," and she thinks of her previous life in Jamaica with longing. Throughout the story, though, Zettie's relationship with her mother anchors her. Her mother is kind and affectionate, and they are doing their best to get through this difficult experience with love and dignity.

In the end, Zettie's mother finds work and is hopeful that they will be able to rent an apartment. Zettie thinks to herself, "With or without an apartment, I've got Mama and she's got me."

The story raises issues about homelessness and poverty, the meaning of home, and whether love can shelter us from social injustice.

Questions Raised

- Why do Zettie and her mother live in their car?
- Can a car be a home?
- Do people need shelter? Why?
- What are the most important things people need in life?
- What does it mean to be homeless?
- Why does Zettie want her mother to drop her off at the corner behind the school instead of in front of the school?
- Why do some of Zettie's classmates call her "Junk Car Zettie?"
- Does Zettie feel safe? What do we need in order to feel safe?
- Can love be a kind of shelter?
- What would a perfect home look like? Do perfect homes exist?

LESSON PLAN
FOUR FEET, TWO SANDALS BY KAREN LYNN WILLIAMS AND KHADRA MOHAMMED

Topics: Ethics; social and political philosophy
Time: 30 minutes to an hour, depending on ages of the children

Objectives

- To consider the experience of being a refugee and the moral obligations owed to refugees

- To examine whether refugees have the right to enter countries of which they are not citizens
- To explore the nature of friendship
- To address the way in which gender impacts experience

Description

Four Feet, Two Sandals tells the story of two girls, Lina and Feroza, and their families, who are living in a refugee camp in Pakistan, having fled the war in Afghanistan. The girls become friends when each finds one sandal from a matching pair. They decide to share the sandals, taking turns wearing them. The story describes the girls' lives in the camp, with long lines for water and the stressful wait for new homes.

Eventually, Lina's family receives permission to emigrate to the United States, and Feroza gives the sandals to Lina, saying, "You cannot go barefoot to America." When she is leaving, Lina gives the shoes back to Feroza, as Lina's mother has saved money to buy her shoes. Feroza then gives Lina one sandal to keep, noting that "it is good to remember."

Questions Raised

- Why do people become refugees? Are countries that can provide safety obligated to allow in people escaping their homelands?
- Do countries have different obligations to their citizens than to other people around the world?
- Why do the girls decide to share the shoes?
- What makes Lina and Feroza friends?
- Can friendship help people to feel more at home when they have fled their homes? If so, how?
- Why are only boys in school in the refugee camp?
- Are Lina's and Feroza's experiences in the camp different than they would be if they were boys?
- Why does Feroza give Lina one shoe at the end of the story? Did Lina do the right thing in accepting the shoe?

LESSON PLAN
AMAZING GRACE BY MARY HOFFMAN

Topics: Ethics; social and political philosophy
Time: 30 minutes to an hour, depending on ages of the children

Objectives

- To consider the effects of racism on identity
- To explore gender stereotyping and its consequences
- To examine what it means to be yourself

Description

Mary Hoffman's 1991 picture book *Amazing Grace* tells the story of Grace, who loves stories and especially loves acting them out. Filled with imagination and dramatic flair, Grace decides that she will play the part of Peter Pan when her teacher tells the class that they are going to perform the play.

One student tells her, "You can't be Peter—that's a boy's name." And then another student informs her, "You can't be Peter Pan. He isn't black." But Grace keeps her hand up to indicate that she wants to play this role.

When Grace goes home and tells her mother and grandmother what happened at school, they tell her that she can be Peter Pan if she wants to do so. "You can be anything you want, Grace, if you put your mind to it," her grandmother says.

Soon after, Grace's grandmother takes her to the ballet to see an African American ballerina play Juliet in *Romeo and Juliet*. After the ballet, Grace dances around her room, telling herself, "I can be anything I want."

After the class meets for auditions, everyone in the class votes for Grace to be Peter Pan. The play is a great success and Grace is an "amazing Peter Pan."

This story inspires discussions about race, gender, role models, the limits to our ambitions, and the importance of imagination.

Questions Raised

- Why do other students tell Grace she can't be Peter Pan because she's black and or a girl?
- Is Grace's grandmother right that Grace can be anything she wants to be?
- Does it help us to hear that we can be anything we want to be?
- If the class hadn't voted that Grace should play Peter Pan, what consequences would that have had for Grace?
- Does being the best mean we always get chosen?
- What does it mean to be "the best?"
- Why did seeing the ballerina make Grace more confident that she could be Peter Pan?
- Can we imagine ourselves doing things that we never see anyone like us doing?
- What is the relationship between how we look and who we are?

LESSON PLAN
PAPERBAG PRINCESS BY ROBERT MUNSCH

Topics: Ethics; social and political philosophy
Time: 30 minutes to an hour, depending on ages of the children

Objectives

- To consider the effects of gender on identity
- To examine gender stereotypes and their consequences
- To reflect about what it means to be yourself

Description

Elizabeth is described as a "beautiful princess," who lives in a castle and wears "expensive princess clothes," and is set to marry Ronald, a prince. "Unfortunately," the story tells us, "a dragon smashed her castle, burned all her clothes with his fiery breath, and carried off Prince Ronald." Elizabeth decides to chase the dragon and save Ronald. As all her clothes have been burnt, she puts on the only thing she can find to wear, a paper bag.

Finding the dragon, Elizabeth outwits him and saves the prince. When Prince Ronald sees her, he doesn't thank her but instead comments on what a mess she looks like and tells her, "Come back when you are dressed like a real princess."

Elizabeth tells him, "Your clothes are really pretty and your hair is very neat. You look like a real prince, but you are a bum."

The story relates that the two did not get married after all.

The book is an effective catalyst for exploring issues around social roles, including gender and class, status and appearance, as well as questions about bravery, gratitude, and moral obligations to others.

Questions Raised

- Why does the story tell us that Elizabeth wore "expensive princess clothes?"
- Does being a princess depend on wearing certain clothes or looking a certain way?
- Why does Elizabeth chase the dragon?
- Is Elizabeth brave?
- How does Elizabeth save Ronald?
- Why doesn't Ronald thank Elizabeth? Should he?
- Does Ronald expect certain things of Elizabeth because she is a princess? Because she is female?
- What does Elizabeth mean when she tells Ronald he is a bum?
- Does Ronald act like a prince? Does Elizabeth act like a princess?
- Does Elizabeth "live happily ever after" without marrying Ronald?

LESSON PLAN
THE OTHER SIDE BY JACQUELINE WOODSON

Topics: Ethics; social and political philosophy; race and racism
Time: 40 minutes to an hour, depending on ages of the children

Objectives

- To consider some of the ways in which racism manifests itself
- To examine how divisions between people get started and are maintained
- To reflect about how small acts of resistance to oppression can make a difference
- To explore the nature of friendship

Description

The Other Side begins as follows: "That summer the fence that stretched through our town seemed bigger." The story is narrated by Clover, who lives in a house on the side of the fence that separates the black townspeople from the whites in the town. Clover's mother tells her not to climb over the fence, because it isn't safe.

That summer Annie, a white girl Clover's age, begins sitting on the fence each day, by herself. When Clover and her friends are jumping rope, Annie asks if she can join, but one of Clover's friends, Sandra, says she can't. Clover recalls, "That summer everyone and everything on the other side of the fence seemed far away. When I asked my mama why, she said, 'Because that's the way things have always been.'"

Clover finds herself always looking for Annie sitting on the fence. One day she comes close to the fence and Annie asks her name, and they begin talking. Annie notes that the fence was made for sitting on. Clover responds that her mother had told her not to go on the other side, and Annie says that her mother says the same thing, but that she hadn't said anything about sitting on it, and the two girls begin sitting together on the fence. Clover's mother observes this but doesn't tell Clover to stop sitting there, and one morning she notes, "I see you made a new friend." Eventually Annie and Clover ask Clover's friends if they can join them jumping rope, and Sandra replies, "I don't care." So Annie and Clover join the group of young black girls playing. When tired, they all sit on the fence together.

The book ends with Annie saying, "Someday somebody's going to come along and knock this old fence down," and Clover responding, "Yeah, someday."

The story's text and illustrations are ideal for raising questions about race and racial identity and about the ways in which small acts can lead to social change.

Questions Raised

- Why did the fence stretch through the town?
- Why wasn't it safe for Clover to climb over to the other side of the fence?
- Why was it safe for Annie to climb over to Clover's side of the fence?
- Why did Annie want to sit on the fence?
- Were Clover and Annie friends?
- Does race define a person? Is it an important part of our identity?
- Why did Sandra say no when Annie wanted to join the jump rope game, but agree to let Annie join them later that summer when she was with Clover?
- What does the fence represent?
- Are there many kinds of fences?

LESSON PLAN
FREEDOM SUMMER BY DEBORAH WILES

Topics: Ethics; social and political philosophy; race and racism
Time: 40 minutes to an hour, depending on ages of the children

Objectives

- To examine the ways in which race affects our experiences and perspectives
- To consider the nature of racism and its moral and political implications
- To explore the relationship between political oppression and freedom
- To investigate the way in which social class can affect friendship and other personal relationships

Description

This picture book tells the story of a friendship between two boys in the early 1960s in Mississippi: Joe, who is white, and John Henry, who is African American. John Henry's mother works for Joe's family. The boys love to swim and they spend time in the creek because the town pool is closed to John Henry. When the boys want ice pops, Joe goes into the store to buy them, because John Henry is not allowed into the store.

After the passing of the Civil Rights Act of 1964, the town pool is required to be open to everyone, but when the boys arrive at the pool, the pool is being emptied and filled with asphalt by a group of African American workers, including John Henry's older brother. Shocked, the two boys watch until the men finish.

When the workers have left, John Henry says, "White folks don't want colored folks in their pool." Joe says, "I didn't want to swim in this old pool anyway." "I did," John Henry responds. "I wanted to swim in this pool. I want to do everything you can do." Joe doesn't know what to say. He thinks to himself, "I want to go to the Dairy Dip with John Henry, sit down and share root beer floats. . . . I want to see this town with John Henry's eyes." At the end of the story, the boys decide to walk together into the store to buy ice pops.

Questions Raised

- Why is the book called *Freedom Summer*? Who is free in the story? Who is not?
- Are Joe and John Henry friends?
- Are Joe and Henry equal?
- Why does John Henry eat in the kitchen at Joe's house while Joe and his family eat in the dining room?
- Why isn't John Henry allowed in the store? Who decides?
- Who controls the town pool? Why is it filled with asphalt after the law requires it to be open to everyone?
- Why is it the African American workers who are filling the pool with asphalt when it is the whites who are making this happen?
- Do Joe and John Henry experience the filling of the pool in the same way?
- Why don't "white folks want colored folks in their pool?" Why is the pool considered the white folks' pool?
- Do people have a right to swim in the town pool?
- What does Joe mean when he thinks that he "wants to see the town with John Henry's eyes?" Is this possible?

• When the boys walk into the store at the end of the story, who is taking the greater risk? Why?

LESSON PLAN
BIRD BY ZETTA ELLIOTT

Topics: Ethics; social and political philosophy; philosophy of art; race and racism
Time: 40 minutes to an hour, depending on ages of the children

Objectives

• To examine the ways in which race affects our experiences and perspectives
• To consider the nature of racism and its moral and political implications
• To explore the relationship between political oppression and freedom
• To reflect about the connection between art and identity

Description

Mehkai, known as Bird, loves to draw and works hard at improving his skills. He draws the things he sees, but most of all he likes to draw birds. His older brother Marcus, a graffiti artist, was the one who taught him to draw. Bird's grandfather doesn't see Marcus' graffiti as art, noting that "real art belong[s] in a museum." Bird admires Marcus' talent, though. He describes going to the park with Marcus and listening to Marcus talk about the sky. Marcus describes a place high above the clouds where "everything is calm and still." He tells Bird that he "sure can't find no peace in the street."

However, Marcus has stopped drawing and stopped going to school. Bird doesn't understand what is happening, but eventually Marcus' drug addiction leads him to steal from the family and they lock him out of the house.

Bird asks his grandfather what it would take to fix Marcus, and his grandfather tells him that some broken things can't be fixed. Marcus dies, and a couple of months later Bird's grandfather also dies. Bird imagines them up above the clouds, where "everything is calm and still," and Bird tells us that he drew a picture of the sun going down, "so I won't forget."

Drawing helps Bird to express his emotions and to make sense of the world for himself. Marcus had stopped making art and instead turned to drugs to deal with the lack of peace and opportunity he experienced. The story inspires thinking about the choices people make in difficult circumstances and the possibility of barriers to alternative choices. The story also raises questions about the way that art can help us understand and survive difficult situations.

Questions Raised

• Is Bird's grandfather correct when he says that Marcus' graffiti is not art? Is art only found in museums?

- Who decides what is art?
- Do the emotions Bird feels when he looks at his brother's art play a role in the decision about whether Bird's brother's graffiti is art?
- How does Bird's art reflect the reality of his situation?
- How do you think Bird's art makes him feel about his family situation?
- Can art change reality?
- Why can't Marcus find "peace in the street?"
- How did Marcus' addiction affect his family? Could the family have done anything to save Marcus?
- What obstacles could have prevented Marcus from making different choices?
- What role does race play in this story?
- Does society have an obligation to those whose ability to make choices is impeded by obstacles?

LESSON PLAN
THE CONDUCTOR BY LAETITIA DEVERNAY*

Topic: Philosophy of art
Time: 30 minutes to an hour, depending on ages of the children

Objectives

- To explore the nature of listening
- To examine what counts as music
- To consider the relationship between silence and sound

Description

This is a beautiful book of illustrations, without words, that begins with a conductor approaching a set of big bulbous trees. He climbs atop one tree and prepares his musicians—then leaves. Slowly, his orchestra begins as he directs a fluttering of leaves to leap from the tree. Momentum builds as the pages turn and you see and hear with your eyes a beautiful symphony of movement as the leaves engage in new patterns, new arrangements, and new relationships. At one point, all of the trees are almost completely naked, the leaves dancing everywhere. The conductor summons the leaves back to their places as the song nears the end. He takes a bow, descends his tree, and plants a new tree upon leaving his natural stage.

The story inspires thinking about whether music can be silent, whether we need our ears to hear, and what listening involves.

Questions Raised

- Can we listen with our eyes?
- Is it possible to listen without using our ears?
- What does it mean to listen?

- Does silence enhance our ability to listen?
- Can music be silent?

*This lesson plan was contributed by Gobe Hirata, who created it when she was an undergraduate at the University of Washington, working with the UW Center for Philosophy for Children, and who is now one of the Center's volunteer philosophy teachers along with being a professional student of philosophy and life.

LESSON PLAN
WHAT IS MUSIC? SILENCE AND SOUND

Topic: Philosophy of art
Time: 45 minutes to an hour, depending on ages of the children

Objectives

- To encourage children to consider what makes something music
- To examine the relationship between silence and listening

Description

This activity is a nice follow-up to the session on Laetitia Devernay's *The Conductor*.

Activity

Organize a live performance of composer John Cage's piece *4'33"* in the school music room (or watch with your students one of the many online videos of it). Don't explain anything about the work to the students before the performance. Cage's work, which was composed for any instrument and consists of the musician playing nothing for four minutes and thirty-three seconds, has three movements—the first is thirty seconds, the second two minutes and twenty-three seconds, and the third is one minute and forty seconds. The performer uses a stopwatch to time the movements.

Ask the students to be perfectly silent during the performance and to reflect about what's going on. Pretty quickly, the students realize that the point is that the musician doesn't play anything. Once the performance ends, broach some of the following questions:

- What is music?
- Is there some quality that anything considered music must have?
- Can any sound count as music?
- Does all music express emotion?
- Is whatever music expresses in the music itself? In the composer? In us, the listeners?
- What makes music pleasurable?
- Why do we listen to sad music?

You can tell the students that the audience that witnessed the first performance of this piece in Woodstock, New York, in 1952, whispered, walked out, and burst into an infuriated uproar at the end.

After that premiere, John Cage said,

> They missed the point. There's no such thing as silence. What they thought was silence, because they didn't know how to listen, was full of accidental sounds. You could hear the wind stirring outside during the first movement. During the second, raindrops began pattering the roof, and during the third the people themselves made all kinds of interesting sounds as they talked or walked out.

John Cage considered this piece to be a "listening experience." Ask the students what they heard during the performance. Usually students point out all kinds of sounds that they heard in the room, to which they would not otherwise have paid attention.

Does the piece count as music? Students tend to be pretty divided in their views about that question.

LESSON PLAN
THE ART LESSON BY TOMIE DE PAOLA*

Topics: Philosophy of art; ethics
Time: 30 minutes to an hour, depending on ages of the children

Objectives

- To encourage children to consider what makes something art
- To examine the nature of creativity
- To explore issues of fairness in school

Description

Tommy, an aspiring artist, is about to have his first art lesson in kindergarten. Tommy practices art all the time but has learned from his sister that true artists never copy, and so he refuses to copy. Finally, the day he has been waiting for arrives, his first day of art class.

Excited, Tommy brings his impressively large set of crayons to class but is devastated when his teacher not only prevents him from using his beloved supplies but also refuses to give him more than one piece of paper. What's more, she expects the students to copy her in creating their art! Tommy finds himself in a frustrating situation, but he finds a way to resolve the issue and compromise with his teacher without sacrificing his creativity.

The story can motivate exploration of aesthetic issues involving art, creativity, and replication, as well as such topics as whether fairness demands that everyone be treated the same way and how we assess the fairness of rules.

Questions Raised

- Why did the teacher only give Tommy one piece of paper?
- Why was Tommy not allowed to bring in his own crayons after the first day?
- Is it fair to say all students must use the same crayons? Is this realistic?
- Is copying art?
- Why did the teacher make everyone copy her?
- Were the art teacher's rules fair?
- Why couldn't all the students just bring in their own crayons?
- Does uniformity stifle creativity?
- Is art a skill to be learned or something else?
- Are there certain qualifications to make one thing art and not another?
- If someone creates a perfect duplicate of, say, a Rembrandt, does this count as art?
- Would it be acceptable to allow more "creative" students more access to art supplies than other students?
- Is replication an art or something else? What would that something else be?
- What are the pros and cons of uniformity? Of individuality?

*This lesson plan was contributed by Gobe Hirata, who created it when she was an undergraduate at the University of Washington, working with the UW Center for Philosophy for Children, and who is now one of the Center's volunteer Philosophy teachers along with being a professional student of philosophy and life.

LESSON PLAN
WHAT IS ART? AN ART ACTIVITY

Topic: Philosophy of art
Time: 30 minutes to an hour, depending on ages of the children

Objectives

- To encourage children to consider what makes something art
- To examine the issue of intentionality in art

Description

This activity is a nice follow-up to the session on Tomie de Paola's *The Art Lesson*.

1. Have each student draw two pictures. One drawing must be a drawing they would call art, and the other one they would not call art.
2. Once the students have finished drawing, ask them to share their pieces and explain what makes one art and the other not. Ask the students listening to the sharing student: Do you think this [intended not to be art] piece could be art? Why or why not?

Questions Raised

- Are both of these images art? If not, which one is?
- How do we define what art is?
- Does the intention of the artist matter? The effort? What other people think?
- Who decides what is art and what is not?
- Can anything be art?

LESSON PLAN
THE COAT BY JULIE HUNT AND RON BROOKS*

Topics: Philosophy of art; metaphysics
Time: 30 minutes to an hour, depending on ages of the children

Objectives

- To examine the relationship between clothing and identity
- To explore the connection between clothing and emotion
- To examine whether fashion can be art

Description

This is a whimsical story about an animate coat that sits atop a paddock, buttoned up tight and stuffed with straw, lamenting, "What a waste of me!" Soon enough, a man comes along and, realizing some value in the coat that is going to waste, concludes, "I could do with a coat like that!" As the man puts on the coat, or rather, the coat puts on the man, the two fly over the city to Café Delitzia where they put on a lively performance for a wonderfully receptive audience.

Questions Raised

- Can what we wear affect us? How does that happen?
- How do we respond to certain clothing, certain textures, lengths of fabrics, colors? What makes certain materials feel in certain ways to us?
- Are certain thoughts possible when wearing some attire, which are more difficult to conceive in other attire?
- Do we wear clothing to reflect our current mood or perhaps to give us some sort of magical ability to take on new tasks, personas, and postures?
- Do we play a role when we wear certain clothing?
- Does a new set of clothes give us a new perspective on the world? A new perspective about ourselves?
- Do we wear our clothes or do, to some extent, our clothes wear us?

Activity: "What We Wear and What Wears Us"

- Bring into the class an assortment of six pieces of unique clothing. For example,
  - A funky coat of swirling fabric with a faux fur trim
  - A small, but wearable children's sweatshirt featuring a cartoon character
  - A hospital gown
  - An alpaca poncho
  - A sparkly hooded plastic sweatshirt
  - A large, striped, collared button-down shirt

  Try to pick garments that will fit all students relatively comfortably and can be worn by both genders relatively equally.
- Draw a name from the class list and ask the first person if they want to try on one of the garments; if they do, allow them to pick which one. It's helpful to have a random way of choosing students, such as names in a hat or on popsicle sticks.
- Continue drawing names until each garment has a wearer.
- Encourage students to take in information from all senses, reflecting on how garments look, feel, smell, sound, etc. Ask the participants to stand in a line in front of the class and display their garments. Allow each student spotlight time to share his or her individual experience with the class. Students enjoy feeling the different materials, posing for their friends, and reflecting on how the clothing makes them feel.
- Ask different questions of each participant such as the following:
  - Why did you choose this garment over the others?
  - How does it make you feel?
  - Can you tell us about the texture?
  - Do you have new thoughts or feelings in this garment that you did not previously have?

Note: Make sure to provide enough time for every student who desires to try on clothing to do so.

*This lesson plan was contributed by Gobe Hirata, who created it when she was an undergraduate at the University of Washington, working with the UW Center for Philosophy for Children, and who is now one of the Center's volunteer Philosophy teachers along with being a professional student of philosophy and life.

Chapter 7

Philosophy in Middle School

Middle-school students grapple with a range of philosophical issues, including identity, ethical choice, and the nature of community. The lesson plans that follow are geared toward middle-school students but most of them can be easily adapted for younger or older students. On topics ranging from freedom to stereotypes to the meaning of leadership, these plans are designed to help middle-school students become effective philosophical thinkers and adept at philosophical discussion. They have been written by academics, teachers, graduate students, and undergraduates, and include activities, readings, and writing exercises.

LESSON PLAN
FREEDOM*

Topic: Freedom
Time: 45 minutes

Objectives

- To develop the skill of listening and responding to others' ideas
- To think about the value of freedom and whether there should be legitimate restrictions on freedom in society

Materials Needed

- One large sheet of paper for each group of 3–4 students
- Instruction sheets for each group
- Pens/markers

Description

Through questions about freedom, this lesson is designed to give students practice participating in philosophical discussions (in both small- and large-group settings).

Students work in small groups to design "free societies," based on their prior knowledge and intuitions about freedom. The questions about freedom that come up during this activity will be addressed by the larger group as students present their societies to the class. The facilitator will track important questions and points on the board.

Introduction

To introduce the concept of freedom, discuss whether and why we consider freedom to be a virtue. Many societies restrict freedom, thinking that it can lead to vice; other societies are convinced that a lack of freedom is more problematic than the potential problems associated with freedom.

After a brief discussion of freedom, students are asked to design "free societies." Each group of three–four students is given an instruction sheet and a large sheet of paper on which they can draw and describe their societies (instructions are below). As the facilitator moves from group to group, he/she should have students note important questions that arise as they discuss how a society might be free. Some examples might include:

- What makes designing a free society particularly challenging?
- What does it mean for a society to be free?

Small-Group Activity

Design a free society!

Your Goals

1. Make the society as *free* as possible.
2. Write at least five guidelines that best promote freedom for your society. These can be laws, procedures, agreements between citizens, etc.
3. Potential issues to consider:
   - Money: Does your society have a currency? How is it used and managed?
   - Food: Who produces the food? What happens if there is not enough food?
   - Families: How are families structured?
   - Government: Is there a government? Who runs the government?
   - Work: Who works? Do people have jobs, or do they make a living without jobs?
   - School: Is school required? If not, do students decide whether they want to go to school?
   - Children and youth: How are children treated in this society? Can they be as free as adults? How old must people be before they can choose what to eat? What to wear? Where to live? Where to work?
   - Justice: What happens if someone doesn't follow the guidelines?

Your society's name: _____

Whole-Class Activity

Each group presents their description and drawing of a free society to the entire class, relating any important questions or problems they considered while they created their society. The facilitator will ask the class to respond to these points and give the class opportunities to ask the presenting group questions about their society, especially as regards freedom.

Some examples of questions the facilitator could ask:

- A says that a completely free society wouldn't be a society at all. Rather, it would just be a group of people. Can a completely free society exist?
- B says that people should be able to self-govern as soon as they are able to talk. Should people be free at this age? Can people be free at this age? Is there anything positive about letting very young children self-govern?
- Is freedom the same thing as having no restrictions or laws?
- Are certain restrictions and laws necessary for the preservation of freedom in society?

Concluding Activity

Poll the class (show of hands): How many students would want to live in the society they created? For those who say "yes," ask them to explain why. For those who say "no," ask them to explain what they would change.

Additional points to consider:

- How important is freedom in a society?
- Are there any values that are more important for or more central to society than freedom?

*This lesson plan was contributed by Sarah Urdzik, who graduated from the University of North Carolina at Chapel Hill in 2013 with a BA in Mathematics and Classics and is currently a middle-school teacher at Trinity School of Durham and Chapel Hill; Donovan Dorrance, a musician from Chapel Hill, North Carolina, who is currently staying in Brooklyn, New York, while occasionally contributing to new works in the field of Philosophy; and Margaret Owens, who graduated from the University of North Carolina at Chapel Hill in 2015 with a BA in Linguistics and Philosophy.

LESSON PLAN
FAIR OR EQUAL?*

Topics: Ethics and fairness
Time: About half an hour

Objectives

- Students will explore the nature of fairness
- Students will examine whether fairness requires that everyone should have the same things

Materials Needed

- List of roles and responsibilities (see below)
- A bag of candy

Description

Begin the exercise by holding up the bag of candy (make sure you have enough for at least one piece for every student) and ask, "What's the fair way to distribute the candy in this bag? Who all should get a piece?"

Usually, students will agree that everyone should get the same number of pieces. (Occasionally, a student will—usually half in jest—claim that he or she ought to get the whole bag; this naturally doesn't fly with his or her classmates and a discussion about why it's not right can ensue.)

After talking about the fair way to distribute the sweets, pass out the candy according to the decision of the group. After giving students a few moments to enjoy their treat, ask, "Is everyone getting the same thing always the fair way? Are there situations in which it's okay for people to be treated differently?"

Field the responses to segue into the roles-and-responsibilities exercise as follows.

Activity

Ask for four volunteers to come to the front of the classroom. Explain that they are going to be working together to build a house. Each of them, though, should have different tools. Pass out to each student a slip of paper, each of which has a different description of the tools he or she has, and ask the students to read aloud what they've received. Here is what they've got:

- (On Slip 1): You have a bulldozer and a dump truck. You are an expert in the use of these machines.
- (On Slip 2): You have a full collection of hand tools, like hammers, drills, and screwdrivers. You are an expert in the use of these tools.
- (On Slip 3): You have a huge supply of bricks and cement. You are an expert bricklayer and cement-mixer.
- (On Slip 4): You have all the paints and brushes anyone could need. You are an expert painter.

Now ask students who they think should do what when the house is being built, and why. Usually, it's pretty obvious, but the discussion can be fairly interesting as the class begins talking about why so-and-so should do such-and-such. (It's also not unprecedented that students will say, for instance, that the painter ought to help do bricklaying, for example, as a way to learn new skills.)

As this discussion dies down, bring a different group of four students to the front of the room and give them slips that read:

- You are the world's greatest dessert chef.
- You are the world's greatest dishwasher.
- You are the world's greatest soup maker.
- You are the world's greatest sandwich maker.

Now say something like: "Okay, it's time to make lunch for everyone. Who should do what?" Again, the discussion is likely to be pretty straightforward, with the class generally agreeing that the tasks should be divvied up according to expertise. (This isn't always the case; again, because sometimes students argue that people should be expected to do whatever is needed or that everyone ought to get good at everything, but most of the time, the consensus is that it's good for everyone if everyone does what he or she does best.)

Time permitting, do one more iteration. This time, bring five students to the front and pass out slips that read:

- You are the world's best rebounder.
- You are the world's best shot-blocker.
- You are the world's best three-point shooter.
- You are the world's best passer.
- You are the world's best free-throw shooter.

Obviously, the question now is, "What is the best way for this basketball team to play?" And again, pretty much just as obviously, students will respond that the players who are good at a given skill ought to focus on that skill. It's worth talking for some time about why this is the case though; there might be different reasons to consider, ranging from something like, "If everyone does what they're good at, the team will win;" to "People have more fun if they do the thing they're good at." In any case, by this third iteration the class will have explored in some depth their positions on when it's appropriate (if at all) for people to have different responsibilities, given that they do have different skills and abilities.

At this point, pass out to all students slips of paper with the phrase "What I do best is . . ." and ask them to fill in the blank. When they've done so, bring a group of four (randomly chosen) students to the front of the room. Ask each student to read his or her slip of paper, and then ask, "If you were building a house, who should do what?" Compare the answer in this discussion to those from the earlier example. What's similar? What's different? Why?

Do the same thing with different groups for the lunch-making and basketball-playing examples. Again, compare similarities and differences and probe together with students as to why they've answered as they have.

Finally, get everyone back in their seats, and have each student read his or her slip out loud. Then have a large-group discussion focused on the question, "Given our skills and abilities, who should do what in our classroom? What's the fair way to divvy up the tasks?" Typically, this leads to an interesting contrast with the other discussions, although sometimes students will want to assert that since they're all good at different things, they all should have different kinds of assignments in the classroom.

Conclusion

The hope is that the students have begun to explore whether fairness always means that everyone should get the same thing. Are there cases in life where it's fair to give some people more (or different things) than others? Often, students will give examples like handicapped parking spaces or extra time in test-taking for people with learning disabilities.

At the end of the discussion, it sometimes works to do a fill-in-the-blank "poem," where students fill in this sentence, "With my special talents, one thing I can do to make the world a little better is . . ."

Here are some sample answers from a fourth-grade class:

- One thing I can do to make the world a little better is play with new friends.
- One thing I can do to make the world a little better is be nice to my brother.
- One thing I can do to make the world a little better is share my toys.
- One thing I can do to make the world a little better is play basketball.
- One thing I can do to make the world a little better is draw and paint.

*This lesson plan was contributed by David Shapiro, Education Director of the University of Washington Center for Philosophy for Children and a full-time faculty member in Philosophy at Cascadia College in Bothell, Washington.

LESSON PLAN
JUSTICE AND FAIRNESS IN SCHOOLS

Topics: Justice and fairness
Time: 50 minutes

Objectives

- To help students distinguish different conceptions of justice
- To foster discussions about justice and fairness relevant to the concerns of young students

Materials Needed

- Dialogue handouts
- A whiteboard

Description

1. Distribute "A Dialogue on Justice" (see below) to class members. Ask for three volunteers who will read and take on the role of characters in the dialogue.
2. Following the reading, ask students to identify different conceptions of justice and/ or fairness raised by the characters in the dialogue. Potential starter questions could include the following:

- What conceptions of justice and/or fairness are Derrick, Elicia, and Timothy presenting to us?
- How are they different?
- How are they similar?

The dialogue presents a number of different conceptions of justice for the class to consider. Students are presented with a communitarian-based conception, an authoritarian conception ("might makes right"), and a majority-based conception.

3. After identifying the different conceptions of justice, begin considering which conception is most defensible to the class. In relation to the example presented in the dialogue, students can be asked to
   - provide specific reasons in support of their chosen conception of justice; and
   - introduce their own conception of justice, or one that is relevant to the case at hand but was not included in the dialogue.
4. To make this discussion concrete, students should be encouraged to focus on the example presented in the dialogue (the uniform policy). This example was specifically chosen after working in schools with uniform policies that many of the students deemed to be unfair. Indeed, this is a vital issue for many students and one that they tend to be very interested in discussing.
5. At the conclusion of the discussion, take time to review the conceptions of justice that came to light. In addition, discuss important elements of agreement and disagreement that emerged during class discussion. List all of these items on the whiteboard.
6. In most cases, no consensus will emerge as to the most defensible conception of justice. This is fine; the concluding goal should be to increase the class' understanding of diverse conceptions of justice and to note important lingering questions for continuing discussion. Examples of these questions could include the following:
   - What is the proper extent of freedom in schools?
   - What kind of decision-making powers should young students have in schools (e.g., uniform policy, curriculum, etc.)?
   - Do we possess/give up certain rights when we enter/leave school?

Handout

A Dialogue on Justice

Derrick: Hey Elicia, did you hear about the new rule just handed down from the school administration?

Elicia: No, what is it?

Derrick: Starting tomorrow all students have to wear uniforms to school.

Elicia: That is not fair, I mean, that is *unjust.*

Timothy: What do you mean by *unjust*?

Elicia: I mean that the students' voices weren't taken into account—that is *unjust.*

Derrick: So it would have been *just* if students had a say in the new rule and supported it?

Elicia: Yes.

Derrick: No way. What is *just* is what is decided by the powerful. The powerful people (in this case, the school administration) say that we need to wear ties and dress pants. Therefore, it is *just* that we wear ties and dress pants.

Timothy: I don't know about that. I have a different understanding of justice. *Justice* is whatever the majority of people in a community think it is. For example, the majority of people in this community (students at this middle school) do not think that having to wear ties and dress pants is just. Therefore, wearing ties and dress pants is not just. What *is* just, then, is wearing what we want.

Derrick: That seems like a dangerous understanding of justice.

Timothy: Why dangerous?

Derrick: Well, on your definition of justice, can't *anything* end up being just?

Timothy: Sure, whatever the majority thinks is just *is* just.

Elicia: What if the majority of folks in this city think the legal enforcement of racial segregation in schools is just? Does that mean legally enforced racial segregation is just?

Timothy: Well . . . maybe not. But if you think my definition of justice and my supporting argument supporting is no good, then what is yours?

LESSON PLAN
STEREOTYPING*

Topic: Stereotypes
Time: 50–60 minutes

Objectives

- Develop a working definition of "stereotype"
- Determine potential problems with stereotyping and discuss whether this practice can be morally permissible

Materials Needed

- Plenty of paper
- Several sets of five different colored pencils or markers
- Timer

Introduction

Ask your students to think about how they define a stereotype. Work in small groups to come up with a basic definition. Have your students write this definition down. After small-group discussion, write each group's definition on the board and discuss commonalities and differences.

Activity

For this part of the discussion, you will use a "silent discussion" technique. Each group should have about five people in it. After reading the example as a class, pose the first question (see below).

Students have one minute to respond to the question(s) on their own piece of paper. After responding, they must pass it to the student on their left. (Feel free to change the order or direction of passing for different questions, so students can respond to different classmates.) Students will pass the paper four times or until it returns to the original person. Then everyone gets time to read what was written on their pages. Be sure to encourage students to respond directly to the statement(s) that have just been made during the writing periods.

Example

Mr. Moore owns a convenience store near a school. He sells lots of candy and school supplies to middle-school students. He has also had a lot of his merchandise stolen. Mr. Moore decided to implement a new policy requiring all students to leave their bags at the front with him when shopping in his store. If a student comes in wearing a large sweatshirt, Mr. Moore asks the student to leave it up front too. He does not ask women with large purses or men with briefcases to leave their bags at the front. When asked why, he tells the students that 90 percent of the people he has caught stealing have been students from the school and he is just trying to protect himself.

- Begin the discussion by asking the following question and completing the silent discussion: *Is this an example of stereotyping?*
- Once your students have discussed the nature of a stereotype, move on to the next question (again using the silent-discussion technique): *Is Mr. Moore's policy morally wrong?*
- How accurate is the stereotype in this case? Does the accuracy of the stereotype bear on whether it is morally wrong or permissible?
- Be sure to point out here that many students that go into the store will not steal from Mr. Moore, but he is treating them as if they will. What if only one student out of one hundred would not steal from him, if given the opportunity? Would he still be treating that one student unfairly?
- To what extent does the fact that Mr. Moore believes he is protecting himself justify his actions?
- It is not difficult to leave one's belongings at the front of the store; however, the policy seems discriminatory. Is discrimination inherently wrong?

Concluding Activity

- To conclude, ask students to raise their hands if they believe stereotyping is always wrong. Have this group write down at least one reason that they think this is the case.
- Ask the other students who think stereotypes will sometimes be morally permissible to come up with either a second example of a time when stereotyping is not wrong or some criterion for determining if stereotyping might be permissible.
- After they have developed their responses, partner students as evenly as possible with students of the opposite group. Give them time to discuss their answers with one another.
- Return as a class and discuss.

*This lesson plan was contributed by Kelsey Satchel Kaul, who graduated from the University of North Carolina at Chapel Hill in 2013 and looks forward to starting his life in Oregon, which he hopes will forever be dedicated to educational and social equity, and Heather Van Wallendael, who graduated from University of North Carolina at Chapel Hill in 2013 with a BA in English and Philosophy and currently works for the Jubilee Catholic Schools Network in Memphis.

LESSON PLAN
FOLLOWING THE LEADER*

Topics: Social and political philosophy; the nature of leadership; the qualities of a good leader
Time: 50 minutes

Objectives

- To help students identify and talk about diverse aspects of leadership, which are reflected, for instance, in the following questions—Must leaders guide action directly? What are the differences between leading by example and leading from behind?
- To help students work toward a definition of good leadership

Materials Needed

- An object that can be hidden
- Whiteboard (or other writing surface) and dry erase marker

Description

A. Choose two volunteers. One will close his or her eyes and the other will lead him or her by the wrist to an object (hidden by the teacher) in the room. The rest of the class will watch silently; they have been asked to take notes regarding the success of this form of leadership, the style of this form of leadership, etc.

B. Choose two different volunteers. One will close his or her eyes and the other will lead him or her with verbal cues (absolutely no physical guidance) to an object (hidden by the teacher) in the room. The rest of the class will watch silently, again, taking notes on this demonstration of leadership, and making comparisons between the leadership and guidance demonstrated in activities A and B.

C. Choose one additional volunteer. The volunteer will close his or her eyes, and the rest of the class will participate in this part of the activity with verbal cues (absolutely no physical guidance), leading the student to an object (hidden by the teacher) in the room. Students may call out randomly and without limit. While giving directions, the class should take notes regarding this form of leadership, comparing it with the leadership demonstrated in activities A and B.

D. General discussion/ Reaction to the activity:

D1. At the end of these activities, discuss the following:
  o How did the first activity (A) compare to the second activity (B)? In what ways were they different? In what ways were they similar?
  o Which activity demonstrated the best example of leadership? Why?
  o Was the third activity (C) an example of good leadership? If not, what qualities made it an example of bad leadership?

(*Note*: Record student answers and major discussion themes on whiteboard.)

D2. Following these initial questions, the discussion should center on comparing the different aspects of leadership demonstrated in the activities. Students can consider the following points and questions:
  o The commonalities and differences between the different examples of leadership.
  o What qualities make for a good leader?
  o What is a definition of leadership that can be developed from our discussion?

*This lesson plan was contributed by Andrew Chirdon, a 2013 Philosophy graduate of the University of North Carolina at Chapel Hill who has left the tranquil pace and balmy weather of North Carolina to serve in the frenetic South Bronx as a family foster-care social worker, and Josh Jones, who received a BA in Philosophy and History from the University of North Carolina at Chapel Hill in 2013.

LESSON PLAN
ON FRIENDSHIP*

Topic: Friendship
Time: 50 minutes

Objectives

• Students will identify and defend the qualities/aspects of a good friend(ship)
• Students will explore which qualities/aspects of a good friend(ship) are the most important and which qualities/aspects are the least important
• Students will learn to identify necessary and sufficient conditions

Materials Needed

• Index cards
• Whiteboard and several different colored dry erase markers

Description

Pass out one index card to each student. Instruct the students to draw, without using representations of people (including stick figures, faces, and the like), a creative representation of a good friendship. Have the students then discuss their drawings in small groups, with each student explaining why his or her drawing is a representation of a good friendship.

Main Activity

I.   Coming out of small-group discussions, tell the students that you'd like to consider the following question as a large group: "What makes a friendship a good friendship?"
II.   Have the students contribute answers to this question based on their drawings.
III.   After discussing their drawings, ask if the students would like to add anything else to the list.
IV.   After a general list is established, move to more specific questions on the nature of a good friendship:
       a. Be sure to give the students about 10 seconds to think of their answers in silence before asking for hands.
       b. Be prepared to acknowledge that several traits on the board are related. It might be helpful to use different colored markers to connect different traits as related to one another. For example, students might identify "trust" as the underlying reason for "feels safe to be around."
       c. If students disagree, be sure to ask them to respond specifically to one another, giving reasons in support of their positions.
V.   *Question #1*: Which of these qualities/aspects might be the most important to a good friendship? Why? This should focus the discussion on what is *necessary* for a good friendship and what is *sufficient* for a good friendship.
VI.   *Question #2*: Which quality/aspect would be the most detrimental if it were absent? Why?
       a. If students seem to agree about a certain trait being *necessary*, turn the discussion to whether or not the trait is a *sufficient* condition. Tell the class that Bill and Bob (or any names you like) are two people that exhibit whichever trait your class has identified as necessary with one another. Ask the class if they can assume that Bill and Bob are good friends. This would be a good time to ask for counterexamples—stories about Bob and Bill in which they do exhibit the trait but are not good friends (perhaps they are actually just coworkers or distant relatives).
       b. Note, you might not identify any sufficient conditions over the course of the discussion, but this is fine!

VII. *Question #3*: If you could have a friend that had all of the listed traits except for one, which trait would you leave out?
   a. This question gets at the *least* important trait. It may be argued that the traits that seem least important may not be *necessary* (and certainly not *sufficient*) traits for a good friendship; thus, it continues the focus of questions 1 and 2.
   b. This could reveal that the created list has only vitally important and/or interconnected traits, so it may be hard (or impossible) to positively answer this question. The distinctions raised will be beneficial nonetheless.
VIII. Alternative/supplemental questions about the list can be posed. The three questions above should provide for a full discussion, but if you have more time (or want to extend the discussion into another class period) feel free to consider any of the following questions:

A. Can nonhuman animals or objects be friends to us? Can they be friends to each other?
   • Refer to the phrase "a dog is a man's best friend." What does the phrase really mean? In what ways do dogs make for better or worse friends than people? Be sure the students relate their answers back to the created list.
B. Consider expressions that seem metaphorical, like "my shadow is my only friend when I feel lonely," and "ice cream is my best friend; she always understands my needs." What is really being expressed here? What traits (on the board) are being referenced?
C. Are there different kinds of friends?
   • This could focus on the differences between friends who are family, family friends, social media friends, school friends, neighbor friends, etc. Answers will likely vary. It would be best to follow up by discussing which traits/qualities from the list are more important for the various kinds of friends identified (perhaps "having fun" is more important for school friends, while "commitment to working through problems" is more important for sibling friends).

Concluding Activity

• Ask the students to review the list of traits written on the board and identify one trait they believe is a strength and one trait that is a weakness for them. Have them write down their answers, but tell them that this can be as personal/private as the students want.
• Put a star against the characteristics the students identified as necessary and circle any they thought were sufficient. Ask if any of your students identified a sufficient condition as a strength? As a weakness? Ask if any student identified a necessary condition as a strength? As a weakness? It is not necessary to have your students share their thoughts aloud, but writing them down would be beneficial (you could even assign a more thorough task with journal entries answering or reflecting on these and similar questions).

*This lesson plan was contributed by Kelsey Satchel Kaul, who graduated from the University of North Carolina at Chapel Hill in 2013 and looks forward to starting his life in Oregon, which he hopes will forever be dedicated to educational and social equity, and Heather Van Wallendael, who graduated from the University of

North Carolina at Chapel Hill in 2013 with a B.A. in English and Philosophy and currently works for the Jubilee Catholic Schools Network in Memphis.

LESSON PLAN
HUMAN NATURE AND THE RING OF GYGES*

Topics: Human nature; moral goodness and evil
Time: 50 minutes

Objectives

- To raise questions about human nature
- To examine what motivates moral behavior

Materials Needed

Worksheet (see below)

Description

Begin by asking the students "What does everyone in this room have in common?" Once "we're all human" is offered (or prompted), ask the students, "What is significant or important about being human?" Likely, the students will bring up intelligence, creativity, technological progress, and, hopefully, morality. If they do not bring up morality, ask them directly about whether our ability to choose morally good or morally bad actions is important. Ask them to raise their hands if they've ever done anything bad. Ask them why people do bad things. Start a list on the board. Similarly, ask why people do good things. Create a list of these as well.

Introduce Plato's story of the Ring of Gyges. Here's a modified version of it:

> Gyges was a shepherd in the service of the king of Lydia; there was a great storm, and an earthquake made an opening in the earth at the place where he was feeding his flock. Amazed at the sight, he descended into the opening, where, among other marvels, he beheld a massive hollow bronze horse, full of holes. He looked into the horse and saw a corpse, larger than most humans, wearing only a ring.

At this point ask the students what they think Gyges did next.
Here's what actually happened in the story.

> Gyges took the ring from the finger of the dead and departed the chasm.
>
> Now the shepherds met together, according to custom, that they might send their monthly report about the flocks to the king. Into their assembly Gyges came with the ring on his finger, and as he was sitting among them he chanced to turn the jewel of the ring inside his hand, and he instantly became invisible to the rest of the company and they began to speak of him as if he were no longer present. He was astonished at this, and again

touching the ring he turned the jewel outwards and reappeared. He made several trials of the ring, and always with the same outcome.

At this point ask the students what they think Gyges would do with his newfound power. They will likely be suspicious of Gyges, not trusting him to act perfectly morally. Ask them why they think he will do immoral things with his power.

Hand out a worksheet with the following three questions:

1. What would you do if you had the ring?
2. What would other people do if they had the ring?
3. What would happen if every single person in the world had such a ring?

Give the students about five minutes to fill this worksheet out, emphasizing that they should be specific and honest in their answers.

Go through the questions one by one, getting several responses for each answer. Ask if anyone said they would get rid of the ring or refuse to use it. Ask if it's even possible for someone to resist doing bad things with the ring. Could there be such a person, or would he or she succumb, to some degree, to the temptation?

Ask the students what this says about human nature. Does this mean we are monsters who need the threat of punishment to do good? Are we actually good? Are we somewhere in between?

After some discussion, take a poll, giving three options: (1) overall, we are morally bad, (2) overall, we are morally good, (3) overall, we are somewhere in between. After the poll, draw a line on the board, as given:

Bad   Good

Ask the students to raise their hands when you've hit the right proportion of goodness to badness in human nature. Start on the left, saying all the students who raised their hands for "bad" should raise their hands again. Slowly move your hand toward the right, making marks on the line when there are spikes of hands.

End by summarizing the views represented by the poll and recapitulating what was discussed in class.

*This lesson plan was contributed by Dustyn Addington, a Ph.D. candidate in Philosophy at the University of Washington.

Worksheet

The ring of Gyges allows you to be completely undetectable. You will never be caught for what you do while wearing the ring.

1. What would you do if you had the ring of Gyges? Be specific.

2. What do you think other people would do if they had the ring of Gyges? Be specific.

3. What would happen if every single person in the world had such a ring? Be specific.

LESSON PLAN
DRAWING A GOOD LIFE

Topics: Aesthetics; values; elements of a good life
Time: 1–2 hours

Objectives

- To prompt philosophical discussion and exploration through artwork
- To have students consider and discuss elements of a good life
- To have students reflect on their own beliefs and value commitments

Materials Needed

Paper and drawing instruments (colored pencils, markers, or crayons)

Introduction

Conceptions of what it means to live excellently (the good life) have long been of interest to philosophers. Although there is no single definition that can encompass all aspects of living well, students are generally quite interested (and invested) in defining important (or necessary) elements of a good life. In addition, by using the drawing activity (described below) students come to recognize implicit beliefs and value commitments they hold about how one ought to live and elements of life that should be prioritized over others.

Activity

1. Begin this activity by providing each student with a sheet of blank paper and drawing instruments. Ask the students to draw a picture, image, or scene of the good life. Keep the instructions broad—the idea is that students should develop an image of their own choosing with minimal influence from others in the class. Students should work on this individually and without (or with minimal) discussion. Students will create a drawing that reflects their understanding of a good life or an important element of a good life.
2. Ask for volunteers; they should come to the front of the room and present and discuss their drawings, noting (1) why they chose to draw it (as opposed to numerous other possibilities for this exercise) and (2) what aspects of a good life the drawing captures.

3. After a few volunteers have presented their drawings the facilitator can prompt a broader philosophical conversation on the qualities and nature of a good life. Potential questions to prompt this discussion include the following:
   - What themes or values were shared across drawings?
   - What do these drawings tell us about our personal conceptions of a good life?
   - Does art offer greater possibilities for understanding a good life than written definitions or texts?
   - What important aspects of a good life were missing from the presented drawings?
   - Is there any quality, experience, or activity, the absence of which would make it impossible for one to live a good life?
   - Is it possible to define any condition of a good life that holds for all persons? Or, does what constitutes a good life simply depend on each individual?

Conclusion

Part of the virtue of this activity is that it is fun and engaging for students. Students will enjoy the relatively unstructured opportunity to draw and illustrate their ideas and values in class. In addition, this activity leads to substantive philosophical discussion and insight into the students' values and beliefs regarding how one ought to live one's life. "Living well" is a central ethical and social/political topic that is also very concrete and accessible for young philosophers. Following the activity, students will have a broader conception of possibilities for a good life and a work of art to take home.

LESSON PLAN
SHALLOW POND AND CHARITY*

Topics: Ethics (charity, morally required actions, supererogatory actions, beneficence)
Time: 50 minutes

Objectives

- Students will consider what special duties we might have to others
- Students will consider the differences between actions that are morally required versus those that are morally permissible
- To provide an exercise in analogical argumentation

Description

Begin by asking the students what they think makes an action "good" and what makes an action "wrong" (or "bad"). Create a list on the board. Some elements brought up to define good actions are that they are directed at helping others, are beneficial in some way, and aren't against the law. For wrong actions, some qualities brought up might include how wrong actions harm others, are selfish, and are cruel in some way.

Introduce philosopher Peter Singer's Shallow Pond case, a modified form of which goes like this:

> Imagine that one day a person is walking past a shallow pond. He or she notices that a child has fallen in and appears to be drowning. To wade in and pull the child out would be easy, but it means that his or her clothes will be ruined. Does this person have any obligation to rescue the child?

Students will often have strong intuitions that the character should save the child. Ask the students what is morally required, if anything.

This should produce a discussion during which students examine whether this action is absolutely morally necessary or not morally required (i.e., a nice, but not morally required, action).

Create a list, from the discussion, of reasons one must help the child and reasons why it may be permissible to choose not to save the child.

Then introduce a second case that runs like this: In a foreign country, a small child is very close to dying of malnutrition. For less than the cost of your clothes, you could donate money and save the child. Are you morally required to do so?

Many students will say that this is not morally required. Often students will explicitly connect the two cases, but, if they do not, draw out the connection. Ask them what makes the two cases different.

After some discussion, have the students write down their views in response to the following question:

What kinds of help are we morally required to give other people?

After a few minutes of writing, ask the students to share their responses with each other in partner groups, and then ask for volunteers to share their responses with the class.

Ask the class what they think of each response, giving them time to articulate their views about the topic.

Supplemental Materials

Peter Singer expresses his view on the Shallow Pond case here: https://www.youtube.com/watch?v=sagg2C30RMk.

*This lesson plan was contributed by Dustyn Addington, a Ph.D. candidate in philosophy at the University of Washington.

LESSON PLAN
PHILOSOPHICAL INQUIRY AND *THE BOOK THIEF*
BY MARKUS ZUSAK

Topics: Ethics; social and political philosophy; identity
Time: Several class sessions

Objectives

- Enhance student awareness of the philosophical suggestiveness of literature and the ways literature can inspire thinking about essential questions
- Explore various philosophical issues emerging from *The Book Thief*
- Develop some basic tools for spotting philosophical topics in literary novels

Introduction

Many middle- and high-school curricula include *The Book Thief*, written in 2006 by Markus Zusak. *The Book Thief* takes place in Nazi Germany, and its narrator is Death. Liesel Meminger, the novel's central character (and the "book thief"), is a child living in a town near Munich with her foster parents, Hans and Rosa Hubermann. The book portrays everyday life in an extraordinarily terrible time, and depicts the ways in which small choices made by ordinary people can carry great ethical weight.

The Book Thief explores many philosophical issues, including the meaning of courage, the nature of friendship, the moral obligations connected to being part of a community, the relationship between character and moral behavior, and the beauty and ugliness of human life. This lesson plan provides prompts for highlighting various passages to inspire inquiry about these philosophical topics. Read the passages aloud with students and then ask them, "What questions does this make you wonder about?" The discussion questions included can be used as prompts for discussion and writing.

Topic 1: The Meaning of Courage

PASSAGE

> When he appeared inside, Mama fixed her gaze on him, but no words were exchanged. She didn't admonish him at all, which, as you know, was highly unusual. Perhaps she decided he was injured enough, having been labeled a coward by his only son.
>
> For awhile, he remained silently at the table after the eating was finished. Was he really a coward, as his son had so brutally pointed out? Certainly, in World War I, he considered himself one. He attributed his survival to it. But then, is there cowardice in the acknowledgement of fear? Is there cowardice in being glad you had lived?
>
> (Zusak, 106–07)

Discussion Questions

- Hans' son calls him a coward because Hans refuses to support Hitler. Is this cowardice?
- Hans implies that he believes he was a coward in the First World War because he was afraid to die. What is the relationship between courage and fear? Can you be afraid and still be courageous?
- Can you be courageous and not be afraid?

PASSAGE

> "I can no longer join," Hans stated.
>   The man was shocked. "Why not?"

Hans looked at the knuckles of his right hand and swallowed. He could already taste the error, like a metal tablet in his mouth. "Forget it." He turned and walked home. . . .

Innocuously, a man walked past. "*Heil* Hitler," he said.

"*Heil* Hitler," Hans replied.

(Zusak, 182)

Discussion Questions

• When Hans tells the Nazi Party member, "Forget it," and when he says "*Heil* Hitler" even though we know he doesn't support Hitler, is he demonstrating a lack of courage?

• What is the relationship between courage and being careful? Between courage and recklessness?

• Does Hans have courage?

PASSAGE

When a Jew shows up at your place of residence in the early hours of morning, in the very birthplace of Nazism, you're likely to experience extreme levels of discomfort. Anxiety, disbelief, paranoia. Each plays its part, and each leads to a sneaking suspicion that a less than heavenly consequence awaits. The fear is shiny. Ruthless in the eyes.

The surprising point to make is that despite this iridescent fear glowing as it did in the dark, they somehow resisted the urge for hysteria.

(Zusak, 199–200)

Discussion Questions

• Is "resisting the urge for hysteria" a kind of courage?

• Does courage always involve action? Can it take courage to do nothing? To remain silent? To think in a particular way? To refuse to care what other people think?

• Can a community be courageous?

Topic 2: The Nature of Friendship

PASSAGE

In one of their basement sessions, Papa dispensed with the sandpaper (it was running out fast) and pulled out a brush. There were few luxuries in the Hubermann household, but there was an oversupply of paint, and it became more than useful for Liesel's learning. Papa would say a word and the girl would have to spell it aloud and then paint it on the wall, as long as she got it right. After a month, the wall was recoated. A fresh cement page.

"You stink," Mama would say to Hans. "Like cigarettes and kerosene."

Sitting in the water, she imagined the smell of it, mapped out on her papa's clothes. More than anything, it was the smell of friendship, and she could find it on herself, too. Liesel loved that smell. She would sniff her arm and smile as the water cooled around her.

(Zusak, 72)

Discussion Questions

- What does Liesel mean when she imagines "the smell of friendship?" Is there a feel to friendship?
- What makes friendship pleasurable?
- How do we recognize friendship? What do we find valuable about it?

PASSAGE

Dear Mrs. Hermann,

As you can see, I have been in your library again and I have ruined one of your books. I was just so angry and afraid and I wanted to kill the words. I have stolen from you and now I've wrecked your property. I'm sorry. To punish myself, I think I will stop coming here. Or is it punishment at all? I love this place and hate it, because it is full of words.

You have been a friend to me even though I hurt you, even though I have been insufferable (a word I looked up in your dictionary), and I think I will leave you alone now. I'm sorry for everything.

Thank you again,
Liesel Meminger
(Zusak, 522)

Discussion Questions

- Does friendship have to be mutual? Can I be a friend to someone even if that person doesn't consider me a friend?
- What do we owe to our friends? Can I be a friend to someone even if they hurt me?
- Are there features that are common to all friendships?

Quote: "If I had to choose between betraying my country and betraying my friend, I hope I should have the guts to betray my country." — E. M. Forster

Discussion Questions

- Do we have greater obligations to our friends than to the larger community?
- What do we do when friendship conflicts with our welfare?
- Do we have different obligations to different kinds of friendship?

Topic 3: Moral Obligations to the Community
PASSAGE

After lodging his form at the Nazi headquarters on Munich Street, he witnessed four men throw several bricks into a clothing store named Kleinmann's. It was one of the few Jewish shops that were still in operation in Molching. Inside, a small man was stuttering about, crushing the broken glass beneath his feet as he cleaned up. A star the color of mustard was smeared to the door. In sloppy lettering, the words JEWISH FILTH were spilling over at their edges. The movement inside tapered from hurried to morose, then stopped altogether.

Hans moved closer and stuck his head inside. "Do you need some help?"

(Zusak, 181)

Discussion Questions

- Why did Hans offer to help Mr. Kleinmann?
- What might be some reasons that many people did not act to help Jews and others during the Holocaust?
- Is everyone who doesn't act in the face of oppression or injustice indifferent?
- What small moral choices do people make in their everyday lives that can lead them to become either resisters or bystanders?

PASSAGE

Somewhere near Munich, a German Jew was making his way through the darkness. An arrangement had been made to meet Hans Hubermann in four days (i.e., if he wasn't taken away). It was at a place far down the Amper, where a broken bridge leaned among the river and trees.

He would make it there, but he would not stay longer than a few minutes.

The only thing to be found there when Papa arrived four days later was a note under a rock, at the base of a tree. It was addressed to nobody and contained only one sentence.

THE LAST WORDS OF

MAX VANDENBURG

You've done enough.

(Zusak, 398)

Discussion Questions

- Why did Max leave?
- Had Hans done enough?
- Are we required to put ourselves in danger to help others? Under what circumstances, if any?
- Is it always wrong to be a bystander? Sometimes wrong? Never?

Topic 4: The Beauty and Ugliness of Life

PASSAGE

It's probably fair to say that in all the years of Hitler's reign, no person was able to serve the *Führer* as loyally as me. A human doesn't have a heart like mine. The human heart is a line, whereas my own is a circle, and I have the endless ability to be in the right place at the right time. The consequence of this is that I'm always finding humans at their best and worst. I see their ugly and their beauty, and I wonder how the same thing can be both. Still, they have one thing I envy. Humans, if nothing else, have the good sense to die.

(Zusak, 491)

Discussion Questions

- What does it mean to have a heart like a line or a circle?
- Does our mortality limit what we can understand?
- Are humans both beautiful and ugly? Are each of the characters in the book both beautiful and ugly? Can you be both? Are we always both?
- Would there be beauty without ugliness?

PASSAGE

I wanted to tell the book thief many things, about beauty and brutality. But what could I tell her about those things that she didn't already know? I wanted to explain that I am constantly overestimating and underestimating the human race—that rarely do I ever simply *estimate* it. I wanted to ask her how the same thing could be so ugly and so glorious, and its words and stories so damning and brilliant.

None of those things, however, came out of my mouth.

All I wanted to do was turn to Liesel Meminger and tell her the only truth I truly know. I said it to the book thief and I say it now to you.

A LAST NOTE FROM YOUR NARRATOR

I am haunted by humans.

(Zusak, 550)

Discussion Questions

- Was Liesel's life beautiful, despite the brutality that surrounded her?
- Can suffering be beautiful?
- Why is Death haunted by humans? Is it due to the capacity of humans to make choices and the choices we make?

Conclusion

Much of literature abounds with philosophical themes. Focusing on specific passages and illuminating their philosophical significance gives students tools with which to begin to read with a better sense of the fundamental larger questions that often underlie literary works and to further develop their own understanding of the broader issues raised by novels like *The Book Thief*. This in turn encourages students to think about their own questions and the ways in which reading literature can help them to examine those questions.

LESSON PLAN
LEGOs OF THESEUS*

Topic: Identity
Time: 50 minutes

Objectives

- Students will gain an appreciation of the question of the identity of an object
- Students will be able to articulate theories about the identity of an object

Materials Needed

- LEGO bricks (about 20 per pair of students).
- For Building Part 1 of the activity, it will be easiest if students have two identical sets of LEGO bricks with which to work

Introduction

This lesson introduces students to the Ship of Theseus puzzle and basic questions of identity. (See Supplemental Materials below for a description of the Ship of Theseus puzzle.) Students begin with an activity that models the Ship of Theseus thought experiment. After some introductory discussion and an introduction to the historical Ship of Theseus thought experiment, the activity continues by modeling Thomas Hobbes' extension of the Ship of Theseus puzzle (also described in Supplemental Materials). Students discuss what Hobbes' addition to the thought experiment suggests, and consider some basic solutions to the puzzle through an interactive lecture.

The Supplemental Materials section at the end of this lesson plan provides a very brief introduction to the problem of identity in philosophy as well as descriptions and primary source references for the thought experiments included in the lesson.

Building Part 1 (10 minutes)

1. Pair students. Give each pair of students about 5 minutes to build a small object (no more than 10 bricks) out of LEGO bricks. Have them name the object. (Naming the object will facilitate the discussion about identity.)
2. After the students have built their objects, ask them to replace one brick from their object with another brick of the same size, shape, and color. Ask them to replace another brick from the original object with a brick of the same size, shape, and color. Have them repeat this until all of the original bricks have been replaced. Instruct the students to keep the replaced LEGO bricks in a pile to the side.

Discussion Part 1 (10 minutes)

1. Have students discuss in their pairs whether or not the object they now have is the same object as the object they originally built. Ask a couple of students to share their thoughts with the group.
2. Explain that this activity models a famous philosophical thought experiment. Introduce the Ship of Theseus thought experiment. Ask the students if they feel the same about the identity of the Ship of Theseus as they do about their LEGO structures.

Discussion Notes

There is a commonsense notion that the identity of an object is defined by what the object is made of. If an object were to be made of different stuff, it would be a different object. The Ship of Theseus and the LEGO activity are prompts to get students to think more critically about that idea. The central question for students to consider is the relationship between identity and material constitution. That is to say, to what extent is the identity of an object bound to the parts from which it is made? In this case, is what makes the Ship of Theseus the Ship of Theseus the wood that it is made from?

Of course, there are complexities to consider beyond a simple answer of "yes" or "no":

- Does the quantity of material replaced bear upon the identity?
  - Is it the same ship after one board is replaced?
  - Is it the same ship after more than 50 percent of the boards have been replaced?
  - Is it the same ship after all boards but one have been replaced?
- Does the amount of time over which the replacement takes place bear upon identity?
  - Is it the same ship if all of the boards were replaced over a hundred years?
  - Is it the same ship if all of the boards were replaced over one day?

These complexities are relevant in thinking about the differences between the Ship of Theseus and the LEGO activity. Differences that might come into the discussion and that are worth mentioning if students do not bring them up are the following:

- Number of pieces. The ship is made of thousands of boards but the LEGO structures are made of only a few bricks. Each LEGO brick replacement represents a much bigger part of the object than each board on the Ship of Theseus.
- Time. The Ship of Theseus was replaced over hundreds of years. The LEGO bricks were replaced in a couple of minutes.

Talking about these differences will help students explore their intuitions about the identity of the objects.

Building Part 2 (5 minutes)

Have the student pairs recreate their original object using the replaced LEGO bricks they put to the side in Building Part 1. At the end, they should have two identical-appearing LEGO objects—one from Building Part 1 and one created out of the LEGO bricks that were replaced during Building Part 1.

Discussion Part 2 (15 minutes)

Briefly introduce Hobbes' extension of the Ship of Theseus, which Building Part 2 models. (See the Supplemental Materials.) Ask the students to discuss the following question in their pairs: Which is the real Ship of Theseus?

Have the pairs then share highlights of their discussions with the larger group.

Interactive Lecture or Discussion (15 minutes)

This interactive lecture is intended to take the form of structuring and clarifying thoughts brought up in Discussion Part 2. Begin by identifying two underlying assumptions we have about identity that come into tension and make the Ship of Theseus an interesting puzzle:

- Assumption 1: Objects can undergo change but remain the same object. This assumption motivates the thought that the Building Part 1 object is *the real object*. For example, I leave an unripe banana on the kitchen counter for a few days, and it changes color from green to yellow and becomes softer and sweeter. Nonetheless, I am inclined to say it is the same banana despite it having undergone changes to the way it looks, feels, and tastes.
- Assumption 2: The identity of an object is connected to its parts. This assumption motivates the thought that the Building Part 2 object is *the real object*.

For example, I am looking at two red playground balls that are the same size and color, the balls bounce the same way, and I can throw them equally far. Nonetheless, I am inclined to say that they are not identical (in the relevant sense of identity here) because the balls are made from different stuff. What makes the ball on the right THAT ball is the particular rubber molecules it is made from. Similarly for the ball on the left; it is THAT ball because of the particular rubber molecules it is made from. Different rubber means different balls no matter how similar they look or behave.

Propose some solutions to the Ship of Theseus in the context of the above assumptions. Students may have come up with some of these approaches in Discussion Part 2, so be sure to connect these solutions to that discussion.

Solution 1: Deny Assumption 2. It is not the pieces that matter for identity, but the history of the ship. Identity is based on spatial-temporal continuity.

Solution 2: Limit the scope of Assumption 1, allowing for identity to persist across some but not all change. One could say sometimes identity is preserved over change and sometimes it isn't. The difficulty is then where to draw the line. Did the ship stop being the Ship of Theseus after the 100th board was replaced, the 1000th board, etc.? This seems arbitrary.

Solution 3: Deny Assumption 1. Commit to the idea that the identity of an object cannot survive change. This view implies that there is a new ship every time a board is replaced—a thousand ships were destroyed and a thousand more created.

Solution 4: Move forward with both assumptions and allow for two Ships of Theseus to be there. (*Note*: This requires one to reject the transitivity of identity. As with transitivity in math, this is the idea that if *a* is identical to *b* and *a* is identical to *c*, *b* must also be identical to *c*. The ship with the replaced boards (*b*) is identical to the original Ship of Theseus (*a*). The ship made later out of the original boards (*c*) is also identical to the Ship of Theseus (*a*). However, the ship made out of the replaced boards (*b*) and the ship made out of the original boards (*c*) are not identical.

Homework/Follow-Up (5 minutes)

Show the following clip from *American Restoration*: http://www.youtube.com/watch?v=nRIH3Nz94S0.

This clip shows a full restoration of two classic toys: a bike and a ride-on train. Both are rusty and in extreme disrepair when brought into the shop. They are restored to pristine condition and are fully functional after the restoration.

Ask the students to write one paragraph on each of the following questions:

• Is the restored train or bike the same object as the original? Clearly state your answer and provide an argument to support it.
• Why do some changes, such as the restoration of the train, enhance the value of an object but others, such as cleaning the patina from an antique gun or piece of furniture, decrease the value? Clearly state your thesis and provide an argument to support it.

Supplemental Materials

Brief Overview of Identity

In nontechnical terms, the question of identity, as discussed by philosophers, is a question about the relationship of a thing to itself. That is to say, what makes a particular object *That* object (as opposed to some other object)? There have been numerous attempts to flesh out this concept over the years. As one might expect, there is no overstating the nuance and level of detail with which philosophers engage this issue, but this lesson focuses on two general approaches:

• The material from which the object is composed provides that object's identity.
• The spatial-temporal history of an object provides that object's identity.

It is worth noting that this lesson does not explore a third major approach to the question that posits that it is the constellation of properties possessed by an object that provides that object's identity.

Ship of Theseus Thought Experiment Description

The Greek historian and philosopher, Plutarch, tells the story of Theseus, the mythical hero and founding king of Athens who slayed the Minotaur. As a memorial of Theseus, the Athenians preserved his ship. Over time, the ship deteriorated and boards were replaced one by one. Eventually, all of the original pieces of the ship were replaced. The question then arose as to whether or not it was the same ship, the Ship of Theseus, or something else. Does the identity of the ship persist even though all of the parts have been replaced? Is it still the Ship of Theseus?

Below is the relevant excerpt from the Plutarch text:

> XXIII. The ship on which Theseus sailed with the youths and returned in safety, the thirty-oared galley, was preserved by the Athenians down to the time of Demetrius Phalereus. They took away the old timbers from time to time, and put new and sound ones in their places, so that the vessel became a standing illustration for the philosophers in the mooted question of growth, some declaring that it remained the same, others that it was not the same vessel.

Life of Theseus, Plutarch. Theoi Classical E-Texts Library: http://www.theoi.com/Text/PlutarchTheseus.html.

Hobbes' Extension of the Ship of Theseus

Suppose that someone saved all of the original pieces of the Ship of Theseus. Years later, the pieces were reassembled exactly as they were in the original ship. There are now two ships:

1. A restored ship crafted over time as original pieces were replaced one by one.
2. A reassembled ship crafted out of the original pieces.

Which one is the Ship of Theseus? Are both the Ship of Theseus? Is neither?
Below is the relevant excerpt from Hobbes:

> For if, for example, that ship of Theseus, concerning the difference whereof made by continual reparation in taking out the old planks and putting in the new, the sophisters of Athens were wont to dispute, were, after all the planks were changed, the same numerical ship it were at the beginning; and if some man had kept the old planks as they were taken out, and by afterwards putting them together in the same order, had again made a ship of them, this without doubt, had also been the same numerical ship with that which was in the beginning; and so there would have been two ships numerically the same, which is absurd.

Hobbes, Thomas. *De Coropore,* in *The English Works of Thomas Hobbes*, ed. Molesworth, Vol. 1, 1839, p. 136.

*This lesson plan was contributed by Stuart Gluck and Carlos Rodriguez from the Johns Hopkins University Center for Talented Youth (CTY). Stuart Gluck received a Ph.D. in philosophy from Johns Hopkins University and is currently the Director of Institutional Research at CTY, and Carlos Rodriguez serves as Assistant Director for Summer Programs at CTY and develops curriculum and provides pedagogical support for CTY's many precollegiate philosophy courses.

LESSON PLAN
SOCIAL MEDIA AND FREE WILL*

Topic: Free will
Time: Several class sessions

Objectives

- Develop a working definition of "free will"
- To show the complexity in determining whether a person truly acts freely
- Become familiar with what philosophers refer to as "internal constraints" to a person acting freely

Introduction

Students will learn about issues pertaining to free will by reading and analyzing a thought experiment. This thought experiment is about Debbie, a student who became "hooked" on her smartphone. It appears to Debbie's friends and family as though she is completely obsessed with using social media, which causes concern. In what follows, students will read a thought experiment that raises serious questions about what it means to act freely and participate in a guided discussion that addresses such questions by analyzing the thought experiment.

Activity

Before asking students to read the following thought experiment, have a short discussion about what it means to act freely. To begin with, you might want to ask students whether they freely chose to attend class. This may lead to a discussion on how one knows when one acts freely. After discussing some of the ideas students raise about whether or not they freely chose to attend class, introduce a simple working definition of free will:

A person is said to act freely if, and only if, he or she could have acted otherwise.

For example, a student might say that she *chose* to come to class today but that she could have instead pretended to be sick and stay at home.

Here, one should point out that it is possible that one could *feel* as though he or she could have acted otherwise, but that given his or her genes, character makeup, and numerous environmental and social factors, it might be unlikely that they he or she truly could have acted otherwise.

Philosophers discuss two types of constraints that can infringe upon a person's having free will: *internal constraints* and *external constraints*.

Internal constraints have to do with various psychological, genetic, or otherwise internal factors that compel a person to have certain preferences or behaviors. For example, a person who is a kleptomaniac has a psychological compulsion to steal things. It could be argued that a kleptomaniac isn't truly free because he/she is compelled to steal, and it is nearly impossible for him or her to act otherwise (not steal).

External constraints are environmental or social conditions that regulate or restrict a person's behavior or that limit the options that are available. An example of this can be illustrated using the original example of deciding to attend class. Suppose a student pretended to be sick, but his parents said that he had to go to school otherwise he would be grounded for six months. One could argue that this student didn't freely choose to attend class—he was forced to attend as he feared his parents' punishment.

Ask students to keep these ideas in mind while reading the following thought experiment. Afterward, discuss the questions as a class.

Debbie and Her Obsession with Social Media

Debbie started using her older sister Dalia's smartphone at the age of 11. She mainly played games, searched for free apps that seemed interesting, and looked through her sister's pictures. One day, Debbie stumbled onto one of her sister's social media accounts. What fun! She looked at all of their family members' profiles, as well as the timelines, posts, and pictures of Dalia's friends. Debbie was in heaven! She decided to open her own account so that she could create her own profile and add her own friends. When Debbie turned 12, her parents bought her a smartphone as a special "preteen birthday surprise."

What Debbie and Dalia's parents didn't know was that Debbie would become completely obsessed with social media. At first everyone just thought that Debbie was excited about getting such a nice birthday present. After a couple of weeks, however, it became apparent that Debbie was glued to her phone so that she could stay on social media 24–7. She would post a picture of what she was wearing to school that day, then another picture of what her mom made the girls for breakfast. Then, during car pool, Debbie would post funny videos of the car ride to school. During school, Debbie would sneak her phone with her on trips to the bathroom so that she could message her friends and see what everybody was up to. During lunch, Debbie would update her status with "selfies" of herself and her friends. After lunch, Debbie would continue to sneak social media trips to the restroom and then look at everyone's posts on the car ride home. Debbie continued to be constantly connected to social media in this manner all day, every day.

After a couple of weeks or so, Debbie and Dalia's parents noticed that Debbie wasn't engaging with her family the way she used to. Instead of talking about what was going on that day in school at the dinner table, Debbie was posting pictures, updating her status, or looking at other friends' posts. The parents in the car pool noticed a change in Debbie, but were reluctant to say anything. One of Debbie's teachers noticed Debbie's frequent trips to the restroom, along with her declining grades and participation, and figured something was going on. This teacher, Mrs. Bloom, waited outside the bathroom stall to speak with Debbie but found Debbie on her phone engrossed in social media. Mrs. Bloom confronted Debbie, sharing her concern and discussing the consequences for using a phone during the school day. Mrs. Bloom had no choice but to contact Debbie's parents. After speaking with Mrs. Bloom, Debbie's parents decided to have a social media intervention when Debbie came home from school that day.

Questions Raised

1. If a person acts freely if, and only if, they could have acted otherwise, is Debbie freely choosing this behavior? Why or why not?
2. What makes a person responsible for her actions? Is Debbie responsible for her social media addiction? Would it be right to blame Debbie for her social media obsession? Why or why not?
3. Should the question of whether or not Debbie is acting freely have bearing on whether or not she should be punished in accordance with the classroom rules?
4. If Debbie is not acting freely, given, say, a genetic predisposition to gravitate toward social media, should she be held responsible for breaking the classroom rules? Should Mrs. Bloom make sure that Debbie suffers the consequences as outlined in the class rules (which strictly prohibit any cell phone use during the day)?
5. What are some practical recommendations for helping Debbie with her addiction to social media? Should her parents take her phone away? Limit her use of the phone? Send her to the guidance counselor? How should the teacher deal with this situation?

Conclusion

Students should walk away from the discussion with a sense of complexity as it pertains to issues of free will. Although we might often feel as though we freely choose to do (or not to do) something, we might be less free than we believe, given internal and external constraints of which we might not even be aware. Students should take away the idea that we can only blame or praise people when they act freely. Does it make sense to hold people accountable for things they did not freely choose to do?

*This lesson plan was contributed by Ayesha Bhavsar, a Ph.D. holder in philosophy with areas of specialization in bioethics and feminist philosophy, whose experience teaching philosophy to seventh graders sparked her commitment to making philosophy accessible to children.

LESSON PLAN
CONVINCE YOUR TEACHER/PRINCIPAL*

Topic: How to write a strong argument
Time: Several class sessions

Objectives

• Formulate an argument
• Learn how to anticipate and respond to objections

Introduction

What is an argument?

An argument consists of a set of reasons that are given with the intention of persuading someone else that a particular action or idea is right or wrong, good or bad, desirable or undesirable, etc. It is a method of trying to convince another person (or persons) that your position on an issue is correct, by using relevant support and evidence.
    Consider the following examples:

Premise 1 (P1). Having the shared responsibility of a class pet would help cultivate more responsible, caring students.
Premise 2 (P2). Responsibility is a character trait that teachers and parents think is important, and is something they would like to see more of.
Premise 3 (P3). Having a class pet would give students a living being to care for, thereby teaching students the true meaning of responsibility.
Conclusion: Therefore, our class should be allowed to get a class pet.

Arguments are combinations of statements that are put forth in a particular structure, that are intended to change or convince the minds of a particular audience. Notice that in the argument given above, the conclusion—our class should be allowed to get a class pet—is supported by specific and relevant reasons (premises) and is a culminating statement meant to convince an audience.

There are three basic elements of an argument: premises, inference, and conclusion.

Stage One: Premises

The basis of persuasive communication is made up of premises, or statements that are necessary for the argument. Premises are the evidence, or reasons that are put forth in a particular structure, aimed at convincing another to accept the conclusion. You will see in the above example that premises are listed as P1, P2, P3, and so on.

Stage Two: Inference

The premises of the argument can be used to obtain further ideas. This process is known as inference. In inference, we start with one or more accepted premises. We then derive a new premise from those preceding it. For instance, in the example above, P3 is an inference based upon the information presented in P1 and P2. It takes the information that has been accepted in P1 and P2, and formulates a new idea that plays a central part in leading us to the conclusion.

Stage Three: Conclusion

The conclusion is the claim that you want the other person or party to agree with. It is drawn from and supported by the premises of the argument. The conclusion is often the final stage of inference. Conclusions are often, but not always, indicated by phrases such as "therefore," "it follows that," "we conclude," "thus," "hence," and so on. In the following exercise, the conclusion will be something that you want to persuade either your teacher or principal of.

Activity

Step 1: Formulate a conclusion

Although the conclusion is the final stage of an argument, it is often helpful to work backward when formulating an argument. First think about something that you think would really benefit you and your classmates. Make it something reasonable, and something for which you can provide strong support.

- Think of one thing that you really want to convince your teacher or principal to grant you and your classmates, something that is both reasonable and defensible. Possible ideas might include longer recess, longer lunch, an extra break, a class pet, a new elective that isn't offered, new playground equipment, etc.
- Formulate whatever it is that you want to convince your teacher or principal of as a conclusion. For example,
  - In light of these reasons, our class should adopt a pet iguana.
  - Therefore, we should have an hour-long recess every other day.
  - In conclusion, lunch period should last an hour instead of a mere half-hour.
  - In sum, our school should offer Philosophy as an elective.

o Hence, the extracurricular budget should include funding for a climbing wall in the school gym.
- Share these conclusions with the class before moving on to the next step.

Step 2: Formulate the body of the argument

What supporting evidence would help convince your teacher or principal to accept your conclusion? Begin by listing all the relevant evidence. Next, arrange the premises so that they flow in a "natural order" from one to the next. That is, the premises should support and lead the audience to the conclusion. Inferences should follow from the premises preceding it, as in the example above.

For example,

P1. Numerous studies show that students that get more exercise perform better academically and are better behaved in class.

P2. At present, students are not getting adequate exercise during the school day, because recess is only 15 minutes long.

P3. Having a longer recess period would provide students the opportunity they need to get enough exercise.

P4. By increasing exercise, students will likely perform better both academically and behaviorally.

Conclusion: Therefore, our class should be allowed to have an hour-long recess.

Step 3: Objections/response to objections

After you have formed your argument, consider possible objections. You might think that acknowledging the objections that the principal or teacher could make will weaken your argument. This is not necessarily the case. In anticipating possible objections, you are able to preemptively respond to these objections and thereby strengthen your argument. Also, in considering objections to your argument, you might realize that you need to revise your argument by rewording one or more premises (or your conclusion). Some arguments are not defensible, or are less defensible than others. If the objections cause you to realize that there are significant weaknesses in your argument, you have two options:

Option 1. Rewrite your argument and form a different, stronger argument.

Option 2. Realize that your argument is not defensible and will rightly be dismissed based upon strong and compelling objections.

One way to formulate objections to a given argument is by challenging the truth of the premises or the plausibility of particular inferences being drawn. The more complex the premise, the more opportunity there is to challenge it, so you might want to go back to your original argument and reframe your premises so that they are more defensible. Keep your premises short, noncontroversial, and based in fact.

Here are some examples of possible objections and responses to objections that could be made from the above example.

Objection 1: A pet is too much of a burden to care for—it will be too much of a responsibility.
Response to objection: A guinea pig, for example, wouldn't be too much work because we can take turns cleaning the cage and feeding it. They don't need walks like a dog does.

Objection 2: Pets are distracting and will make it difficult for students to focus during class.
Response to objection: A guinea pig can be kept in a cage and can be taken out to hold and play with only during recess and certain agreed-upon times.

Objection 3: Pets can be dangerous.
Response to objection: Unlike snakes and hermit crabs, which can be dangerous, guinea pigs don't bite or scratch. They are friendly, meek creatures.

Objection 4: There isn't enough support to prove that having a pet will cultivate a sense of responsibility.
Response to objection: I know of several cases where students became more responsible by caring for a pet. For example, consider the transformation we see in many of the students in Mrs. Bloom's, Ms. Wright's, and Mr. Chase's classes.

Step 4: Role play

Have students form pairs. Each student will present his or her argument to the other student who will pretend to be the teacher/principal. The student playing the teacher/principal will then formulate an objection to the student's argument. Allow the student to respond to the objection, and go back and forth until all relevant objections have been discussed. At this point, the student presenting his or her argument should take a moment to revise his or her work, if additional objections have been raised. Switch roles, and repeat the role-play exercise.

After students have had the opportunity to revise their drafts in light of newly raised objections, they may submit their final draft to the teacher/principal.

*This lesson plan was contributed by Ayesha Bhavsar, a Ph.D. in philosophy with areas of specialization in bioethics and feminist philosophy whose experience teaching philosophy to seventh graders sparked her commitment to making philosophy accessible to children.

Supplemental Materials

Weston, Anthony. *A Rulebook for Arguments* (4th ed.). Indianapolis: Hackett Publishing, 2009.
Hurley, Patrick. *A Concise Introduction to Logic*. Belmont, California: Wadsworth Publishing, 2011.

LESSON PLAN
LOGIC CHARADES*

Topic: Four common deductive arguments
Time: Several class sessions

Objectives

• Students will learn four new vocabulary terms: statement, argument, conclusion, and premise.

- Students will be able to name, describe, identify, construct, and creatively enact their own examples of deductive arguments of the following forms: modus ponens, modus tollens, hypothetical syllogism, and disjunctive syllogism.

Materials Needed

- Props and costumes (not necessary but fun) for enacting any of the skits
- Construction paper and markers to make signs
- Copies of the handout (see Supplemental Materials section below).

Description

An argument is a deductive argument when we can arrive at the conclusion solely on the basis of information contained in the *premises* (the reasons, evidence, or support given for each conclusion).

Introduction

In philosophy, an "argument" does not mean the kind of fight you get into with your brother or sister, classmate, or parents (e.g., getting upset and calling the other person names).

In a philosophical context, an *argument* is a sequence of statements used to support, provide evidence for, prove, or back up a conclusion. In order to convince another person (or persons) of a particular position, we create arguments to establish and provide support for our position.

- A *statement* is a sentence or a claim that asserts something is either true or false.
- A *conclusion* is a statement that is supported or backed up by other statements.
- The statements that provide reasons, evidence, or support for the conclusion are called *premises*.

For example, Rebecca might argue for a later bedtime by offering strong support for *why* her parents should let her stay up an extra half-hour (see example below).

> *Rebecca: Due to the fact that I had to wake up at 6:00 a.m. in order to be ready in time for car pool, my bedtime has always been 8:30 pm. Given that Mrs. Green is now in charge of morning car pool, she comes at 6:30 am and I have an extra half-hour to sleep in. Now, I can go to bed a half-hour later and still get the same amount of sleep. Therefore, I should be allowed to stay up until 9:00 p.m.*

Premises and conclusions are often easy to spot because they follow words that act as indicators, or guide-posts, giving the reader notice that a premise or a conclusion is about to appear in the body of the text. (Conclusion indicators and premise indicators are addressed in the accompanying handout.)

First, identify the conclusion:

Therefore, (conclusion indicator) I should be allowed to stay up until 9:00 p.m. Second, what are the premises that work to support the conclusion?

P1. Due to the fact that (premise indicator) I had to wake up at 6:00 a.m., my bedtime has always been 8:30 p.m.

P2. Given that (premise indicator) Mrs. Green is now in charge of car pool, I have an extra half-hour to get ready in the morning.

P3. I can go to bed a half-hour later and get the same amount of sleep as before.

Activity 1

1. Give students the handout (see Supplemental Materials). Have students complete numbers 1–5 and review the answers as a class. Have students do number 6 and then share their examples with the class. Explain that P1, P2, etc. is shorthand for Premise 1, Premise 2. When they are proficient in being able to identify parts of an argument and also provide their own examples, move on to other kinds of deductive arguments.

2. We will learn four types of arguments. These four argument forms are all *deductive* arguments, which means that we can arrive at the conclusion *solely* from the information provided in the premises.

Type 1: Modus ponens

Arguments in the following form are called *modus ponens.* The "P" and the "Q" can stand for any statement you choose, just be sure to keep your "P's" and "Q's" consistent throughout a given argument.

P1. If P is true, then Q is true.
P2. P is true.

_____

Therefore, Q is true.

When we substitute "P" for "it rains" and "Q" for "we get to watch a movie" the argument would look like this:

P1. If it rains then we get to watch a movie.
P2. It is raining.

_____

Therefore we get to watch a movie.

Type 2: Modus tollens

Another argument form, *modus tollens*, is of the following form:

P1. If P is true, then Q is true
P2. Q is not true.

_____

Therefore, P is not true.

When we substitute our "P's" and "Q's" a modus tollens argument might look like this:

P1. If I do all of my chores, then I get a new puppy.
P2. I didn't get a new puppy.

_____

Therefore, I didn't do all of my chores.

Type 3: Hypothetical syllogism

Hypothetical syllogism is of the following form:

P1. If P is true, then Q is true.
P2. If Q is true, then R is true.

_____

Therefore, if P is true, then R is true.

This argument form can be expressed using common language. Consider the following example:

P1. If I finish my homework then I can log onto Facebook.
P2. If I can log onto Facebook, then I can instant message Avi.

_____

Therefore, if I finish my homework, I can instant message Avi.

Type 4: Disjunctive syllogism

Disjunctive syllogism can take two (very similar) forms. These are:

P1. Either P is true or Q is true.
P2. P is not true.

_____

Therefore, Q is true.

Similarly, disjunctive syllogism could also take the form where Premise 2 states that Q is not true. For example:

P1. Either P is true or Q is true.
P2. Q is not true.

_____

Therefore, P is true.

When we substitute our "P's" and "Q's" it would look like this:

P1. Either Esther is a drama queen or Michael has a mean sense of humor.
P2. Esther is not a drama queen.

_____

Therefore, Michael has a mean sense of humor.

OR, using the same example, disjunctive syllogism could also look like this:

P1. Either Esther is a drama queen or Michael has a mean sense of humor.
P2. Michael does not have a mean sense of humor.

_____

Therefore, Esther is a drama queen.

3. Ask students to make their own examples of each of the four argument forms on the handout. Have students share their examples with the class, or come up to the board and write their examples on the board. Let the class determine whether the examples are done correctly, and if not, determine what would be needed to fix the example. Once students are proficient in understanding how these four forms work, have them do the following activity.

Activity 2

1. Each student will make four signs using construction paper and markers. The name of an argument form should be on the front, and the structure of the form should be on the back.
2. Next, for the capstone activity, students will create skits that enact each of these forms.
   • First, form small groups depending upon class size. Write the names of the forms on small pieces of paper and put these in a hat or bucket. Each group will draw two forms from the hat and *keep it secret.*
   • Groups should go to private corners of the room or perhaps work in the hall to ensure that other groups do not know which argument form they drew. Each group will develop two skits (using props and costumes if provided) that illustrate the argument forms they drew. Encourage students to make these funny, as it can be easier to remember things that make you laugh.

An example of a skit could be the following:
Suppose a group wants to enact hypothetical syllogism in front of the class.

One student might pretend to be a dog trainer, another student the dog in training, and the third student the dog owner. The dog owner says to the trainer: "All my dog wants to do is play dead all day. I brought him here for training because my neighbor tells me that if Bailey (the dog) plays dead all day he will only eat fruit rollups." The trainer attempts to get the dog to roll over, shake, and do a few other tricks, but all the dog does is play dead.

The trainer responds to the owner: "Well, if Bailey will only eat fruit rollups, then all the other dogs will want to be his best friend." At this point, the dog sits right up and says to both the owner and the trainer: "In this case, if I play dead all day then all the other dogs will want to be my best friend! Sounds like a plan!"

P1. If P is true, then Q is true.
P2. If Q is true, then R is true.

_____

Therefore, if P is true, then R is true.

3. Finally, each group will perform their first skit and the audience will hold up their sign *at the end* of each skit, showing which one they think it is. It is important that students don't call out answers but hold up signs. After all the groups have presented their first skit, each group will present their second in the same manner.

*This lesson plan was contributed by Ayesha Bhavsar, a Ph.D. in philosophy with areas of specialization in bioethics and feminist philosophy, whose experience teaching philosophy to seventh graders sparked her commitment to making philosophy accessible to children.

Supplemental Materials

A couple of additional resources are as follows:

Weston, Anthony. *A Rulebook for Arguments* (4th ed.). Indianapolis: Hackett Publishing, 2009.
Hurley, Patrick. *A Concise Introduction to Logic*. Belmont, California: Wadsworth Publishing, 2011.

Handout: A Little Logic

Conclusion Indicators
Therefore, thus, so, hence, in conclusion, consequently

Premise Indicators
Because, since, assuming that, given that, the fact that, due to the fact

Note: Not all premises or conclusions will be introduced by these indicators. There are additional indicators that are not included here, and often one must determine the conclusion and premises from contextual cues.

Exercise 1

Circle the conclusion and underline each of the premises in the following arguments:

1. It is true that $2 \times 3 = 6$, and it is also true that $6 \times 1 = 6$. Thus, we can conclude with certainty that $(2 \times 3) = (6 \times 1)$.

2. All dogs love to chew on shoes. Bailey is a dog. Therefore, Bailey loves chewing on shoes.
3. Mario's parents let him watch movies that are rated PG-13. I will be thirteen in less than two years, and I am very mature for my age. Given these facts, I should also be allowed to watch movies that are rated PG-13.
4. Today we have a grammar quiz that I haven't studied for. I need an A on the quiz or my parents won't let me get on Facebook for a week. So, today I need to spend lunchtime studying instead of sitting with my friends.
5. Everyone either loves Mrs. Harper or they think she is a boring teacher. I don't love her. Consequently, I think that she is a boring teacher.

Come up with your own argument and label the premises/conclusion!

Exercise 2

Come up with your own examples! Be as creative as you like. Just make sure you follow the exact form provided in substituting your "P's" and "Q's."

Modus ponens: Your example of modus ponens:

P1. If P is true, then Q is true
P2. P is true

_____

Therefore, Q is true

Modus tollens: Your example of modus tollens:

P1. If P is true, then Q is true
P2. Q is not true

_____

Therefore, P is not true.

Hypothetical syllogism: Your example of hypothetical syllogism:

P1. If P is true, then Q is true.
P2. If Q is true, then R is true.

_____

Therefore, if P is true, then R is true.
Come up with two examples of **Disjunctive syllogism:**

P1. Either P is true or Q is true.   Your example:
P2. P is not true

_____

Therefore, Q is true.

P1. Either P is true or Q is true.   Your example:
P2. Q is not true.

_____

Therefore, P is true.

Chapter 8

Philosophy in High School

As we hope is clear from previous chapters, philosophical practice need not be delayed until high school. Children possess philosophical interests and are capable of contributing to philosophy sessions in diverse ways from a young age. However, high school can be an opportune time to introduce philosophical inquiry if students have not had previous experience with philosophy in school. High school students are thinking seriously about identity, the nature of the good life, the meaning of happiness, issues of justice and fairness, and many other philosophical questions.

In this chapter, we provide a selection of lesson plans that can be used to practice philosophy with high school students. Responding both to the development and greater educational experience of adolescent students, many of these lessons provide opportunities for sustained and prolonged examination of philosophical topics, questions, and problems. These lessons also include a more explicit focus on reasoning and argumentation skills, in-depth discussion of ethical, social, and political issues, and pedagogical strategies for structuring productive high-school philosophy classes. These philosophy lessons are not exhaustive; indeed, there are numerous other areas that can be tackled with adolescent students. Rather, we present lessons in this chapter—written by classroom teachers, academics, and graduate students—as useful examples of introducing philosophy in a high school setting.

LESSON PLAN
ARGUMENTS AND PHILOSOPHICAL REASONING*

Topics: Arguments and philosophical reasoning
Time: 50 minutes

Objectives

- Introduce students to philosophical arguments
- Explore the types of logical reasoning used to investigate philosophical issues

Materials Needed

- Chalkboard or whiteboard
- Computer and projector or equipment to watch short video clips from the web

Introduction

This lesson can be used at any time in a philosophy course, for a meeting of a philosophy club or discussion group, or for a workshop, but, because it introduces students or participants to the method of how philosophers approach philosophical questions, it is especially appropriate as the first lesson or experience. It is intended to get students or participants to recognize that philosophical reasoning takes place in the form of argumentation. This lesson, however, stops short of providing tools for evaluating philosophical arguments. Therefore, if you are using this as the first lesson in a class or for the first meeting of a philosophy club or interest group, it would be natural to follow it up with some lessons on critical thinking or logic to provide a more complete foundation in philosophical reasoning. In turn, those lessons could be followed by explorations of philosophical content, in which you would use the method of philosophical reasoning to address specific philosophical questions or topics.

Activities

Am I Your Teacher? (10 minutes)

1. Begin by writing "I am the teacher of this class" (or "I am the presenter" or whatever would be most appropriate for your setting) at the bottom of the board with a line drawn above it. Ask the students or participants to show by raising hands how many of them think this statement is true. Presumably, all of them will. If so, ask them why they think this. As they give reasons, write the reasons on the board above the line. Once there are a large number of reasons on the board, ask them what everything written on the board together is called. The purpose is to illustrate that an argument is being made.

Textbox 8.1

I told you that I am the teacher.
I am standing at the front of the class.
I am leading this exercise.
I am the only adult in the room.

――――――――――――――――――――――

I am the teacher of this class

2. Ask the students or participants why they think you had them do this as the first exercise when exploring philosophy. Lead a brief discussion. A few points to try to develop during the discussion include the following:
   - What you have written on the board is an example of an argument.

- Arguments are the way we think and reason—when we're reasoning something out, what we're doing is forming a series of arguments in our heads.
- Philosophy is essentially a process of thinking systematically about difficult and interesting questions, and a primary component of philosophy centers on making and evaluating arguments.

What Is an Argument? (10 minutes)

1. Begin this activity by showing the Monty Python clip, "The Argument Clinic." The clip can be found at: http://www.youtube.com/watch?v=kQFKtI6gn9Y
2. After showing the clip, ask:

What are the two different concepts of "argument" presented in the skit?

The two concepts are:

- Mere contradiction or a dispute ("Yes it is . . . No it isn't . . . Yes it is . . . No it isn't . . .")
- (Proposed by the customer) "A collected series of statements to establish a definite proposition."

When we talk about arguments as used by philosophers, we are talking about an argument in the latter sense. Again, doing philosophy is essentially a process of making and evaluating arguments.

Parts of an Argument (10 minutes)

1. Return to the "I am the teacher of this class" argument. You'll use it as an example to illustrate and help explore what arguments are and how they work.
2. In a group discussion, explore the parts of an argument. As you do so, it will be helpful to develop the following points and to introduce the following terms:

Ask what parts constitute an argument. What are its basic building blocks? Arguments are composed of sentences. In fact, they are made up of a particular type of sentence, known as a proposition.

Proposition: A declarative sentence that has a truth value. In other words, a proposition is a sentence that can be either true or false. To be precise, propositions express facts about the world that can either be true or false. Examples include "Today is Monday," and "It's raining outside."

Question: Are there kinds of sentences that are not propositions? Answer: Yes. Questions, commands, exclamations, etc., are all types of sentences that are not propositions because they lack a truth value. Examples include "Go open the door," and "What is today's date?"

Typically, most of the propositions in an argument state facts or provide information which support the claim being made. These propositions are known as premises.

Premise: A proposition serving as a reason for a conclusion.

The claim being made is known as the conclusion of the argument.

Conclusion: A proposition that is supported or entailed by a set of premises.

Arguments always have one conclusion, but the number of premises can vary quite a bit. The "I am the teacher of this class" argument has several premises.

Question: Can there be an argument with only one premise? Answer: Yes. For example, "Bill is an unmarried male. Therefore, Bill is a bachelor."

Question: Can there be an argument with no premises? Answer: Yes. For example, consider an argument with no premises and the following conclusion: "It is either Monday in Tokyo or it is not Monday in Tokyo."

It's worth noting that adding premises doesn't necessarily add support for a conclusion. For example, the argument above with no premises is in fact a compelling argument, since it always has to either be Monday or not be Monday in Tokyo.

3. Now we can say what an argument is in a more precise way:

   Argument: An argument is a set (a collection) of propositions in which one proposition, known as the conclusion, is claimed to derive support from the other propositions, known as premises.

4. To summarize:
   o Arguments are the way we think and reason—when we're reasoning something out, what we are really doing is forming a series of arguments in our heads.
   o Though "argument" can also mean a dispute in common use, that's not the sense in which we mean it when doing philosophy.
   o Arguments consist of a conclusion and (almost always) some premises.
   o The conclusion is what the argument is meant to support as being true; it's the claim being made.
   o The premises provide support for the conclusion.
   o There can be any number of premises, from 0 to an infinite number (but having more premises doesn't necessarily mean there is more support for the conclusion!).
   o The premises and conclusion are propositional statements; that is, they are sentences that express facts (propositions) about the world that may be true or false.

Argument Dissection (10 minutes)

The "I am the teacher of this class" argument is in normal form. That's just a fancy way of saying that the premises have been collected together in a list with the conclusion following them. Often, we separate the conclusion from the premises by drawing a line between them (or by putting in the symbol "∴," which means "therefore," before the conclusion) to make it very clear which proposition is the conclusion. Usually arguments written in English prose are not so simply presented. The conclusion may be stated first, or for stylistic reasons it might not be at either the beginning or the end of the prose. Converting an argument from English prose into normal form allows us to clearly pick out the premises and conclusion.

How can we identify the premises and conclusion of an argument in ordinary prose? It can take some judgment, but we are usually guided by indicator words. The propositions in arguments are often accompanied by words that indicate whether that proposition is a premise or a conclusion.

As a group, brainstorm to come up with words or phrases that might indicate that the proposition they introduce is a premise or a conclusion. The following lists provide some of the most common premise and conclusion indicators.

> **Premise Indicators:** since, because, for, in that, as, given that, for the reason that, may be inferred from, owing to, inasmuch as
>
> **Conclusion Indicators:** therefore, consequently, thus, hence, it follows that, for this reason, we may infer, we may conclude, entails that, implies that

With that background in hand, the next activity will help everyone see that arguments are in fact all around us and to identify more easily the structure of those arguments, which is an important first step in evaluating whether we should be convinced by the argument.

1. Hand out to each student or participant a couple of arguments you have found in editorials, blogs, philosophy texts, or wherever. Ask them to rewrite the arguments in normal form, identifying the premises and the conclusions.
2. When done, ask everyone to pair up. Each person should show his or her partner the original arguments and the rewritten arguments in normal form. Each pair should then discuss whether or not the premises and conclusions were correctly identified. Walk about in the room and answer questions.

Evaluating Arguments (10 minutes)

This is a fun activity to help everyone start thinking about how to evaluate whether we should be convinced by an argument. Begin this activity by showing the Monty Python clip, "She's a Witch!" The clip can be found here: https://www.youtube.com/watch?v=zrzMhU_4m-g.

Begin a discussion about whether people are convinced by the argument provided in the video clip. Try to focus the discussion on whether the premises provide good reasons for believing that the conclusion is correct. Note that until the characters in the video clip actually use the scale, they don't know whether some of the facts asserted in the premises are true. That's often the case in exploring philosophical questions. What's important is the logical relationship between the premises and the conclusion. Hypothetically, if all the premises were to turn out to be true, would they then make it likely that the conclusion would also be true? By asking that question, we can evaluate the reasoning in an argument. Philosophers often focus the most on this step. If the reasoning in an argument is good, then we can go on to ask whether the premises are in fact true. Often that requires empirical investigation (and so may require the aid of scientists or other specialists). If both are the case—the reasoning is good and the premises are true—only then should we assent to the conclusion.

After a few minutes, pause the discussion. Ask the students to write a paragraph defending why they are or are not convinced by the argument in the video clip. Remind everyone that the paragraph should, of course, take the form of an argument!

If this lesson is being used for a one-time event, you can ask some volunteers to read their paragraphs and then resume a discussion about what they learned. If you are using this lesson as part of a class or a series of meetings, you can always ask the students or participants to write the paragraph at home and bring it with them to the next meeting. You can then discuss their paragraphs and what they learned from the exercise. If you are teaching a formal course, you can have the students turn in their paragraphs as an assignment.

Follow-Up and Conclusions

If this lesson is part of a course or a long sequence of meetings, it would be worthwhile to follow up with another lesson or two on how to properly evaluate arguments. How that is done will depend on how formal or informal you want to be in thinking about logic, and also how long you want to spend on an introductory philosophical reasoning unit.

Supplemental Materials

There are a number of excellent textbooks and resources on arguments, critical thinking, and logic. For example, reading the first two chapters of the following logic textbook would prepare you thoroughly for leading this lesson:

Hurley, Patrick. *A Concise Introduction to Logic* (12th ed.). Stamford: Cengage Learning, 2015.

(As an aside, reading the third and fourth chapters of the Hurley text would prepare you well for a potential follow-up lesson on distinguishing deductive from nondeductive arguments and evaluating arguments.)

A supplementary text with a more informal discussion of arguments is the following:

Weston, Anthony. *A Rulebook for Arguments* (4th ed.). Indianapolis: Hackett Publications, 2009.

The following brief magazine article was written by the authors of this lesson and, in a fun way, explores how philosophers investigate philosophical questions:

Gluck, S. and Rodriguez, C. "The Philosopher's Toolbox," *Imagine* 17.4 (2010): 20–21.

(Available online here: http://www.nxtbook.com/nxtbooks/imagine/20100304_SFF/.)

*This lesson plan was contributed by Stuart Gluck and Carlos Rodriguez from the Johns Hopkins University Center for Talented Youth (CTY). Stuart Gluck received a Ph.D. in philosophy from Johns Hopkins University and is currently the director of Institutional Research at CTY. Carlos Rodriguez serves as assistant director for Summer Programs at CTY and develops curriculum and provides pedagogical support for CTY's many precollegiate philosophy courses.

LESSON PLAN
DROP THE BALL*

Topics: Logic and practical reasoning; inductive versus deductive knowledge
Time: 5–15 minutes

Objectives

• To illustrate two possible sources of knowledge
• To introduce the difference between inductive and deductive reasoning

Materials Needed

A small, unexpected object, for example:
• A Sir Isaac Newton doll
• A baby spoon

Description

To demonstrate the difference between inductive versus deductive reasoning, or to introduce differences at the heart of rationalist versus empiricist epistemology, try this exercise.

1. Hold an object at arm's length and tell your students that, in three minutes, you will open your fingers. Ask students what they predict will happen. It helps if students are in a playful mood when working with abstract questions, so the object could be something whimsical or weird, like a headless doll.
2. Most students will say the object will drop (while some, encouraged by the headless doll, lighten the mood further with ridiculous predictions—but they'll be wrong).
3. At this point, declare to students that they seem pretty sure it will drop; ask them what makes them so certain.
4. Most students will say something along the lines of "That's what happens," and "That's the way it's always happened." Someone will say, "It's gravity."
   These are the two kinds of answers you're looking for. You need both kinds.
5. Explain that students making their predictions based on repeated experiences are reasoning *inductively*: they are drawing conclusions from repeated events. Students making their predictions based on a rule like gravity are reasoning *deductively*, using if-then thinking—if objects attract each other, then Earth will attract this headless doll.
6. Announce that you are now going to open your fingers and then everyone will see if the class is right. The object goes to the ground and the lesson is almost over.
7. Elaborate on what students have seen. You might at this point draw an upside-down triangle to represent inductive reasoning—many experiences leading to one conclusion—and a right-side-up triangle to represent deductive reasoning—one premise leading to numerous applications. This may also lead to a discussion about empiricism versus rationalism. Empiricism is the view that sense experience is the ultimate source

of all knowledge, while rationalism is the position that knowledge is gained independently of sense experience, through reason. Empiricism relies especially on inductive reasoning for its path to truth, and rationalism exclusively on deductive reasoning.

*This lesson plan was contributed by David Grosskopf, who cochairs the English department at Roosevelt High School in Seattle, Washington.

LESSON PLAN
WHAT DO WE FIND BEAUTIFUL?*

Topics: Beauty, as well as subjectivity and objectivity
Time: 90 minutes

Objectives

- To explore the nature of beauty
- To examine the significance of beauty in music

Introduction

Students should be given a week to do the following assignment (though it can be revised as needed to fit your time constraints):

Pick as many "beautiful" songs as you are old. So, for example, if you are 16 you will pick 16 of the songs you feel are the most "beautiful." Please make a list of these, and then write a paragraph for each song, detailing why you think they are the most beautiful songs ever created. After you have done this, please pick one song that you believe is "the opposite of beautiful," that you might term "ugly." Please also write a paragraph for this song, detailing why you think it is ugly.

Emphasize that the songs have to be the *most beautiful* songs of all time. Students are asked to bring, on the due date along with their completed assignment, their songs with them via iPod, phone, CD, or other device, and told that they will have a chance to play some of them. Make sure to have the facilities to play different mediums on the due date.

Activity

When students come together on the due date, divide them into groups of four or five. Ask students to share, in their small groups, what songs they chose that were beautiful and why. You can walk around and listen to the groups' conversations.

After about fifteen–twenty minutes (based on how you feel the group discussions are going), ask the students to share with their groups the "ugly" song they chose and explain why. Give this part of the activity somewhere between five–ten minutes, and again listen to each group's discussions.

Bring the class back together in one large group and ask the students whether, when they shared their beautiful songs, they found they chose some of the same ones. What were they? Why did they think they were beautiful? Did anyone else in the class pick those songs? If it turns out that there are a few songs about which the class shares the belief that they are beautiful, ask if students would like to play those songs. When a song is played, listen to the whole piece, unless it is particularly long (in which case you can ask the student to choose a segment to play). When the song is over, ask the student who played it why he or she thought it was beautiful if they haven't done so already. Ask the rest of the class if they thought the song was beautiful and why. Generally, a few students will volunteer ideas about the song and address why they think it is beautiful.

Questions Raised

As students address the whole class, listen to find places to ask follow-up questions about beauty. If you keep your ears open, the questions will come easily, and the context will call forth particular queries, but here are a few possible questions:

- What exactly is beauty?
- Is there something in music that needs to happen in order for you to find a song "beautiful"? What? Why?
- Is there a quality to this piece of music you find beautiful and that you recognize as happening in other places as well? So, for example, you say that this song makes you cry. Does every time you cry mean that you are experiencing beauty? Why or why not? (There are many different variations to this question.)
- How did you recognize the beauty of this song? Was it a feeling? A sensation? A thought? What was the process you went through to get to the belief that this song is "beautiful"?
- Why do you think other people might not see this song as beautiful? Is the song beautiful in itself, or does it depend wholly on the listener? If no one ever heard Beethoven's Fifth Symphony, for example, might it still be beautiful?
- What is the difference between subjectivity and objectivity? Can there be an objective beauty or is beauty always in the eye of the beholder?

After the groups have reported to the class, ask the whole class for volunteers to play a song they consider beautiful. Before they play it, ask them why they think it is beautiful. Continue this process and discussion until there is about twenty minutes left of class time. Then turn to the "ugly" songs and again ask the whole class if anyone wants to play their "ugly song." Repeat the format used for the beautiful songs by asking the students why they think various songs are ugly before they play them, and then open it up for discussion after it is played. Generally, the class will explore the relationship between beauty and ugliness and examine such topics as the connection between sadness and beauty, violence and ugliness, the song's music and its lyrics, etc.

At the end of the class, thank the students for sharing what they believe is beautiful. This can be a very personal exercise for students. When they describe why they find certain music beautiful and talk about the songs they love, they are sharing parts of themselves. The activity is often very moving and meaningful to the students, and elicits complex discussions about what makes something beautiful, the relationship between beauty and ugliness, and the objective or subjective nature of beauty.

*This lesson plan was contributed by Terrance McKittrick, a philosophy teacher at Nova High School, a public alternative school in Seattle, Washington.

LESSON PLAN
AFFIRMATIVE ACTION IN UNIVERSITY ADMISSIONS (1)*

Topics: Affirmative action and constitutional classifications
Time: Approximately two 80-minute class periods

Objectives

- Comprehend the Court's ruling and reasoning in major affirmative action cases
- Engage with a central topic in applied ethics and the philosophy of law
- Synthesize and evaluate the arguments in the affirmative action debate
- Demonstrate improvement in critical thinking skills by developing conclusions supported by reasons while avoiding fallacious reasoning
- Demonstrate intellectual empathy while engaging in the debate surrounding affirmative action

Materials Needed

Before the class begins,
- Copy the list of potential candidates, "The Final Four" (see below)
- Make a card for each student in the class with a number (1–14) on each card
- Determine which candidate will correspond to each number but do not share with students until the appropriate time in the lesson

Introduction

This lesson plan on the topic of affirmative action is intended to illustrate how philosophical concepts and analysis can be integrated into a typical US government course curriculum, or any class exploring this issue. The lesson uses Rawls' "veil of ignorance" in a hypothetical university admissions activity to motivate the arguments in the Affirmative Action debate, and encourages students to shed their often self-interested views about the topic in favor of a reasoned analysis of the arguments both in favor of and against Affirmative Action. In this lesson, philosophy is used as a tool to achieve subject matter objectives and to develop good reasoning skills.

Activity

Day 1: Entering The Veil of Ignorance

1. Introduce students to the basic facts of *Regents of the University of California v. Bakke* case. Ask students for their initial responses.
   Regents of the University of California v. Bakke—In the early 1970s, the medical school of the University of California at Davis devised a dual admissions program to increase representation of disadvantaged minority students. Sixteen of

the 100 seats for that year's incoming class were set aside for African American students. Special candidates, however, did not have to meet the 2.5 grade point cutoff and were not ranked against candidates in the general admissions process. Allan Bakke was a white male who applied to and was rejected from the regular admissions program in 1973 and again in 1974. Though he had a 468 out of 500 score in 1973, he was rejected, since no general applicants with scores less than 470 were being accepted at that time, but minority applicants with lower grade point averages and testing scores were admitted under the special admissions program. Bakke filed suit, alleging that this admissions system violated the Equal Protection Clause and excluded him on the basis of race.

For more information and teaching materials, see: http://www.streetlaw.org/en/landmark/cases/regents_of_the_u_of_california_v_bakke.

2. This initial discussion should be short but should allow students to express their beliefs and feelings about the issue. Teachers should use this initial discussion to draw out themes that will come up in the remainder of the lesson.
   o For example, a student might say something like, "Denying Bakke admission on the basis of his race is just as discriminatory as excluding minority students just because of their race; neither can control their racial identity." From this comment, you can highlight the idea that maybe punishing or rewarding someone based on factors beyond their control is impermissible. It can be interpreted as arbitrary from a moral or procedural point of view. Other concepts to highlight might include the notion of rights, compensation for past injustices, the purpose of a university, and the meaning of equal protection under the laws.
3. Provide students with a copy of "The Final Four." Explain to students that an admissions officer is tasked with selecting the final four students for admission to a prestigious university from the 14 candidates shown in the chart. Actively encourage students NOT to begin thinking about who they would select; instead, ask students to think of a reason why an admissions officer would want to admit each of the students. Students should give at least one reason for each potential candidate. Reasons can include economic, geographic, and racial diversity; leadership potential; high scores/grades; potential financial benefit to the university; benefit of a different perspective, etc.
4. At this point, distribute a card to each student with a number 1–14 on it. Explain to students that this number corresponds to one of the fourteen applicants, but they don't know which one. This part of the activity is meant to mirror Rawls' veil of ignorance. Essentially, the veil of ignorance is a tool Rawls uses to discover those principles of justice we would agree to (a hypothetical social contract) if we were ignorant of certain relevant facts about ourselves including our gender, race, socioeconomic status, etc. This method of developing just principles of government eliminates our potentially selfish motivations and, Rawls believes, will lead us to support principles of justice that will be most beneficial to those least well off. When the veil is lifted, we might find that we are one of the least advantaged citizens and this makes us think about justice in a different way.

   In this application of the veil of ignorance, students know the basic facts of the situation but they don't know relevant facts about themselves (race, gender, scores, family, etc.). Students should discuss which of the reasons they developed in step 2 are fair or just reasons for determining who the final four admitted students should be.

- It will be helpful here to return to the "fairness discussion" (step 2). Should students be rewarded for characteristics that are interpreted as morally or procedurally arbitrary (characteristics over which they have no control)? For instance, is it justifiable to consider Scholastic Aptitude Test (SAT) scores in university admissions processes (for which some students benefit from prep classes and tutors) but not geographic diversity? Is it justifiable to consider a student's legacy status but not his or her race? Is a person's intelligence quotient (IQ) a factor over which s/he has no control?
- Remind students that they are still under the veil of ignorance, and instruct them to apply the fair and just reasons from step 3 to select the four admitted students.
- Reveal the corresponding numbers and let students know "who they are" from the list of candidates.
- Conclude the class by allowing students to reflect on the process. Was this a fair way of determining the principles by which the selection should be made?

Day 2: Motivating the Arguments in the Affirmative Action Debate

1. Begin the class by reviewing the major points raised in the discussions from the previous day.

    Explain that today the class will be analyzing the major arguments for and against Affirmative Action. To prepare for a reasoned discussion, briefly explain some common fallacies and psychological error tendencies in reasoning. Tell students to be on the lookout for fallacious reasoning in their own arguments as well as the arguments of others. Some of the fallacies or psychological error tendencies that occur frequently in discussions on this topic are the following:
    - Confirmation bias (a tendency of people to search only for that information that confirms what they already believe to be true);
    - Straw man (attacking a misrepresentation or the weakest interpretation of the opposing argument);
    - Hasty generalization (coming to a hasty conclusion based on insufficient evidence);
    - False dilemma (considering only limited alternatives when there is at least one other option).
2. Using the online *Stanford Encyclopedia of Philosophy*'s entry on Affirmative Action (see link below), discuss the following arguments in favor of and against Affirmative Action:

    In Favor:
    a. Affirmative Action does not violate the justice done by equal opportunity because it equalizes opportunities in a system rife with inequality.
    b. There is no actual harm suffered by those denied admission in Affirmative Action programs. There is a difference between benign and malign discrimination.
    c. Affirmative Action serves as compensation for past exclusion from universities.
    d. There is a social utility achieved by Affirmative Action programs.
    e. The whole system of tying economic reward to earned credentials is indefensible. Justice is not harmed because we are not rewarding or punishing persons for factors that are beyond their control.

f. The Integration Argument. The leadership of a state ought to represent the states' population. As the state's premier training ground for leadership, universities ought to admit a racially and ethnically representative class to conform to this representational goal. It is directly connected to the purpose of a university and the legitimacy of a civic society.

Against:

a. Affirmative Action violates rights.
b. Affirmative Action confounds justice by subordinating merit, conduct, and character to race.
c. Using race as a means to an end where race doesn't matter doesn't make sense.
d. The Equal Protection Clause must mean the same thing for White Americans as it does for Black Americans.

3. Conclude the class by asking students to develop the beginnings of their own arguments either for or against Affirmative Action while avoiding fallacies and psychological error tendencies. Divide students into groups of four and present their arguments to their groups for discussion.

Additional Questions Raised

1. What would fair and just principles look like in the university admissions process?
2. Is it just and fair to reward someone for factors that are arbitrary from a moral point of view? If so, which factors can rightly be considered beyond one's control?
3. What is the responsibility of government to right past wrongs committed by that government?
4. What are the benefits of a diverse collection of people studying together?
5. Should the leadership of a legitimate civic society roughly reflect the demographics of its members?
6. Is it ever okay to infringe on someone else's rights to redress a past wrong? To achieve a greater good/end?
7. What are some of the common fallacies committed in the Affirmative Action debate and how can we avoid them in favor of a well-reasoned discussion on the issue?

Supplemental Materials

Fullinwider, Robert, "Affirmative Action," *The Stanford Encyclopedia of Philosophy*, http://plato.stanford.edu/archives/fall2014/entries/affirmative-action/.

The idea of using Rawls' veil of ignorance came from Ronald Green, a student of Rawls. A description of Green's initial Rawls Game can be found on pages 4–8 in William Soderberg's, *The Game of Philosophy*, University Press of America, 2000.

Rawls, John. *A Theory of Justice*. Cambridge, MA: Harvard University Press, 1971.

*This lesson plan was contributed by Allison Cohen, who currently teaches AP Government and a Philosophy elective at Langley High School in Virginia and is a member of the board of directors of PLATO (Philosophy Learning and Teaching Organization).

Table 8.1

Brief Description of Applicant	Class rank, top__% of class	Did they go to a: *really good school; +average school; –bad school	SAT score	Letters of rec. were: *stellar, special +good, but predictable; –fine, but not really that good	*Essay really stood out, stellar
Talented athlete, key member, and leader of three Varsity sports teams	10%	*	1900	+	
White son of a farmer from Iowa	2%	–	2000	*	*
White resident of a wealthy Boston suburb	5%	*	2150	+	
Black American from New York City	2%	*	2050	*	
Hispanic American from Texas	1%	–	1900	*	*
Asian, accomplished concert pianist	5%	*	2200	+	
Son of alum, three generations back	10%	*	2000	+	
Black American from Georgia	1%	+	2100	*	
White resident of a wealthy DC suburb, daughter of a lawyer and a hill staffer	2%	*	2150	+	
Son of a big donor	20%	*	2000	–	
Community service advocate	10%	+	2050	*	*
African who grew up in Sudan— overcame political repression, immigrated to the United States with his parents, struggled with the English language the first two years	5%	+	1950	*	*
Black American, resident of wealthy Chicago suburb, son of a neurosurgeon	5	*	2150	+	*
White son of an Appalachian coal miner	1	–	2100	*	*

LESSON PLAN
AFFIRMATIVE ACTION IN UNIVERSITY ADMISSIONS (2)*

Topics: Affirmative Action and constitutional classifications
Time: Approximately two 80-minute class periods

Objectives

- Understand and comprehend the classifications the US Supreme Court uses in its Equal Protection analysis
- Apply the constitutional classifications to basic fact patterns in the three major Supreme Court decisions on Affirmative Action in university admissions
- Comprehend the Court's ruling and reasoning in major Affirmative Action cases
- Synthesize and evaluate the arguments in the Affirmative Action debate
- Demonstrate intellectual empathy while engaging in the debate surrounding Affirmative Action
- Engage with a central topic in applied ethics and the philosophy of law

Introduction

Explain to students that sometimes the government decides that it is necessary to treat certain classes of citizens differently. For instance, many states decide to prohibit any person under the age of 16 the ability to obtain a driver's license, no matter how well a particular 15-year old can drive. But most people, including the Supreme Court, would say that it is okay to treat these two classes of citizens (those over and those under the age of 16) differently. At the same time, it would be unjust to deny persons driver's licenses based on their race. This lesson will explore what the Equal Protection clause of the Fourteenth Amendment means and how the Supreme Court applies the Equal Protection Clause to Affirmative Action cases.

Day 1: The Supreme Court and Affirmative Action

1. If you used the previous lesson on Affirmative Action, begin class by reviewing some of the students' arguments. Did they encounter arguments that made them think about the issue in a different way? If you did not use the previous lesson on Affirmative Action, simply review the basic facts of the case *Regents of the University of California v. Bakke* and ask students to briefly discuss.

   Regents of the University of California v. Bakke—In the early 1970s, the medical school of the University of California at Davis devised a dual admissions program to increase representation of disadvantaged minority students. Sixteen of the 100 seats for that year's incoming class were set aside for African American students. Special candidates, however, did not have to meet the 2.5 grade point cutoff and were not ranked against candidates in the general admissions process. Allan Bakke was a white male who applied to and was rejected from the regular admissions program in 1973 and again in 1974. Though he had a 468 out of 500 score in 1973, he was rejected, since no general applicants with scores less than 470 were being accepted at that time but minority applicants with lower grade point averages and testing scores were admitted under the special admissions program. Bakke filed suit, alleging that this admissions system violated the Equal Protection Clause and excluded him on the basis of race.

   For more information and teaching materials, see: http://www.streetlaw.org/en/landmark/cases/regents_of_the_u_of_california_v_bakke.

2. Lecture/Discuss:

   In order to determine when it is okay for the government to treat a particular class of citizens differently, the Supreme Court devised three tests: the rational basis test, heightened scrutiny, and strict scrutiny. Use the brief descriptions below to explain each test and why strict scrutiny is always applied when a classification occurs on the basis of race.

   Rational Basis Test: A law that classifies and treats people differently will pass the rational basis test if the law is *rationally related* to a *legitimate* state interest. A law that classifies based on age will be subject to this test. In our example above, the state has a rational and legitimate interest in not allowing a 10-year old behind the wheel of a car.

Heightened Scrutiny: Under this test, the law must serve an *important* government interest. Recognizing a long history of gender discrimination, the Court subjects laws that classify on the basis of gender to heightened scrutiny.

Strict Scrutiny: However, if the class of citizens in question has been "deliberately subjected to severely unequal treatment or society has used [the classification] to render people politically powerless," then that class is deemed a suspect class and strict scrutiny applies to the law. Under strict scrutiny, the state must show a *compelling* government interest AND that there is no less restrictive way (must be narrowly tailored) to accomplish this compelling purpose. Any law that classifies on the basis of race is subject to strict scrutiny.

Explain that the University of California needed to show it had a compelling interest to enact its program of racial preference in the case of *Regents of the University of California v. Bakke* and if successful, it would have to show that the program was the least restrictive way to achieve that compelling interest.

3. Present the four reasons given by the University of California and ask students whether they think any one of the four could qualify as a compelling interest; not just an important interest, but a compelling one. Divide the class into groups of four–five students and allow them a few minutes to discuss. It might be helpful to review the arguments in favor of and against Affirmative Action located in the previous lesson plan. Ask each group to report a summary of their conclusions to the class. Take a bit of time to go through each reason individually and discuss the possible merits of each of these arguments made by the university:
   a. To reduce the "historic deficit of traditionally disfavored minorities in medical schools and the medical profession."
   b. To counter "the effects of societal discrimination."
   c. To increase "the number of physicians who will practice in communities currently underserved."
   d. To obtain, "the educational benefits that flow from an ethnically diverse student body."

4. Using the links below as a resource, review the Court's decision in *Bakke* with a focus on the compelling interest found in (d); namely, that the interest in preserving the First Amendment's freedom of speech on a university campus raises the interest in (d) to a compelling one. Also point out to students that the Court determined that a quota system was not the least restrictive means available to achieve that interest. Powell noted, "The diversity that furthers a compelling state interest encompasses a far broader array of qualifications and characteristics of which racial or ethnic origin is but a single though important element." So, using a quota system that focuses solely on race is not the least restrictive means to achieve diversity. Race can be considered as a so-called "plus factor" to achieve this diversity, but quotas are unconstitutional.

Link to the decision in Bakke: http://www.law.cornell.edu/supremecourt/text/438/265.

For a helpful analysis of the decision, see: http://plato.stanford.edu/entries/affirmative-action/.

Day 2: Applying the Court's Reasoning in *Bakke*

1. Review and be sure that students understand how strict scrutiny was applied in *Bakke*.
2. In this part of the lesson, students will apply the Court's reasoning in *Bakke* to three more recent cases. Using the link below, locate Street Law's "Case Summary" for *Gratz v. Bollinger, Grutter v. Bollinger, and Fisher v. University of Texas.* Divide the class into three groups of four–five students and assign each group one case. Provide the groups with a summary of their case (from the Street Law link below). Ask the groups to apply the reasoning in *Bakke* to the facts of their case. What would they decide? Once the groups have completed their analysis, bring the class together and have the groups present their conclusions and their reasoning. Finally, discuss the actual rulings of the Supreme Court with students (summaries of the Court's ruling are also found in the link below).
   Street Law's resource library: http://www.streetlaw.org/en/resource_library.
3. To conclude the lesson, divide the class into three groups. Have students rearrange the desks in the classroom so there is a circle in the center of the room big enough for one group. The remainder of the students will sit outside of that circle. Before class, type each of the five questions (given below) on a piece of paper, fold the papers and place them in a container. The first group to sit in the inner circle should pick one paper out of the hat and discuss the question typed on it. Be sure to manage the time for discussion so that each of the three groups will be able to discuss at least one question. At the conclusion of each group's discussion, ask the other members of the class to repeat what they thought to be the most important points that were raised. You may also allow them to ask the "discussion group" any questions to clarify points that were made.
   - Are there arguments in the Affirmative Action debate (discussed in the previous lesson and referenced in Day 1 of this lesson plan) to which the students feel the Justices haven't adequately responded?
   - Do they see future decisions by the Court on this issue going in a different direction? If so, based on what sorts of considerations?
   - What is the responsibility of government to right past wrongs committed by that government?
   - Should the leadership of a legitimate civic society roughly reflect the demographics of its members?
   - Is it ever okay to infringe on someone else's rights to redress a past wrong? Achieve a greater good/end?

Supplemental Materials

Fullinwider, Robert, "Affirmative Action," *The Stanford Encyclopedia of Philosophy*, http://plato.stanford.edu/archives/fall2014/entries/affirmative-action/.

The idea of using Rawls' veil of ignorance came from Ronald Green, a student of Rawls. A description of Green's initial Rawls Game can be found on pages 4–8 in William Soderberg's, *The Game of Philosophy*, University Press of America, 2000.

Magleby, D. (ed.). *Government by the People* (24th ed.). Pearson, 2011.

Rawls, J. *A Theory of Justice*. Cambridge, MA: Harvard University Press, 1971.

Links to a summary of the facts, decisions, and recording of the oral arguments can be found online at the following sites:

Regents of the University of California v. Bakke: http://www.oyez.org/cases/1970-1979/ 1977/1977_76_811.

Gratz v. Bollinger: http://www.oyez.org/cases/2000-2009/2002/2002_02_516.

Grutter v. Bollinger: http://www.oyez.org/cases/2000-2009/2002/2002_02_241.

Fisher v. University of Texas at Austin: http://www.oyez.org/cases/2010-2019/2012/ 2012_11_345.

*This lesson plan was contributed by Allison Cohen, who currently teaches AP government and a Philosophy elective at Langley High School in Virginia and is a member of the board of directors of PLATO (Philosophy Learning and Teaching Organization).

LESSON PLAN
I LOST MY COOL*

Topics: Stoicism; ethics
Time: Approximately one to two class periods

Objectives

• Apply Stoic ethical principles to a personal situation
• Consider the benefits and drawbacks of Stoic ethical principles

Materials Needed

Handout (see below)

Introduction

The teacher should engage in a brief review of basic Stoic principles at the beginning of class. A cogent review of Stoic thinking should include the embrace of reason as the guide for one's moral life, as opposed to emotions, which are fleeting and unpredictable. For the purposes of this lesson, the teacher should also introduce the Stoic belief that controlling the events of the world is a fruitless undertaking because much of what happens in the world is beyond an individual's control. What is needed, instead, is a personal acceptance of the determined laws of the universe. What a person can control is his or her reaction to these laws. The more a person is guided by acceptance of external forces, the more a person's character is made stronger as he or she faces his or her own mortality. These principles should be introduced the day before the activity.

Activity

1. Tell students to choose a partner and face each other with their desks. Hand out "I lost my cool" handout (see below). Tell students to read the handout and write their story (10–15 minutes).
2. Tell students to exchange papers and read their partner's story.
3. Instruct each student to write a response to his or her partner from a Stoic perspective, which explains how *he or she should have* acted (10 minutes).
   o It's important that students assume the persona of a Stoic as best they can, even sharing direct quotes from famous Stoics like Aurelius and Epictetus. Students' abilities to provide relevant advice will be dependent on how thoroughly the teacher has introduced Stoic principles in advance of the lesson.
4. Ask for volunteers to read the stories and the Stoic responses.
5. Engage students in question/answer as stories are read.

Potential Questions Raised

- What are the advantages of setting aside emotions when reacting to life's challenges? What are the disadvantages?
- What are the difficulties in following Stoic principles?
- Is Stoicism an attractive moral theory? Why or why not?

Conclusion

This lesson usually spills over into an additional day. Try to get as many students to share as possible. Engage students with the larger tension between free will and determinism, or the power of individuals to act out of free will versus the conspiring forces of the world that might determine actions and outcomes independent of free will. Additionally, shape the discussion toward the question of whether we should integrate emotions into our moral lives. The chief value of this lesson is that it asks students to reflect upon their moral actions and the impact those actions have on other people and, more important, on their own characters.

Supplemental Materials

The Handbook of Epictetus, N. P. White (trans.), Indianapolis: Hackett, 1983.
The Meditations of Marcus Aurelius, George Long (trans.), New York: Collier & Son, 1909–1914.

"I lost my cool"

Think of a situation you have had recently where you reacted very strongly to somebody who did something hurtful to you. Select a situation where your reaction was so strong and emotional that it ended up hurting the other person and perhaps you felt bad about it later. It could have happened at home, at work, or at school. You can select a highly dramatic situation but you can also choose one that is more mundane and could happen any day, to anyone. Again, make it a situation where you felt personally hurt, angered, or wronged and those feelings led you to react in a way that was ultimately embarrassing to you and/or hurtful to the other person.

Choose a situation that will be appropriate to share with class.

Once you have identified your situation, write it up in one detailed paragraph, making sure you answer the following questions:

1. What was the situation? Describe it.
2. How did you react? Describe it.
3. How was your reaction hurtful to the other person? To yourself? Describe it using specifics (focus on the negative consequences that resulted).

*This lesson plan was contributed by Dan Fouts, who teaches philosophy and government at Maine West High School in Des Plaines, IL and is a member of both PLATO and the American Philosophical Association Committee on Pre-College Instruction in Philosophy.

LESSON PLAN
SOCIAL CONTRACT THEORY: CREATING A COOPERATIVE LEARNING ENVIRONMENT*

Topics: Social contract theory; applied political philosophy
Time: 2 class periods of 50 minutes each

Objectives

- Students will learn the basics of classic social contract theory
- Students will then apply this theory to create a cooperative, inclusive classroom environment by writing and ratifying their own class constitution

Materials Needed

- John Locke's *Second Treatise on Government*, chapters 2 and 8. An alternative is James Rachels' *The Elements of Moral Philosophy*, chapter 11, "The Idea of a Social Contract" (see full citations below)
- A questionnaire (see below)
- Poster board for displaying the finished constitution
- *Optional*: online discussion forum; wig and gavel

Introduction

This lesson teaches students about self-government by using social contract theory to create a class constitution. The lesson encourages students to argue their positions in order to convince their peers how a classroom should run. Since everyone is responsible for formulating and ratifying their constitutions, students are encouraged to participate in class from the first day. Furthermore, as students argue for and vote on their constitutions, they must inevitably address a number of political and philosophical problems, such as the danger of the tyranny of the majority, the meaning of consent, and the issue of how to enforce their contract. Thus, by the end of the exercise, students have learned the basics of social contract theory, the value of compromise and productive negotiation, and the need to make logical arguments to support their views.

Activity

Inform students on the first day that the class is going to write a constitution that will govern how they and the teacher will conduct the course throughout the school year. They will decide the content of this constitution by establishing a social contract.

1. The first step is for students to fill out a questionnaire that allows the teacher to get to know each student a little better. While each teacher should tailor the questionnaire according to his or her needs, it should include the following four questions, which will form the basis of the classroom constitution.
   * Question 1. My favorite teacher always used to . . .
   * Question 2. I believe that as a student I am responsible for . . .
   * Question 3. I don't like it when other students in my class . . .
   * Question 4. I would also like you to know that . . .

   Collate the responses by grouping together similar answers and noting how many times students give the same or similar responses. Students will often give their own personal preferences when answering these questions. The teacher should group the students' answers according to general headings that relate to specific rights and duties in the class. For example, a student's comment that expresses a dislike for others talking out of turn would be placed under the general heading of respect. Occasionally, students will give frivolous responses, but these are often quickly thrown out by other students when they debate the articles of their constitution.

2. Before handing out the collated responses, instructors should introduce the students to social contract theory, either by having them read selections from Locke or by giving a brief, summary lecture. Social contract theory holds the following views:
   * Locke's social contract theory starts with the claim that human beings originally lived in a *state of nature,* where they had perfect freedom from external authorities.
   * The state of nature is dangerous and inconvenient. While one's *natural rights* to life, liberty, and property still exist, no one is sure how to enforce and apply these rights fairly and impartially in the absence of an authority.
   * To escape the state of nature, people *contract*, or mutually agree, to give up their perfect freedom in order to guarantee these natural rights and live in a fair and just society.
   * The *social contract*, therefore, establishes the rules governing a society or state; these rules are legitimate because the governed themselves have mutually and freely *consented* to them.

3. Tell the students to imagine that they are currently in a state of nature. For example, ask them to suppose there are no rules governing their classroom and that each student is perfectly free to pursue her own self-interest during this time. Emphasize that each individual is perfectly free, so that "no one can be put out of this estate and subjected to the political power of another without his [or her] own consent" (Locke, §95). Ask them what the class would look like if they were to stay in this state of nature. How conducive would this class be to their academic success? Most will see that it is in their own self-interest to have rules. Once they realize this, they will likely raise such questions as the following:
    * Should all the rules be decreed by the teacher?
    * Should students have any voice in how the class runs?
    * Do they as students have any inalienable rights, such as the right to receive additional help from the teacher when they don't understand a concept, or the right to express their opinions without fear of ridicule from other students?

4. Explain next what a social contract means, emphasizing that they will have to give up some of their perfect freedom in order to have guidelines and rules for the conduct of the class. Students will, therefore, have to negotiate and compromise with each other to function together day to day in the course.

5. Break the students down into four- to five-person teams, and distribute the collated answers to the students' questionnaires. Have each group appoint a scribe to create a document that contains all their choices, breaking the rules into three categories of rights and obligations:

    (a) the teacher;

    (b) the citizen-student; and

    (c) the civil classroom.

    Each category corresponds to one of the three articles of the constitution. Each team must negotiate and reach agreement on their top three responses to each of the questions. They should also feel free to write a new response if they think that something essential is missing from the lists. Stipulate that each team must aim at unanimity at this stage of the exercise, but if a group is really deadlocked, then they should either abandon the responses about which they can't agree or include them all. Often times, the other groups will have selected the principles that have caused the deadlock anyway.

6. Reconvene the entire class and invite each group to report on its choices. At this stage, the students should critique each proposed rule. As they negotiate the articles of their constitution, the following problems inevitably arise and must be addressed:
    * How many rules should each article have?
    * Should rules be chosen by a simple majority, a two-thirds majority, or unanimity?
    * Does majority rule quash minority rights?
    * Who's going to enforce the rules?
    * Can the constitution be amended later in the class?

    Students generally have strong opinions on all these matters, and they often will be willing to try to convince each other of their positions. The instructor should referee and ask questions, not guide them to a predetermined outcome. Nevertheless, it is important to remind them that everyone, including the teacher, will have to live with the rules they choose.

7. On the second day of class, hold a constitutional convention in which students will ratify their constitution. Consider the following example of an actual, student-written constitution.

SAMPLE STUDENT CONSTITUTION

Article I: The Teacher

The teacher of this course should always strive to:

1. Be organized, consistent, clear about expectations;
2. Review material before tests;
3. Show relevance to the modern world whenever possible;
4. Be open-minded and flexible;
5. Give opportunity for student feedback on the teacher.

Article II: The Citizen-Student

Students of this course should always strive to:

1. Be prepared and organized;
2. Pay attention;
3. Participate and try to be curious about learning;
4. Be comfortable taking risks;
5. Take the class seriously.

Article III: Civil Society

All members of the classroom community should:

1. Be respectful. Respect means
   - No pressuring or hazing others;
   - Not being disruptive;
   - Not being arrogant;
   - Being accepting of others.

At the end of the lesson, explain to the students how they have now done what Locke was describing: they have moved from a state of nature to a civil classroom society based on mutual consent.

Conclusion

Using social contract theory to have the students create their own constitution encourages student ownership of their education. The exercise not only teaches students

Locke's contractarianism, but it also shows them how it can be used practically to create a classroom environment that will foster their education. Students learn the value of arguing for their views, as they quickly see that giving an opinion without a good reason often carries little weight with their peers. Students often carry this lesson with them into subsequent discussions throughout the course. Students also learn autonomy and responsibility because the lesson turns students into legislators for their course. They, thereby, see what it means "to be a law unto themselves," instead of having rules imposed upon them. They also see the need to take personal responsibility for the rules that they have written.

Supplemental Materials

1. Instructors may find the following sources useful when planning this lesson:
   Locke, John. *Second Treatise of Government and A Letter Concerning Toleration*. Mineola, New York: Dover Publications, Inc., 2002.
   Rachels, James. *The Elements of Philosophy*. New York: McGraw Hill College, 1999.
2. The *Stanford Encyclopedia of Philosophy*'s entry on social contract theory provides helpful information on social contract theory and John Locke's political philosophy.
   http://plato.stanford.edu/entries/contractarianism/.
   http://plato.stanford.edu/entries/locke-political/.
3. Sample Questionnaire
   Below are the questions that can be used on the questionnaire. This questionnaire has been adapted from Johns Hopkins University's Center for Talented Youth program, where it was used as an icebreaker exercise for a logic course.

Preferred Name:_____

Please take the time to answer the questions below. Your responses will help give me a better idea of who you are and how I can be effective as your teacher this year. We'll also be using some of these answers to develop a classroom "social contract." ALL ANSWERS ARE ANONYMOUS! But, I may share answers without identifying you with the class.

COMPLETE THE FOLLOWING SENTENCES:

1. My favorite teacher EVER always used to . . .
2. I believe that as a student I am responsible for . . .
3. I don't like it when other students in my class . . .
4. I would also like you to know that . . .

*This lesson plan was contributed by James Davis, who teaches history and philosophy at Boston University Academy and is a member of the board of directors of PLATO (Philosophy Learning and Teaching Organization) and the editorial board for *Questions: Philosophy for Young People*.

LESSON PLAN
APPLIED ETHICS—GENETIC ENHANCEMENT*

Topics: Genetic enhancement; application of ethical and political theory; analyzing arguments
Time: Two 80-minute class periods

Objectives

- Students will identify arguments in favor of and opposed to genetic enhancement
- Students will appreciate the complexity of distinguishing between enhancement and treatment
- Students will evaluate arguments for cogency
- Students will develop their own conclusions on the issue of genetic enhancement
- Students will apply ethical and political theory to a contemporary debate

Activity

Day 1: Enhancement versus Treatment
Before class, make two signs. One sign should read "Enhancement" and the other "Treatment." Hang the signs in opposite corners of the classroom.

1. Explain to students that one of the distinctions ethicists draw in the genetic enhancement debate is between enhancement and treatment. Enhancement can generally be understood as improving upon an already healthy body. Treatment can generally be understood as restoring a person back to a typical state. This introductory activity is meant to illustrate some of the potential difficulties in drawing this distinction. Students will then explore what this distinction might mean for the debate surrounding genetic enhancement.
2. Read the following activities (see below) aloud and instruct students that, for each activity, they should decide whether or not it is an enhancement or a treatment. Students should stand by the sign that corresponds with their answers. Discuss selected responses as a class. Emphasize that they are not deciding whether they approve of the activity but whether they think it is a treatment or enhancement.
   - Taking vitamins
   - Taking human growth hormones
   - Getting vaccinated for diseases
   - Adding whey protein to a breakfast shake
   - Taking Viagra for a medical issue
   - Taking Viagra recreationally
   - Manipulating memory-linked genes to improve one's memory
   - An athlete goes to Europe to seek treatment not approved in the United States to recover from an injury more quickly
   - Laser eye surgery
   - Taking Ritalin or Adderall for attention-deficit hyperactivity disorder (ADHD)

- Taking Ritalin or Adderall to improve concentration while studying for a test
- Drinking energy drinks to stay awake while studying
- Taking hormone-replacement therapy to retard the effects of aging
- Getting braces
- Removing a birthmark
- Getting a facelift
- Whitening your teeth
- Genetically altering the height of a child who is well below the norm but not due to any medical problem
- Genetically enhancing the musculature of someone with multiple sclerosis (MS)
- Genetically enhancing the musculature of an increasingly immobile person as he or she ages
- Genetically enhancing the musculature of a talented athlete who possesses the skills but not the body type to get an athletic scholarship to college
- Genetically altering an embryo to improve the musical abilities of the future child
- Genetically altering an embryo to resist cold and flu viruses
- Raising the IQ of someone from 120 to 130 through some future scientific advancement
- Raising the IQ of someone who was a genius but suffered a head injury in a car accident back to their genius-level IQ

3. Inevitably, in the discussion about whether an activity is considered treatment or enhancement, the idea of returning someone to, or helping someone attain, a normal state will come up. Ask students: What does it mean to be normal? What is a normal state? Would widespread genetic enhancement change what is considered normal?

4. Present the following scenarios and ask students what their reactions would be. These examples are taken from Michael Sandel's article, "The Case Against Perfection," *The Atlantic*, April 2004, http://www.theatlantic.com/magazine/archive/2004/04/the-case-against-perfection/302927/.

- Consider an athlete who is not blessed with great natural gifts but manages, through striving, grit, and determination, to excel in his or her sport.
- Consider an athlete who is beautiful to watch simply because he or she naturally excels in a sport.
- Both of these athletes display their gifts with grace and effortlessness.
- Now, imagine we find out that both players took performance-enhancing drugs. Whose actions would we be more bothered by? Would we think that the athletic ideal of *effort* or *gift* was more deeply challenged? Discuss with students what their response to these scenarios tells us about what they (and society as a whole) value.
- Students will typically start with the argument that performance-enhancing drugs give an athlete an unfair advantage. But Sandel notes that what we really value in athletes is excellence and it is the case that some athletes are better endowed genetically than others through no effort of their own; they were simply born with those gifts. Students should then be challenged to think about why enhanced genetic differences produce unfairness, but natural genetic differences do not.

5. Now ask students to think about and respond to the following hypothetical scenarios:
    *   Imagine that you are a seventeen-year-old senior in high school. You are an accomplished musician and earned a scholarship to a prestigious university, based on both your academic performance and your musical abilities. You then find out that your parents genetically engineered you when you were an embryo to improve your IQ and to foster musical abilities. Both your talent and your interest in music are the product of this genetic engineering. How would that make you feel?
    *   Now imagine that you are a seventeen-year-old senior in high school who wants desperately to study science in college. However, science has never come easy to you and your grades are not quite good enough to get into the colleges of your choice. You then find out that your parents could have altered your genetic makeup to ensure that you would possess the talents and skills to excel in science. They could have done this at the age at which you started to express a real desire in the sciences (assume that this might be possible one day). Would you be upset that they did not provide this for you? Would you want to receive the treatment at the age of seventeen?
    *   Imagine that you decided to pursue the treatment in #2. You went on to a great graduate school and earned a PhD from a prestigious university. You are now a successful molecular biologist and making lots of money. Do you think you would find yourself less able to sympathize with another person in your circumstance who decided not to have the treatment and is now struggling to find employment?
6. At this point, ask students to brainstorm and note on a piece of paper or in their journals some of the potential benefits of genetic enhancements. Then ask students to brainstorm some of the potential problems with genetic enhancements. They are not taking a position yet; they are simply starting to consider the arguments that might be made. Discuss students' responses in a general way.

For homework, ask students to read Nathaniel Hawthorne's short story, "The Birth-Mark." The story can be found online at: http://www.lem.seed.pr.gov.br/arquivos/File/livrosliteraturaingles/birthmark.pdf.

Day 2: Analyzing the Arguments

1. Begin class with a discussion of Hawthorne's short story "The Birth-Mark." (See the link below, in the Supplemental Materials section of this lesson plan, for a nice discussion by Albert Whitaker of the story and the role it played in the President's Council on Bioethics.) Divide the students into small groups of four or five and ask them to discuss the following questions. They may also add questions and insights to this list. Once the groups have had ample time to discuss the story, ask the groups to share some of their thoughts with the class.
    *   Is Aylmer a good scientist? In what ways? What do the volumes of Aylmer's scientific library suggest?
    *   Is Aylmer a good person?
    *   What does the story say about our drive to mastery/perfection?

- Part of science seems to explain and provide understanding and another part seems to be concerned with amending and ameliorating. What does this story tell us about the relationship between nature and the scientist?
- All of us struggle at one point or another with what the genetic lottery denied us; what insights does the story provide us?

2. Keeping the desks in small groups of four or five students, provide half of the groups with a brief description of arguments in favor of genetic enhancement and the other half of the groups with a brief description of arguments against. A brief summary of some of the arguments and counterarguments found in Sandel and Kamm (links to their articles can be found in the Supplemental Materials section of this lesson plan) is included. In these small groups, students should discuss each of the arguments to make sure they fully understand them. They should then discuss how strong they think the argument is and come up with possible counterarguments where appropriate.

Arguments Against:

- Genetic enhancement violates the right to autonomy: by choosing a child's genetic makeup in advance, parents deny the child's right to an open future. It would point children toward particular choices (Sandel).
  - But this wrongly implies that in the absence of a designing parent, children are free to choose their characteristics for themselves. But none of us chooses his or her genetic inheritance (Sandel). Whether it's the parent or it's nature, the child still doesn't have a choice in the matter. Children are either at the mercy of their parents or the genetic lottery.
- Genetic enhancement would create two classes of human beings: those with access to enhancement technologies and those who must make do with their natural capacities (Sandel).
  - But this doesn't get at what is wrong with enhancement itself; it is the effect of an unjust distribution of enhancements. If the unjust distribution could be remedied, we would still be left with the debate about whether genetic enhancement is morally acceptable (Sandel).
- Genetic enhancement undermines effort and erodes human agency (Sandel). If I get an A on my calculus test, was it because of my effort and hard work or the enhancement my parents provided? Do I congratulate myself or thank the doctor?
- Genetic enhancement creates a desire to mastery that misses an appreciation of the gifted character of human powers and achievements (Sandel).
  - But suppose a scientist works to find a cure for blindness. Let's also suppose that she is motivated by a desire for mastery; does this make her efforts impermissible? Presumably not. Good ends seem to outweigh the intention. We can judge the scientist's character as lacking but still find that the end (curing blindness) is permissible (Kamm).
- Genetic enhancement would disfigure the relation between parent and child, and deprive the parent of the humility and sympathies that an openness to the unbidden can cultivate (Sandel). Parents may lose the idea of accepting love, affirming the being of the child, and focus too much on transforming their child, seeking perfection (Sandel).

    ○ But if it's okay to hire tutors, pay for SAT prep classes, and hire personal train-ers for their children, why is genetic enhancement any different?
- We would begin to view our talents as achievements for which we are respon-sible instead of gifts for which we are indebted. This would transform the moral landscape in three fundamental ways (Sandel).
  - ○ As parents gain the ability to control various aspects of their child's genetic makeup, they would begin to lose the humility of accepting children as they come to them. This humility acts as a check on the impulse to control our children (Sandel).
  - ○ Genetic enhancement would result in an explosion of responsibility. We would begin to attribute less and less to chance and more to choice. This opens the door to blaming some for not choosing to enhance themselves in some way. We would bear an increased burden for the talents we have or don't have (Sandel).
  - ○ But does one have to do everything that might make oneself better? If not, then we are not at fault (Kamm).
  - ○ Genetic enhancement would erode solidarity. The more chance plays a part in our talents and gifts, the more reason we have to share our fate with, to under-stand the plight of others (Sandel). Why do the successful owe anything to the less fortunate? Because they see their gifts as the product of good fortune and not as deserving them in a strict sense (Sandel).
  - ○ But isn't it also true that many people desire to help others out of a sense of respect and concern for the value of other persons and not because they do or do not deserve their fate (Kamm)?
  - ○ Allowing genetic enhancement would mean that there are fewer instances of people who are badly off and therefore fewer people who would need assis-tance (Kamm).

Arguments in Favor:

- As long as there is no state coercion, people should be free to design their chil-dren or themselves. The result would be in everyone's interests. People will be free to pursue their own preferred life goals and not be bound by nature's unfair distribution of talents and assets (Rawls, as analyzed by Sandel).
  - ○ But what sorts of characteristics would we be selecting and deselecting? Is there a problem with this? What sorts of traits would begin to disappear?
- We would have the ability to cure disease, prolong life, ameliorate suffering, and help people to excel in their endeavors (President's Council on Bioethics).
- Making a moral distinction between genetic enhancement and treatment doesn't seem to capture what might be morally worthy about genetic enhancement. If we can find a cure for a terrible illness only if we enhance the intelligence and memory of our best scientists, then it seems that this enhancement might be morally permissible (Kamm). The importance of discovering treatments might rest on the enhancement of intelligence.
- Not everything that nature provides is sacred and deserving of honor. Nature is also responsible for cancer, AIDS, and earthquakes. If we are permitted, as San-del seems to suggest, to interfere with the "bad" parts of nature, then it seems as

though it would be permissible to extend our life span and prevent certain aspects of the aging process (Kamm).

- ○ Related to this argument is the point that what some see as an impediment worthy of treatment, others might see as a gift.
    - • What is the relevant difference between parents providing voice lessons to strengthen their child's vocal cords and providing a drug or genetic manipulation that achieves the same end?

3. Once students have had time to work through all of the arguments, mix up the groups so that new groups are formed. Each new group should include students who studied the arguments in favor and students who studied arguments against. Each member is responsible for presenting the most important points from their prior group's discussion to their new group. At the end of this part of the activity, each student should be familiar with all of the arguments.

4. Bring the students back to a full-class discussion by asking them to select the two arguments they found most convincing.

5. To conclude this lesson, have students reflect on some of the issues raised in this debate. How would they start to think about resolving those issues? For homework, ask students to write letters to the Presidential Commission for the Study of Bioethical Issues, outlining their reflections on the issue. What recommendations would they make as we continue to develop genetic enhancements and start to make decisions about their availability to consumers? If they are having trouble, you might suggest the following considerations:
   a. Treatment versus Enhancement
   b. Changes made before the child is born and changes made after
   c. Genetic modification versus drugs that don't permanently alter one's genetic code

Supplemental Materials

Kass, L. *Beyond therapy: Biotechnology and the pursuit of happiness.* Washington, DC: President's Council on Bioethics, 2003.

Hawthorne, N. *The Birth-Mark*, 1843.

Kamm, Frances. "Is There a Problem With Enhancement?" *The American Journal of Bioethics* 5.3 (2005): 5–14.

Whitaker, A. "Neoconservative Nathaniel: Bioethics and 'The Birth-Mark'," Retrieved February 9, 2015, from http://www.hawthorneinsalem.org/ScholarsForum/MMD2448.html.

This lesson was also inspired by John Arras and his presentation at the National Endowment for the Humanities (NEH) Summer Institute, *Epic Questions: Mind, Meaning and Morality*, and Courtney Campbell's presentation at the 16th International Conference for Ethics across the Curriculum.

*This lesson plan was contributed by Allison Cohen, who currently teaches AP Government and a Philosophy elective at Langley High School in Virginia and is a member of the board of directors of PLATO (Philosophy Learning and Teaching Organization).

LESSON PLAN
JUSTICE AND UTOPIA*

Topics: Plato's Ring of Gyges thought experiment; justice; John Rawls' veil of ignorance
Time: Approximately one or two class periods

Objectives

- Introduce students to questions of justice as presented in Plato's *Republic*
- Allow students an opportunity to apply concepts of justice in a specific situation
- Reinforce the difficulties of obtaining the ideal of justice
- Provide opportunities for critical thinking with debate and writing

Materials Needed

- Description of the story of the Ring of Gyges
- Handout on the characteristics of Rammeka (a fictional society)
- Worksheet for small-group discussion and individual reflection

Description

Begin with an explanation of Plato's goals in the *Republic*. Explain briefly how Plato attempted to define the just individual and the just society. Plato argues that happiness for the individual and harmony for the state necessitate justice. The instructor will connect these issues to a contemporary theory of justice (Rawls) and current issues of inequality.

To motivate the issue of justice as it relates to individual action, provide students with Plato's Ring of Gyges story (see link in Supplemental Materials) either as a homework assignment or handout. After the story has been read to the class, questions that the class could consider include:

- Imagine for a moment that you were in possession of such a ring. How would you use it?
- If you had a perfect guarantee that you would never be caught or punished, what would you do?
- If there were two persons in possession of the ring—one just and one unjust—what, if any, differences in behavior might occur in their uses of the ring?
- Do other works of modern fiction raise similar issues to those found in the Ring of Gyges (e.g., the "ring to rule them all" from *Lord of the Rings* and the "Deathly Hallows" from *Harry Potter*)?

To begin a broader conceptual discussion of justice, explain that students will now attempt to create principles for a just and fair society (as influenced by John Rawls' *A Theory of Justice*). Students should imagine that they do not know anything regarding their identity other than that they are rational beings. In Rawls' work *A Theory of Justice*, this is what he calls the "original position" or veil of ignorance, which serves as a starting point to decide on the fairest principles for a new society.

- Students will be divided into groups of four to five to complete a worksheet to decide on the principles for the society of Rammeka, which has a history of discrimination against minorities and has the general demographics indicated on the handout (see handout in Supplemental Materials—this can be copied for students or written on the board). Students should be reminded that they have the percentage chance (as indicated on the handout) of being those specific members of society and will need to abide by the rules decided by their small group. Note: percentages are NOT cumulative and can overlap (e.g., a person could be disabled, female, and a veteran).

The worksheet should have the following questions:

1. What would you do with the ring of Gyges? Explain. What do you think most people would do with it?
2. Define justice (*note*: the term itself or a synonym should not appear in the definition).
3. Decide how you would address the following policies from the "original position," under a veil of ignorance. This means the only characteristic you possess is rationality; you have no idea of your gender, age, ethnicity, religious attitudes, political party affiliation, etc.
   - An expansive social welfare system (old-age pensions, universal health care, accident and disability insurance, unemployment insurance, etc.)
   - 75 percent tax on estates over $1 million (to fund the above)
   - Affirmative action (based on race and gender)
   - Same-sex marriage

After students have had an opportunity to make decisions and air any differences, survey group decisions and challenge groups and individuals to defend their reasoning to the rest of the class.

- To conclude this portion of the lesson, explain Rawls' three Principles of Justice. Rawls claimed that these three principles, listed in order of importance, would follow logically from being in the original position:

1. Equal right to liberty consistent with that of others;
2. Fair equality of opportunity for position and offices;
3. Any social or economic inequalities must benefit the least-advantaged members of society ("the Difference Principle").

Rawls conceives of justice as synonymous with fairness, so under a veil of ignorance, legislators will establish basic principles to follow, possibly as individuals who lack advantage, status, or have been subjected to discrimination in the past. Invite students to react to Rawls' conclusions and the principles themselves.

To conclude, students should consider the following questions, which can be written out on a worksheet and/or presented as a final class discussion:

- Is Rawls' thought experiment an appropriate way of creating a just society? Why or why not?
- Is pursuing a perfectly just society a worthy goal?
- How would you define justice?
- To what extent can society realize your definition in practice? What limits the goal of creating a perfectly just society?
- How might your responses above connect back to the Ring of Gyges story?

Supplemental Materials

Description of Plato's "Ring of Gyges" (http://sites.wofford.edu/kaycd/plato/).
Rawls, John. *A Theory of Justice* (rev. ed.). Cambridge, MA: Belknap Press, 1999.
F.M. Cornford (trans.), *The Republic of Plato*. Oxford, UK: Oxford University Press, 1951.

*This lesson plan was contributed by Chris Freiler, who has taught at Hinsdale Central High School in Illinois since 1993, with emphasis on AP European History and Philosophy Honors.

HANDOUT
CHARACTERISTICS OF RAMMEKA

Note: Rammeka has a tradition of discrimination against various minority groups.

53	percent female
23	percent Catholic (Christian)
63	percent Protestant (Christian)
2	percent Jewish
2	percent Muslim
2	percent other faiths
22	percent poor
3	percent rich
11	percent veteran
8	percent gay/lesbian
10	percent Asian
12	percent African American
14	percent Latino
2	percent homeless
7	percent unemployed
6	percent disabled
27	percent professional
35	percent blue collar
18	percent elderly
9	percent ill
6	percent agnostic/atheist

LESSON PLAN
THE CASE OF KITTY GENOVESE: MORAL RESPONSIBILITY
AND THE BYSTANDER EFFECT*

Topics: Ethics; moral and collective responsibility; praise and blame; bystander effect
Time: 1 hour

Objectives

- To have students engage with ethical issues related to moral and collective responsibility, including the nature and extent of these responsibilities
- To have students engage with the topic of bystander intervention and moral intuitions related to the case of Ms. Genovese

Materials Needed

- Copies of *The New York Times* article on Ms. Genovese's death and relevant circumstances (http://www2.southeastern.edu/Academics/Faculty/scraig/gansberg.html)
- Copies of an additional *Washington Post* review on two books that address witness statements (http://www.washingtonpost.com/opinions/kitty-genovese-the-murder-the-bystanders-the-crime-that-changed-america-by-kevin-cook-and-kitty-genovese-a-true-account-of-a-public-murder-and-its-private-consequences-by-catherine-pelonero/2014/03/14/f0a7ca6e-a3a5-11e3-a5fa-55f0c77bf39c_story.html)

Description

1. Begin by asking students whether they would feel responsible to help each other in the case of seeing someone get bullied at school, and why or why not.
   - Some students will say yes or no for varying reasons (e.g., it would be an undue personal risk to intervene; it would be important to help someone being bullied; there is no responsibility to a stranger, but if I knew the person then there may be responsibility to help). The goal is to get students thinking about their ideas of social and moral responsibility (i.e., the social and moral expectations we have for people in society) in a familiar setting.
   - Additional questions to ask students include the following:
     o Would students tell a teacher or someone in authority about bullying if they did not feel comfortable to or desire to intervene personally?
     o Will ending individual acts of bullying also end the phenomenon of bullying?
   - This discussion should last for around 10 minutes, and no formal conclusion is needed—just get the students used to thinking about issues of moral responsibility.
2. Next, have the students read aloud *The New York Times* article that details the fatal attack on Ms. Genovese. The article alleges that 38 bystanders did nothing to help her survive repeated assaults.
3. Ask students to write down their thoughts for a few minutes regarding this scenario and answer the following questions:

- What would you have done if you were one of the neighbors who could have called 911 or gone down to help her?
- Do you think the bystanders should have called the police, gone down to stop the attacker, or do you think that doing nothing was the right decision?
- Why don't people help other people in need in some cases?

4. If the class has more than twelve students, divide students into groups and have them discuss their responses to the three questions, including how they came to their answers. Otherwise, go around the room and have each student give their responses to the three questions and discuss the reasons for their answers.

    - During this discussion you can push students' reasoning some, particularly about the second and third questions. One key issue for students to consider is their idea of the limits of people's responsibilities to others. A way to help facilitate this consideration is comparing cases where students generally agree about having and not having a moral obligation to help someone in need and comparing how students came to those positions. This reading and discussion should last around twenty to thirty minutes.

5. After going through their moral intuitions about the case, reveal to them the information from the *Washington Post* article, namely that there were people who did call the police and that there was confirmation that two people witnessed the attack yet did not assist at all. The group can read through the article in its entirety if time permits, or you can simply reveal the new information that some people did try to help Genovese.

    - Following this new information, ask students again what they would have done if they were one of the neighbors who could have called 911 or otherwise helped Ms. Genovese. You may be surprised to see some students change their positions regarding their willingness to help Ms. Genovese and others hold their positions with new resolve. This discussion should last around ten—fifteen minutes.

6. Toward the end of the period, bring the discussion back to the original example of bullying and ask the students to consider the similarities between the Genovese case and a classmate being bullied. Would they reconsider intervening, even if it meant telling a teacher? Why or why not?

    - Some students will make a distinction between moral and social responsibility in bullying and a life-or-death scenario. This is a relevant distinction to consider because they appear to be distinct situations (e.g., insulting someone versus putting a gun in someone's face), but there are a lot of similarities between a life-or-death situation and bullying, particularly considering how bullying often involves the use of physical and emotional attacks. Bullying, in particular cyberbullying, has generated more news recently with a rise of student suicides and students bringing weapons to school (which are life-or-death situations).
    - Assess this distinction with the group and conclude by discussing the moral significance of this distinction and whether responsibility to act differs depending on the situation. For example, is moral responsibility to help others contingent on the severity of the situation (certain discomfort versus possible death) or are we always obligated to help others in need? This involves assessing how well students understand this distinction and how their responses might change depending on the context and their conception of the extent of moral responsibility.

Additional Key Questions

- When, if ever, should we put ourselves at harm's way to help someone else?
- Should we take a victim's desire for help into account when deciding whether to intervene (e.g., what if the victim of bullying doesn't want our help?)
- Are our responsibilities as bystanders to intervene taught to us?
- Would our feelings regarding our responsibility to intervene change if Kitty Genovese was a friend or relative of ours?
- Should we punish people who don't intervene to save or help someone in need?

What does this case show compared to other cases where strangers do act to save someone? For example, does this highlight different approaches to social and moral responsibility? Or is it possible people did not fulfill their responsibilities in the Genovese case?

*This lesson plan was contributed by John Torrey, who is a graduate student in philosophy at the University of Memphis with interests in philosophy of education, African American philosophy, and social and political philosophy centered around issues of justice.

LESSON PLAN
THE WORDS WE LIVE BY*

Topics: Ethics; beliefs/maxims and defining terms; the nature of the unexamined life
Time: 40 minutes

Objectives

Students will be able to:

- Consider what the mission of their school should be
- Be inspired to look deeply into—and question—the meanings behind statements that may have been taken for granted or not even noticed
- Think critically about the functioning of a school: ideals, patterns, rhythms, silliness
- (Begin to) articulate a philosophy of education

Materials Needed

A motto or mission statement, if the school or district has one. If not, you might include in this activity a little research project using the Internet, along the lines of "What's the best high school mission statement or motto out there?" A quick Google search reveals hundreds of mottos and mission statements from public, private, and parochial schools, on the elementary-, middle-, high-school, and university levels, from all over the world. Have the students choose the motto/mission statement they think best exemplifies their school.

Introduction

This activity can be done as a stand-alone lesson or as part of many different units. In this exercise, students examine something that has been around them, probably unexamined, as long as they have been in the school.

Activity

"We are going on a little field trip." Students leave their bags and notebooks in the class-room, and the class walks together to find an area where the school motto is featured.

If the motto or mission statement is in the hallway, ask: "You walk past this three, five, seven times every day, so you have been within a dozen feet of it many times. How many of you have never noticed it before?" Some will raise their hands—perhaps a third of the class. Even if nobody raises his or her hand, it is an opportunity to discuss Socrates' statement that "The unexamined life is not worth living," or, perhaps better, "The examined life is more rewarding than the unexamined life."

Note: If there is no motto displayed in your school, pick something else in the hall-way, like a piece of art or poster.

Around this time, the students start to become aware that the class is standing in the hallway having a discussion, which doesn't exactly happen every day. Some look around nervously as their friends and teachers and the janitors and the principal might walk by.

- Additional questions about philosophies of education: Have you held discussions in the hallway before? Is this a place that values public intellectual activity? Or do we tend to respond to individual questions while sitting in seats in rows? Some of what we hope to do is challenge the way things are "always done." We may determine, after that examination, that the always-done way has merit and we may determine that there are *better ways than* or at least *serious questions we can ask about* those traditional patterns.
- Additional question for personal consideration: If you are a little uncomfortable having people watch you have a discussion here in the hallway, why?

Now ask: "Do you think this motto/mission statement accurately represents what this school believes in and tries to do?" A variety of answers will come out about the motto of your school or the one the class has chosen as the best possible one. Pursue some of the Yes-tending ones and some of the No-tending ones.

- Protocol worth establishing before discussion starts on this: the names of individual teachers and students are not to be mentioned disparagingly in discussions. If a student has a critique of an educator or peer, he or she can frame it anonymously— "One teacher I had last year only lectured; we did not have a single discussion."
- Additional questions about philosophies of education: Does the motto apply to some classes more than others? Is it broad enough? Is it something that we should aspire to? Does it aim too high or too low?

Now ask: "What is missing from this motto?" Or: "What should the motto focus on more and/or what should it focus on less?" Attempt to progress from assessing the motto to improving it. Of course, the second question, above, demands that the students consider the motto in light of the education they have experienced, while this third question adds to that by asking them to articulate an ideal.

- Additional questions about philosophies of education: This is the perfect opportunity for the students to start thinking about other concepts they think the school's motto *should* hold or represent. Imagination? Creativity? Experience? Growth? Wisdom? Collaboration? Citizenship? Justice? Diversity? Reason? Discipline? Challenge? What are the values of the community, and what are the values that are most appropriate for a (this) school in particular, as compared with other elements in a community? What, indeed, are the values of *education*?
- Context: Ask: "Is this motto less (or would it be less) accepted/relevant now than it might have been for your parents' or grandparents' generation?"

Finally, pose the question: "Should this matter?" or "Should a school have a motto/mission statement at all?"

If the motto is displayed in an expensive way, you might discuss the reasons for paying hundreds, maybe thousands, of dollars to have such a thing embedded in the lobby wall—regardless of whether most students notice it.

Can a motto articulate the values of a community, and focus people on an ethos? What if there is controversy: if a motto creates dissension, would it be better to back off and not have it at all?

Conclusion

Walk back to the classroom. Conclude the class by facilitating a discussion about the following questions:
- What are the purposes of education?
- Is "the unexamined life" less interesting and less challenging than the examined life? Why or why not?

*This lesson plan was contributed by Carl Rosin, who lives in Pennsylvania with his wife, two daughters, and two dogs, and is invigorated by the constant challenge of working with young people as a high-school teacher of English, interdisciplinary studies, and philosophy.

LESSON PLAN
THE ETHICS OF "STOP SNITCHING"*

Topics: Ethics; justice; codes of silence
Time: 80 minutes or more, which may cover one or two class periods

Objectives

Students will be able to:

- Speak in an informed way about the ethics of "Stop Snitching" and related "codes of silence"
- Compare complex scenarios, identifying and evaluating significant distinctions between them
- Analyze the ways in which language can divert observers from a rational approach into a more emotional approach
- [Optional] Understand and be able to compare virtue-based, duty-based, and consequentialist normative theories
- [Optional] Apply various systems of ethics to a specific real-world situation

Materials Needed

- Handout on the "[Blue] Code of Silence" from the Serpico case—January 24, 2010, *The New York Times* excerpt (included below)
- Supplemental background material on "I Am Darren Wilson" bracelets—link to September 26, 2014, *Los Angeles Times* article explains how solidarity and trust are complicating factors in the relationships among law-enforcement officers and between those officers and the public they serve
- Supplemental background material on another interesting "code of silence" story: the extended report on Adam Schoolcraft titled "Right to Remain Silent," reported September 10, 2010 on *This American Life*

Introduction

This lesson begins with a scenario that tends to put young people on one side of the conflict, followed by a scenario that tends to put them on the other. This lesson can be part of a larger ethics unit in which three major categories of normative ethics are studied: virtue ethics (Plato and Aristotle and the cardinal virtues), duty-based or deontological ethics (Immanuel Kant and the categorical imperative), and consequentialist or teleological ethics (Jeremy Bentham and utilitarianism).

If this is a stand-alone lesson, those terms and names are not required.

If you do want to make this lesson part of a larger ethics unit, an optional segment is included at the end of this plan. You can also introduce the categories of normative ethics in a general way without using the names of philosophers or terms like "deontological" or "utilitarianism." The concepts that are necessary for the larger discussion are essentially the following: the cardinal virtues of wisdom, fortitude, temperance, and justice; the idea of "acting in a way that one would will to be universal"; and the broader, consequentialist concept of determining rightness by measuring the relative good and harm for the various stakeholders.

Activity

1. Explain the concept of the "Blue Code of Silence" or "Blue Wall." An example could be that of Frank Serpico, who was a New York City police officer who was disgusted at widespread corruption within the force and became a famous whistle-blower, only to be shot at in a drug bust, in an event that investigators suspected may have been a setup. From a New York Times story by Corey Kilgannon:

> In 1967, Mr. Serpico began telling what he knew to high-ranking officials at police headquarters and City Hall. He presented names, places, dates and other information, but no action was taken. Frustrated, he and a friend on the force, David Durk, a graduate of Amherst College who had become an officer in 1963 after quitting law school, contacted a reporter for the *New York Times*.
>
> The front-page story by David Burnham on April 25, 1970, pressured Mayor John V. Lindsay to form the Knapp Commission, before which Mr. Serpico testified that "the atmosphere does not yet exist in which an honest police officer can act without fear of ridicule or reprisal from fellow officers."
>
> The commission carried out the most extensive investigation of police wrongdoing in the city's history and exposed a pattern of entrenched corruption and cover-up that helped usher in reform.
>
> "It was terrifying in those days—they were really sticking their necks out," recalled Mr. Burnham, who now works at a data-gathering and research firm. "We really shamed the city, and things really changed."
>
> Mr. Serpico does not exactly agree. He believes the department still does not acknowledge its internal problems because the leadership's top priority is to avoid scandal.
>
> "I hear from police officers all the time; they contact me," he said. "An honest cop still can't find a place to go and complain without fear of recrimination. The blue wall will always be there because the system supports it."

Question: What do you think about the idea of the "Blue Code of Silence," which suggests that police officers must keep each other's secrets out of a sense of loyalty, even if those secrets cover illegal actions? Is such a code justified?

Important Note: *Police Chief* magazine emphatically decries the idea that such a code is widespread or that it would be supported by other officers if it were. The example is not meant to impugn law enforcement, only to suggest an example that many students would be likely to find repugnant. It is worth noting, especially for younger students who may be unduly influenced by a single example, that even the worst-case scenario that played out in Serpico's story is an outlying point and not necessarily representative of the police as an organization.

Have students briefly write down their positions and reasoning—these are not to be handed in and read by the instructor, but they will be useful for the sake of comparison with subsequent examples.

- Devil's advocacy can help develop a robust discussion here. For example, if the first student comment suggests that the risks to law-enforcement officers excuse them for being especially unforthcoming to the outside world, the instructor should inquire about the risks to the public if officers "cover up" for each other. By the same token, if the first comment suggests that law-enforcement officers should always share internal information, the instructor should inquire about whether the dangers of the job and the fact that many in society may be hostile to law enforcement should not make it more important that police are able to trust each other, and perhaps that they are correct not to entrust outsiders with information that may easily be taken out of context.

- It is likely that the events of August 2014 in Ferguson, Missouri, and succeeding events will come up. Unarmed African American teenager Michael Brown was shot and killed by policeman Darren Wilson, whose identity was withheld for several days by the authorities. Later, police officers were seen wearing "I Am Darren Wilson" wrist bracelets. Many such incidents have been in the news since.

2. Explain "Stop Snitching": the concept that it is wrong to provide information to the police to help them solve a crime. This is a "code" that is reasonably common among teens and in communities where there is a suspicion of authority figures. *Optional case to consider, if the students want or need an example:*

Student X, a freshman, is changing in the gym locker room, when student Y, a large, popular senior, comes in. Y opens a locker, takes money out of a wallet, and puts the wallet back. Y turns to X and whispers, "You do know that snitches get stitches, don't you?" Y leaves.

X later finds out that student Z has had $50 stolen from his gym locker. The principal makes an announcement over the intercom, asking if anyone has any information about the crime. After the bell rings at the end of the day, Y passes X in the hall. Y stares at X menacingly.
What should X do?
Whether or not you use the optional case, go on to the next question.

Question: Is "Stop Snitching" an ethical code that should be followed?

Have students briefly write down their positions and reasoning—these are not to be handed in or read by the instructor, but they will be useful for the sake of comparison. If you shared the optional case, you can ask them what they would do if they were student X.

3. Continue to a more general discussion. The key to this discussion is this follow-up question about the two scenarios, which the students may raise on their own (but which certainly should be raised before long, as you start drawing the topic together): How are the two scenarios—the "Blue Code of Silence" and the "Stop Snitching"—similar? How are they different?
- Introduce the idea of *significant distinctions*, essential in philosophical discussions. This is especially useful if some students have two different responses to the two scenarios. What are the salient elements that distinguish one scenario from the other? Challenge the students who say "Yes" to one code and "No" to the other code to discriminate between them. Some distinctions will be trivial; which distinctions are significant, and why?
  ○ Police sworn to uphold the law, so a higher standard?
  ○ Risk of physical danger to the individual, real or perceived?

- Another generative digression involves diction. How does this topic shift if the word "Witness" is used instead of "Snitch?" "Whistleblowing" versus "Ratting out?" As philosophers, we have to be aware of the power of language in biasing us and be prepared to show discipline in our own selection of words.

Optional Final Segment

Introduce the class to (or remind them of) the categories of virtue-based, duty-based, and consequence-based ethics. Divide the students into small groups—four or two would be ideal—and ask each group to assess how "Stop Snitching" would be assessed within the context of the following:
- The four cardinal virtues (wisdom, fortitude, temperance, justice)
- The categorical imperative ("act in a way that you would will to be universal"—this can be alternately phrased as "treat each person as an end in himself or herself, never as the means to an end")
- Consequentialism, in that consequences determine the ethical quality of an action
This should take ten to fifteen minutes.

To wrap up, the final discussion should aim at drawing a conclusion about the "Stop Snitching" concept. Select groups to share virtue-based, duty-based, and consequentialist analyses, then discuss alternative ideas that other groups may have.

The point of using these lenses is to help the students understand ways of perceiving problems in society, assess potential solutions, and articulate angles that well-meaning people should consider. Therefore, this is both an ethics lesson and an argumentation lesson. What it is *not* is a moralizing lesson: the goal is not to tell the students that *they should take one or another approach*, only that they should understand why they are favoring the approach they are favoring, and what forces and criteria are at work in their own processing of this applied ethics situation.

*This lesson plan was contributed by Carl Rosin, who lives in Pennsylvania with his wife, two daughters, and two dogs, and is invigorated by the constant challenge of working with young people as a high-school teacher of English, interdisciplinary studies, and philosophy.

LESSON PLAN
SOCRATIC SEMINAR*

Topic: Socratic seminars
Time: Blocks of 1.5–2 hours or two 40-minute classes

Objectives

Students will:

- Read and notate primary source readings (prior to seminar)
- Ask for clarification as necessary (identify areas of challenge)

- Evaluate texts/arguments through prompts from teacher, comments by other students, or their own analysis
- Respond critically and analytically to ideas expressed by other students
- Use text to support dialogue
- Use respectful communication skills that recognize differences in opinion and analysis that facilitates progress in class understanding of the text and encourages all students to be involved

Materials Needed

- Large index cards for student names (fold in half to stand up on the desks)
- Primary source text with line numbers (suggested every five lines) (see below)
- Teacher questions with appropriate line numbers (see below)
- Seating/grading chart for recording student contributions
- Rubric (see below)

Introduction

A Socratic Seminar is a group discussion about a written text to evaluate the truth of an opinion, theory, or argument. Depending on the text, a Socratic Seminar can be used as an introductory lesson, a multiple-perspective analysis, or a summative assessment for any unit of study. The fundamental idea is that the leader of the discussion will use straightforward questions to guide the group to a logical conclusion. This lesson builds on that idea, but encourages the teacher to ask a question and allow the students to comment and question among themselves to reach a conclusion before prompting them with the next question.

Teacher questions focus on fundamental ideas, individual premises of an argument, and how they connect to each other. A sample text and questions are provided in the Supplemental Materials, and the procedure is outlined below.

Procedure

- Set up chairs in a circle.
  - Have students sit in the same place both days if this is a multiple-day activity (easier to document participation).
- Have students display their names (this is needed to encourage students to properly engage with other students during the discussion, if students don't already know each other's names).
- Remind students of appropriate behavior in a Socratic seminar:
  - Required number of times a student must contribute (see rubric)
  - Questions and comments are best when supported by text or specifically related to previous comments by peers
  - While the questions will be posed by the teacher, most of the dialogue should be carried on by the students. Therefore, they will need to call on each other—and they should be conscious of those that have spoken and those who haven't.

Activity

- Sample passage from Plato's *Republic,* Book VII—"Allegory of the Cave" (full text citation available in Supplemental Materials)

    ○ ☐ **Socrates:** Behold! Human beings living in an underground den, which has a mouth open towards the light and reaching all along the den; here they have been from their childhood, and have their legs and necks chained so that they cannot move, and can only see before them, being prevented by the chains from turning round their heads. Above and behind them a fire is blazing at a distance, and between the fire and the prisoners there is a raised way; and you will see, if you look, a low wall built along the way, like the screen which marionette players have in front of them, over which they show the puppets.
    ○ ☐ Socrates: Last of all he will be able to see the sun, and not mere reflections of him in the water, but he will see him in his own proper place, and not in another; and he will contemplate him as he is.
    ○ ☐ Socrates: There will be no end to the troubles of the state or indeed of humanity itself until philosophers become kings or until those we now call kings really and truly become philosophers.

- Sample Questions
    ○ What are some of the symbols we need to identify?
        ▪ Cave—society, the visible world we live in, what we perceive with our senses, in beginning we only know the environment and what people teach us
        ▪ Chains—controls put on us by government, society, ourselves; if we blindly accept these, then we remain prisoners in our cave
        ▪ Prisoners (and the one that gets out)—members of society
        ▪ The sun—the intellectual rebirth, ultimate truth/good, real (no shadows)
    ○ What role do you think Plato wishes for the prisoners who leave the cave? Why?
- Start the seminar by asking for any words or concepts students need to have explained, and encourage other students to clarify.
- Using teacher-generated questions to prompt discussion, continue to focus on developing the author's argument. Allow students to respond and guide the discussion. Teacher facilitation might be necessary to redirect the flow of the discussion, but not by providing the students with "the answer." In addition, students should be reminded to call on their peers to encourage direct communication between students. Teacher facilitation might be necessary to encourage some students to participate or prevent others from dominating the discussion.
- Document student participation on seating chart as seminar progresses. Documentation should reference the type of participation, including answering a teacher's question, answering a peer's question, commenting on a peer's contribution, asking a question, commenting with original information, and commenting by referring to the text.

Questions Raised

A Socratic Seminar is very student driven. The questions should lead to a logical conclusion, but the goal is also to encourage and facilitate student questioning and

Table 8.2

	Excellent (100)	Good (85)	Fair (70)	Unsatisfactory (55)
Conduct	Comments encourage others to participate Comments at least five times Speaks to everyone Discusses instead of debating Comes prepared	Comments encourage others to participate Comments at least three times May tend to only address teacher Discusses and debates Comes prepared	Comments demonstrate frustration with other members of class Comments once Only addresses teacher Tends to debate rather than discuss Comes unprepared	If participates, may be argumentative Does not comment Easily distracted May use inappropriate language and speak about individuals, not ideas Comes unprepared (no notes, pencil, text)
Speaking/ Reasoning	Understands questions before answering Cites evidence from text Expresses complete thoughts with complete sentences Comments are logical and insightful Comments makes connections to previous comments	Responds to questions voluntarily Cites evidence from text when asked Comments indicate thought given to issue, but might miss subtler points Comments are logical and follow conversation Comments implies connection to previous comments	Responds to questions, but might need to be called on Does not cite text evidence Comments may not incorporate relevant ideas Contributions might not progress logically from conversation Comments are minimally connected to previous comments	Extremely reluctant to participate, even when called upon Does not cite text evidence May speak unclearly or express incomplete ideas Comments are illogical or meaningless in reference to dialogue Little or no connection made to previous comments
Listening	Pays attention to details Identifies faulty logic in a constructive manner Takes analytical notes during seminar	Generally pays attention Attempts to evaluate arguments/ideas presented by others Takes summative notes during seminar	Pays attention sporadically Does not ask for clarification when needed Takes few notes during seminar	Appears uninvolved in the seminar Comments display complete misinterpretations of questions or comments of other participants Takes no notes
Reading	Thoroughly familiar with text Prepared with questions/comments in margin and underlining Possible contradictions identified and analyzed	Has read text Underlining with some comments/questions in margin Notes show summary/questions, not analysis	Appears to have read text, but in a superficial way Text is only underlined Notations not evident	Does not demonstrate comprehension of text No notations on text No attempt at getting assistance with text

analysis. If there still seem to be unresolved issues at the end of the seminar, be sure to address them in future classes.

Conclusion

While the Socratic Seminar serves as a measure of the students' understanding of the text provided and the central ideas with relation to an overall unit of study, additional follow-up activities are also possible. Examples include the following:

- Write a personal reflection about the process used in a Socratic Seminar and/or have a class discussion about the seminar process. This is usually beneficial after the first time it is used in a class.
- Write a personal response to arguments presented by the author and in the class discussion.
- Summarize the author's argument in a logical manner (using premises and conclusion).
- Compare the author's argument to others presented in class prior to the seminar.

Supplemental Materials

Paul, Richard and Linda Elder. *The Thinker's Guide to the Art of Socratic Questioning*. Foundation for Critical Thinking, 2006.

Plato. *The Republic*. Christopher Rowe (ed. and trans.). Penguin Classics, 2012. (Reading selection supplied above is a cut version adapted for use in the classroom.)

*This lesson plan was contributed by Mary Moran, who teaches social studies (Debate, Introduction to Philosophy, and Introduction to Research) at Jericho High School in New York, where she also coaches both the award-winning debate team and nationally recognized Ethics Bowl team.

LESSON PLAN
IN-CLASS ETHICS BOWL*

Topic: Ethics
Time: Two 40-minute classes

Objectives

- Student Ethics Bowl competitors will:
  - ○ Work collaboratively in groups of two teams of five to six students per team
  - ○ Analyze multiple ethical dilemmas
  - ○ Identify relevant actors, issues, and philosophical theories
  - ○ Develop and present a cohesive case about the right action(s) to take in the situation presented
  - ○ Identify and describe potential areas of disagreement/alternative solutions and explain why they were not selected

o Actively listen and question an opposing team's presentation of their case in a critical, but productive, manner
o Interact in a productive, collegial, and respectful manner
• Three student judges will:
o Actively listen to presentation of case and critique
o Critically question students who presented the case. Questions should challenge assumptions made, application of theories, consistency of thought and flexibility in response to critique by other team
• Student note-takers (if needed due to size of class or group) will:
o Accurately record presentation, critique, and responses to judge questions for both cases
o Provide the class with a summary of each case, the ultimate decision that was reached, and the relevant theories used

Materials Needed

• Prior to Bowl:
o A useful general description of ethics designed for High School Ethics Bowls—to use as supplement to in-class teaching (see Supplemental Materials below)
o Copies of cases (given to students to prepare) from the National High School Ethics Bowl archives (sample case provided below)
• For Bowl:
o Scoring criteria (available on the National High School Ethics Bowl website)
o Score sheet (available on the National High School Ethics Bowl website)

Introduction

This lesson can engage students in the process of dissecting and discussing ethical issues. In a philosophy course, this activity can be used several times throughout a unit about ethics/applied ethics or it can be a culminating activity for the whole unit. In addition, this activity can be modified to fit into other courses to facilitate full-class or small-group discussions related to specific ethical topics or issues.

Issues that have been included in former Ethics Bowl cases are related to student lives, the role of government in the lives of citizens, and international relations. There are many cases available, so that the Bowl can be tailored to specific topics and/or levels of student knowledge or interest. The National High School Ethics Bowl case archive lists many useful cases: http://nhseb.unc.edu/nhseb-rules/case-archive/.

General Description

Two cases will be distributed to the teams at least one week prior to the in-class Ethics Bowl. Each case will have "study" questions at the bottom to facilitate preparation, but those will not be the questions used in class. To prevent rote preparation, each team will not know which case they will be presenting and which they will be critiquing. Judges/note-takers should not get the cases until the day of the activity.

Activity

Sample Case (from the Regional High School Ethics Bowls 2015):

"Copying Homework"

Gabriella and Vivian have been friends for a long time and are now juniors in high school with aspirations to attend top universities. They have four classes together, including three AP classes. Two of their AP courses have tests scheduled the same day, and homework is assigned in their fourth common course the day before they must take the tests. It is just a simple worksheet, but it must be submitted for a grade. Gabriella is annoyed that she has to take time away from studying for the tests, but does the worksheet in 30 minutes. Vivian, however, studies all evening and the worksheet just slips her mind.

The next day, Vivian realizes that she has forgotten to complete the homework. She knows that getting a zero on an assignment will hurt her overall average and the teacher does not accept late homework. She asks Gabriella if she can copy her answers to the worksheet.

Gabriella is sympathetic and wants to help her friend, but she is worried that she could get in a great deal of trouble for letting Vivian copy her work—after all, it's considered cheating. Gabriella is also frustrated because she took the time to complete the worksheet while Vivian did not. It seems unfair that Vivian will receive the same credit as all of the students in the class who did the homework. At the same time, it is just a menial worksheet and doesn't seem the same as plagiarizing an essay. The benefits Vivian will receive if Gabriella lets her copy the worksheet seem to far outweigh the triviality of the rule being broken and she doesn't want to see Vivian's grade damaged over a silly worksheet. Moreover, if Gabriella says no, she knows that it will really hurt her friendship with Vivian.

Study Questions

1. Would it be morally permissible for Gabriella to allow Vivian to copy the worksheet? Why or why not?
2. Does the fact that Gabriella and Vivian are good friends influence the ethical analysis of whether copying is morally permissible? Explain.
3. Is it ever morally permissible to break rules in order to help a friend? If so, what must the conditions be?

Preparation Prior to the Bowl

Students should discuss the case and develop a consensus about the right course of action for the two girls. Guidelines for discussion could include asking them to identify the stakeholders in this situation (all of the people involved), how each of the stakeholders is impacted, and what would constitute the moral actions of each stakeholder.

Prompting students to think about motives, short- and long-term outcomes, and the relationships between different people involved will also help them develop a thorough answer.

Students can use outside research to enhance their presentation, but they should focus on the fundamental issues raised by the case. Direct students to think about and analyze the ethical decisions that need to be made in the situation presented.

The Bowl

- Seating should be arranged so that the two teams of five—six students are facing each other, but still able to communicate within the team between the separate parts of the presentations or during the judges' questioning.
- Judges should be able to see both teams, but if space/numbers are an issue, then the judges/note-takers can form a circle around the two teams.
- At the start of the Ethics Bowl, flip a coin to determine which team will be Team A (presenting the first case). The team that wins the toss will decide to be either Team A or Team B, without knowing which case is going to be the first case.
- Distribute the case to all members of the class with the NEW question at the bottom. Read the question to be answered out loud to the class. This is a critical component because the students must adjust their preparation to specifically address this new question.
- The activity can follow the National High School Ethics Bowl time limits or the times suggested below (adapted for class time). Make sure that the only people talking are the ones presenting or questioning. In addition, all members of the class should be quiet during prep time, except those team members who are preparing.
    - Determining Team A/Team B and presentation of case/question—3 minutes
    - Prep time for presenting team—2 minutes
    - Presentation of case—5 minutes
    - Prep time for critiquing team—2 minutes
    - Critique of team that presented—4 minutes
    - Prep time for presenting team—2 minutes
    - Response to critique by presenting team—4 minutes
    - Questioning of presenting team by the judges—10 minutes
    - Total time—32 minutes (this allows for time to set up the circle, general directions, and some summary conversation, if necessary/desired)
- This time frame will allow for one case to be presented, critiqued by the opposing team, and questioned by the judges in one forty-minute period. The other team will do the same on the following day.
- After providing the students with the case and the question, the presenting team should summarize their position. Their final position should include identifying all of the stakeholders, answering the question asked, providing reasons for their position and, perhaps most importantly, discussing other possible resolutions of the question and explaining why they did not choose those options. This part of their answer can also include any struggles or disagreements they had in reaching their group decision. For example, most groups will probably decide that cheating would be wrong, but they probably have done it themselves at some point during their school career (or been tempted).
- The other team will then respond to the presentation. They should NOT present their own opinions, but use their ideas to help the first team clarify their position. Posing questions and/or asking for more detailed support for the first team's reasoning are encouraged.
- The first team will then respond to the constructive criticism. This response can include both clarification or more detail and incorporation of ideas or suggestions from the other team.

- The last part of the Bowl focuses on the judges' questions. These questions are only asked of the presenting team, and can serve to ask the team to clarify its position if the class feels this is necessary. Questions can also be asked about the applicability of the presentation team's response in other similar (or different) hypothetical situations. Finally, if the students developed some moral rules in their presentation, questions can challenge the applicability of those rules. For example, is it ever morally permissible to break a rule to help a friend? Can you give a situation when this might be the case?
- This activity has a natural end to it, but students can also be asked to write a personal reflection. Prompts can include the following:
  - Did they agree with the decisions reached by the class? Why or why not?
  - What was the strongest argument used? Explain.
  - Present an alternative solution and defend it.
  - What was your personal reaction to this experience in general?

Supplemental Materials

"Case Archive." *National High School Ethics Bowl*. NHSEB, n.d. Web. February 2, 2015, http://nhseb.unc.edu/nhseb-rules/case-archive/.

Connolly, Peggy et al. *Ethics in Action: A Case-Based Approach*. Malden: Wiley-Blackwell, 2009.

Deaton, Matt. *Ethics in a Nutshell: An Intro for Ethics Bowlers* (2nd ed.). 2013. *National High School Ethics Bowl*. Web. February 2, 2015, http://www.ethicsbowl.org/uploads/3/3/1/4/3314659/ethics_in_a_nutshell_an_intro_for_ethics_bowlers_deaton.pdf.

Rachels, Stuart and James Rachels. *The Elements of Moral Philosophy* (6th ed.). New York: McGraw, 2010.

*This lesson plan was contributed by Mary Moran, who teaches social studies (Debate, Introduction to Philosophy and Introduction to Research) at Jericho High School in New York, where she also coaches both the award-winning debate team and nationally recognized Ethics Bowl team.

Part IV

IDENTITY, SOCIAL INEQUALITY, AND PHILOSOPHICAL PRACTICE

Chapter 9

Philosophical Recognition and Identity: Recognizing the Child

In part III we provided numerous examples of ways to introduce and practice philosophy with young people. These elementary, middle-school and high-school lesson plans are informed by an educational approach that values questioning, dialogue, and collaborative learning in the classroom. This approach regards young people as developing persons capable of philosophical insight and active thinking, and we referred earlier to the ways in which regarding children in this way gives them the opportunity, in a very real sense, to see themselves differently. In this chapter, we consider the potential contributions of a philosophical education for the development of positive forms of identity in young learners.

Dewey understands education as having value in two related senses. First, education is a "necessity of life," a practice through which finite beings ensure social continuity between generations through the transmission of language, beliefs, ideas, and principles (Dewey, 2011, 5). Seen in this light, the value of education lies in its relationship to human flourishing. Second, Dewey argues, the value of education can also be located experientially in the "vital interests" and "powers and purposes" we possess as learners (Dewey, 2011).

In this sense, the primary significance of education arises within the learner's own desire to know, the human inclination to exercise and refine one's capabilities in the world. In their accounts of a "meaningful" education, precollege philosophers often make reference to both senses of educational value: a process of engaging with questions, concepts, and practices central to the human condition and an avenue for harnessing the vital interests of students such that their learning emerges from self-directed exploration of ideas and concepts.

We will argue that practicing philosophy with children illuminates an additional realm of educational value; namely, identity formation. Philosophical practice with young students can be performed as an act of *recognition,* such that children are given opportunities for the development of positive relations-to-self (acquiring important forms of self-regard, such as self-confidence and self-esteem).

In turn, these relations-to-self are essential for the development and exercise of important forms of agency across numerous realms of human action. Given the integral relationship between a positive self-concept and the exercise of various forms of agency, our discussion in this chapter will serve, in part, as a call for increased empirical research on the connection between philosophical work with children and identity formation.

THE VALUES OF PRECOLLEGE PHILOSOPHY

Philosophers have argued for the greater inclusion of philosophy in precollege education for decades, often by linking philosophical education with greater meaning, rationality, and reflection in schools. Lipman employs this approach in *Philosophy in the Classroom* and *Thinking in Education*, arguing that "redesigning" the American educational system should involve introducing philosophy and, with it, "maximum meaningfulness and rationality" into the basic structure of schooling (Lipman, 1980, 3; 2003, 14). According to Lipman, we should introduce a curriculum and pedagogy that is rich with meaning as opposed to remaining beholden to instrumentally valuable testing and related curricula.

This will involve educating learners for "reflective thinking," thinking that is "aware of its own assumptions and implications" and that prepares students to be conscious of reasons, evidence, and logical argumentation in support of or against a conclusion (Lipman, 2003, 26). This form of thinking (and related skills) will thrive in a "meaning-laden" educational system that, at its core, provides opportunities for students to become active discoverers of meaning with greater intrinsic motivation to learn and be reflective thinkers (Lipman, 1980, 9).

In discussing the value of philosophical work in schools, Matthews focuses on adult-child interpersonal relationships, and argues for the importance of establishing authentic collaborations between teachers and students such that they become coinquirers in the educational process. In Matthews' *Dialogues with Children*—in which he recounts numerous examples of philosophical encounters with children in classroom settings—the potential value of establishing adult-child philosophical collaborations becomes clear.

Education can be made more meaningful through redesign of curricula and classes, but also, and perhaps more immediately, in the interpersonal orientation we take toward children in our educational interactions. If we enter these interactions harboring assumptions about the children's deficiencies and with the belief that the adult should exclusively direct the learning process, then we also overlook numerous possibilities for authentic collaboration with children (Matthews, 1992, 52). Conversely, if we establish philosophical relationships with children that create space for genuine exchange, acknowledge children's contributions to the learning process, and seek to engage them in dialogue, we can discover radically different possibilities for adult-child educational interactions. That is, the orientation we take toward educational interactions with children can either aid or inhibit the child's potential to contribute to the educational process, as well as our ability to see this potential.

Developing a related account of the value of philosophical education, Haynes and Murris highlight the significance of *authenticity* in adult-child communication through "more inclusive" and more "meaningful experiences of learning, via communities of inquiry," arguing that "we cannot seriously engage with children in authentic searches for understanding if we have already determined that they lack the authority to speak from their experience or the competence to make choices about which questions to pursue." Instead, by choosing to interact with children in a way that is inclusive and respectful, which acknowledges and helps develop their contributions to the learning process, we "can have a profound effect on a child's ability to work with others, to develop a confident and grounded voice, and, above all, to flourish and learn" (Haynes and Murris, 2012, 155–56).

PHILOSOPHY, IDENTITY, AND RECOGNITION

It is well-documented that young learners can enhance their academic skills through their participation in precollege philosophy programs. Numerous empirical studies show students' advances in skills ranging from critical thinking to communication and higher-order reasoning following sustained participation in precollege philosophy (Sprod, 1997; Morehouse and Williams, 1998; Walker, Wartenberg, and Winner, 2013). These findings are significant in their own right and can be marshaled to make a strong case for introducing philosophy in schools. However, the discussions above—from Lipman and Matthews to Haynes and Murris—provide us with an opportunity to consider an additional, underexplored value of precollege philosophy.

Compared to the impacts of precollege philosophy on academic skills, other important domains of child development—such as positive identity formation and social and emotional development—have not been widely examined. There has been some work in this area: for example, Biggeri and Santi discuss the significance of philosophical work with children in relation to interpersonal educational relationships that "re-shape the potential capability set of the child and enhance or reduce agency" (Biggeri and Santi, 2012, 378). The capabilities and agency of children can be enhanced through substantive interactions with adults and peers, in which they are recognized in "their active role in decision-making and deliberation about things that are worthwhile," thereby "contributing to their self-confidence, self-respect, and self-esteem" (Biggeri and Santi, 2012, 385). These aspects of positive identity can be developed in children's participation in philosophical communities of inquiry:

> The shared experience of being part of a CoI [Community of Inquiry] increases and enriches the process of building an identity in an interpersonal context in which each and every agent is recognized as a valuable thinker, with his/her own original cognitive style, typology of knowledge and life expertise. (Biggeri and Santi, 2012, 387)

In addition to the work of Biggeri and Santi, Trickey and Topping argue that philosophical inquiry "can yield significant gains in academic self-esteem" including a "significant reduction in dependency and anxiety and of greater self-confidence and self-efficacy" (Trickey and Topping, 2006, 608–09). Alongside their own research on philosophy and positive identity development in middle-school children, Trickey and Topping (2004) developed a systematic review of educational research on precollege philosophy programs. The review—spanning decades of empirical research on the educational impact of philosophy with children—documents numerous areas of positive child development resulting from the introduction of philosophical education and pedagogy in schools. Positive benefits include advances in reasoning and critical thinking, as well as less-explored areas of identity formation. For our purposes, it is significant to note that documented benefits of precollege philosophy include student gains in self-confidence, self-esteem, and social and emotional development (Trickey and Topping, 2004, 373–75).

At this point, we should say more about why this area of development—children's positive identity formation in relation to the appraisals of significant others—merits greater consideration as a focus of precollege philosophy research and educational work. First, given the relative underrepresentation of research in this area, we have much to learn in regard to potential connections between philosophy, education, and identity development in childhood. To the extent that we do consider these connections and find relevant positive (or negative) impacts of philosophy, we will have additional grounds on which to advocate for philosophy in precollege classrooms. Second, positive identity development is fundamental to children's abilities to regard themselves as and, in turn, to be, capable people, both within and beyond the classroom. Without a positive relation-to-self, children are hindered in the exercise of numerous forms of agency that presuppose self-confidence or self-esteem, from speaking up in class and interacting with peers to exercising more robust forms of moral and political action in the world. Thus, positive identity formation has far-reaching implications for both how we come to understand ourselves and, ultimately, how we live and perform our lives. Understanding children's abilities to develop in these vital areas will, we contend, include understanding the kinds of interpersonal recognition that help children to develop important forms of self-regard and a positive relation-to-self.

To take an example from the classroom context: children's capacities for expressing philosophical concerns and engaging in dialogue with others can be exercised at early ages, or can remain inactive and undeveloped. The difference between these two possibilities will hinge, in large part, on children's educational environments (supportive and caring, or intimidating and stressful) and the kinds of recognition (or lack thereof) that they receive from educators and peers (whether they are inclusive and responsive to children's concerns and interests, or dismissive and uninterested). When children are engaged as competent contributors to the learning process, they have the opportunity to regard themselves as "philosophers," as "intelligent," as "capable." In turn, these self-conceptions, as supported and sustained over time by significant others, can lead to real changes in the child's identity and ability.

Our attention to the significance of identity and recognition in precollege philosophy is influenced by the work of Charles Taylor (1994) and Axel Honneth (1995). For both Taylor and Honneth, positive recognition is a condition of the possibility of a developing person's ability to pursue meaningful forms of action in the world. This claim is based on a related conception of human development as an essentially *dialogical* (as opposed to *monological*) process:

> [A] crucial feature of human life is its fundamentally *dialogical* character. We become
> full human agents, capable of understanding ourselves, and hence of defining our identity,

through our acquisition of rich human languages of expression. . . . But we learn these modes of expression through exchanges with others. People do not acquire the languages needed for self-definition on their own. Rather, we are introduced to them through inter-action with others who matter to us. . . . We define our identity always in dialogue with, sometimes in struggle against, the things our significant others want to see in us. (Taylor, 1994, 33)

We are, from a young age, dependent on the appraisals of others, and these apprais-als—whether positive or negative—inform our "relations-to-self" (Honneth 1995, 94–95).[1] Taylor and Honneth discuss this dependence in terms of important forms of self-regard (self-confidence, self-respect, and self-esteem) that develop through our interactions with significant others. As developing persons, we have a "constitutional dependence" on experiences of recognition such that forming a positive relation-to-self is "dependent on the intersubjective recognition of one's abilities and accom-plishments" (Honneth, 1995, 136).[2] In other words, development and the formation of a positive identity is a process in which we depend on supportive and affirming relationships with significant others.

The work of Honneth and Taylor brings into focus important *relational* aspects of identity development and agency more generally. We are interested in the relevance of this relational conception of development for understanding the impact and out-comes of our philosophical collaborations with children. We use the term *philosophi-cal recognition* to describe the process of acknowledging and being responsive to children in our educational interactions as developing, but nevertheless philosophical, persons. We turn to the concept of philosophical recognition, in part, because our own fieldwork and experiences with children have shown us that the manner in which we approach and respond to children in the classroom has a substantial impact both on the quality of the session and children's own conceptions of their roles and abilities as participants.

If we actively listen to children and demonstrate (with words, with body language, and with patience) that we respect them as persons capable of contributing valu-able questions and insights to the discussion at hand, then children are more likely to feel cared for and self-confident in their ability to speak to us and to each other. Conversely, if we fail to listen and/or we act in ways that overlook children's con-tributions, we are demonstrating (even if unintentionally) that we do not fully value their ideas or, perhaps more significantly, that they are not worth listening to. We have become more conscious, for example, of how our own missteps as educators can derail a discussion with children—how speaking too much, failing to listen, or neglecting to provide children with opportunities for authentic, unscripted encounters can impact how the children feel about the learning environment and affect their con-fidence and willingness to contribute.

Our understanding of philosophical recognition and its significance in childhood education and development is also influenced by the empirical work of social psy-chologists in educational contexts, such as the research conducted by David Cole. Cole studies the *looking glass phenomenon* in childhood—the impact of others' appraisals on the formation of a child's self-concept. In a series of studies with elementary-school children, Cole examined the degree to which significant others' evaluations of children correlate with and predict changes in children's self-perceived competence (Cole, 1991; Cole et al., 2001). Commenting on this research, Cole writes,

> One's conception of self is constructed out of the perceptions of others. That is, we see ourselves and thus learn about our competences and incompetences from the interpersonal feedback we receive. The opinions and feedback from others constitute the looking glass through which we construct a self-image. (Cole et al., 2001, 378)

Following Cole and the work of other social psychologists (Measelle et al., 1998; Nelson et al., 2005, 2007), we gain an additional empirical basis for taking into account relational and recognition-based development in childhood. We can see that children develop identities—whether negative or positive—in relation to the perceptions of significant others (parents, friends, teachers, and others). This development will also be influenced by many different adult-child and peer interactions in educational and other contexts and, therefore, it is essential that we consider the influence of positive (and negative) recognition in schools.

CHILDREN AND MISRECOGNITION

The significance of philosophical recognition—and recognition in educational interactions more generally—becomes clearer through consideration of its antithesis, *misrecognition*. Taylor is again instructive:

> A person or group of people can suffer real damage, real distortion, if the people or society around them mirror back to them a confining or demeaning or contemptible picture of themselves. Nonrecognition or misrecognition can inflict harm, can be a form of oppression, imprisoning someone in a false, distorted, and reduced mode of being. . . . Misrecognition shows not just a lack of due respect. It can inflict a grievous wound, saddling its victims with a crippling self-hatred. Due recognition is not just a courtesy we owe people. It is a vital human need. (Taylor, 1994, 25)

If a positive relation-to-self is dependent (in part) on recognition and treatment by others, so, too, is a negative relation-to-self. To be denied respect as a person can lead to one internalizing a conception of one's own inferiority that, in turn, hinders one's capabilities as a human actor. Honneth discusses the "denial of recognition" as a harm to persons in relation to their positive self-understanding, in some cases going so far as to "bring the identity of the person as a whole to the point of collapse" (Honneth, 1995, 131–32). As is the case with positive recognition, then, misrecognition can have significant impacts on a person's life, particularly so in the case of developing children. Children can be especially vulnerable to forms of misrecognition that hinder the emergence of positive self-regard, self-perceived competence, and agency in numerous domains (Cole, 1991; Cole et al., 2001; Honneth, 1995). If positive identity formation is not supported from a young age, the repercussions can stretch throughout a person's life, potentially carrying forward a negative self-perception that limits a person's capabilities.

We can begin to grasp the potential harm of misrecognition in childhood more concretely by examining negative prejudicial treatment of children in epistemic contexts. In *Epistemic Injustice: Power and the Ethics of Knowing* (2007), Miranda Fricker provides a helpful framework for understanding how one's social identity (as woman, as black, as old or young, etc.) impacts one's social status as a "knower," as possessing or lacking epistemic credibility.

Fricker argues that testimonial interactions (i.e., verbal communication through which knowledge is exchanged between a speaker and hearer) are intertwined with power relations and social identity such that speakers and hearers are often in unequal positions of epistemic advantage or disadvantage. Certain kinds of speakers (those in epistemically privileged positions) are generally regarded as knowers and are heard and believed by hearers; others (those in epistemically disadvantaged positions) are often not heard and instead receive credibility deficit in testimonial interactions. Identity prejudice against particular groups functions through stereotypes and "a set of background assumptions," which hinder a hearer's willingness to regard a given speaker as a knower (Fricker, 2007, 36). Fricker cites numerous examples of prejudicial stereotypes that can impact a speaker's epistemic credibility:

> Many of the stereotypes of historically powerless groups such as women, black people, or working-class people variously involve an association with some attribute inversely related to competence or sincerity or both: over-emotionality, illogicality, inferior intelligence, evolutionary inferiority, incontinence, lack of "breeding," lack of moral fibre, being on the make, etc. (Fricker, 2007, 32)

Negative identity prejudice (e.g., the woman as overemotional or the black person as intellectually inferior) can discredit a class of speakers, distort a hearer's perception of the speaker in question, and ultimately lead to a breakdown in testimonial exchange. The result is that many speakers are subject to *testimonial injustice*; due to prejudice and negative stereotyping, they are not recognized as epistemically credible, are not heard by others, and are thereby harmed as persons (Fricker, 2007, 28).

The potential harms due to testimonial injustice are manifold. Given the centrality of rationality to conceptions of human value and identity, being treated as irrational in testimonial interactions undermines people in "their very humanity" (Fricker, 2007, 44). As Fricker writes, "when someone suffers a testimonial injustice they are degraded *qua* knower, and they are symbolically degraded *qua* human" (Fricker, 2007, 44). In addition to this primary harm, Fricker identifies "practical" and "epistemic" harms resulting from testimonial injustice. For one, a hearer can be practically harmed—in professional or legal contexts, for example—if others do not regard him or her as competent or epistemically trustworthy. Moreover, recipients of testimonial injustice—particularly when this injustice is persistent and systematic—can lose confidence in their own competence and abilities and become severely hindered as epistemic agents. This epistemic injury then inhibits "the development of an essential aspect of a person's identity," namely, as a rational person deserving of respect from others (Fricker, 2007, 54). The danger here is that the victim of testimonial injustice

actually comes to resemble the prejudicial expectations placed upon her. Describing
this possible harm, Fricker writes,

> The prejudice operating against the speaker may have a self-fulfilling power, so that the
> subject of the injustice is socially *constituted* just as the stereotype depicts her (that's what
> she counts as socially), and/or she may be actually *caused* to resemble the prejudicial ste-
> reotype working against her (that's what she comes in some measure to be). When either
> constitutive or causal construction occurs, we have a case of identity power operating
> "productively" . . . identity power at once constructs and *distorts* who the subject really
> is. (Fricker, 2007, 55)

Taken together, the implications of testimonial injustice are significant, damaging a
person's confidence, agency, and identity. Given the extent of these harms, Fricker
classifies testimonial injustice as an act of "oppression," one that can run "both deep
and wide in a person's psychology and practical life" (Fricker, 2007, 58).

Fricker provides us with a useful framework for understanding misrecognition *qua*
negative prejudice in epistemic contexts—people can be subjected to negative stereotypes and identity prejudice and then internalize these forms of prejudice such that
they accept a negative relation-to-self and are hindered as epistemic agents. However,
Fricker's examples of testimonial injustice do not take children into account, focusing
instead on the impact of epistemic prejudice in the lives of adults. Applying Fricker's
account to children, Karen Murris (2013) discusses the prevalence and impact of testimonial injustice on children in educational contexts. As Murris notes, in addition to
race, class, and gender, age "has significant impact on how much credibility a hearer
affords a speaker, and when and how s/he is silenced systematically" (Murris, 2013,
249). Prejudicial stereotypes and "collective naturalized conceptions" of children as
"unknowing, irrational and immature" can influence adults' perception of children as
lacking epistemic credibility and agency (Murris, 2013, 249).[3] The "deficit model of
childhood"—the view of children as essentially *less-than* adults (less rational, less
intelligent, less capable, etc.)—involves a narrow conception of the experience of
childhood, which can lead the adult to overlook (or misrecognize) the rich lived experiences, capabilities, and diverse interests of children as a social group. Murris argues
that these negative conceptions of childhood extend to educational contexts where
adult-child communication is commonly structured such that the child is not heard or
regarded as an active participant:

> Characteristic of most communicative exchanges between adult and child in school is
> children presenting to adults what the latter want to hear, not necessarily what children
> themselves genuinely believe in. The routine asking of closed, rhetorical questions by
> teachers is a mere symptom of a deeper engrained epistemic orientation that profoundly
> influences how we speak and regard what it means to think *with* children. Even when a
> serious and well-intentioned effort is made by teachers to encourage children's authentic
> speculations, the listening is a listening out for or rehearsal of what teachers already
> know. Teachers' self-identity as epistemic authorities constitutes a serious barrier to hear-
> ing the child's voice even when room is deliberately made in class to listen to children's
> ideas. (Murris, 2013, 249)

This method of classroom communication effectively silences children, failing to regard them as "knowers" (a role reserved for the teacher) and, ultimately, failing to hear children's contributions.

As based on a negative prejudicial conception of childhood, this structuring of adult-child communication can lead to a range of harms. First, children are harmed insofar as they are subject to epistemic prejudice (as irrational, as incompetent, etc.) or simply overlooked as persons capable of providing meaningful contributions in educational contexts. This orientation deprives children of opportunities for authentic participation in the classroom and elsewhere, and results in lower motivation, comprehension, and learning. Framed as misrecognition, the ensuing harm can lead children to take on negative relations-to-self and impede development and performance of a range of actions that rely on positive self-regard.

The impact of child-focused misrecognition has been documented as especially relevant for socioeconomically disadvantaged children and children of color in schools (Rosenthal and Jacobson, 1992, 51–52). Children primarily regarded as disadvantaged, difficult, or lacking in intelligence are generally not expected to learn or perform well academically and, in turn, are affected by these expectations such that they can end up fulfilling the "prophecy" (Rosenthal and Jacobson, 1992, 53). In *Savage Inequalities: Children in America's Schools* (1991), Jonathan Kozol provides additional evidence of this phenomenon, documenting the impact of prejudice that can "diminish the horizons and aspirations of poor children, locking them at a very early age into the slots that are regarded as appropriate to their social position" (Kozol, 1991, 93).[4] When children are subjected to misrecognition and regarded as incapable or incompetent in educational (and other) contexts, they can view themselves through the same deficient lens, thereby negatively impacting their abilities and aspirations.

Adults, too, are harmed by child-focused prejudice and misrecognition insofar as we miss out on the knowledge that children can provide by creating (perhaps unknowingly) an imbalanced educational relationship. When learning is enacted as a process by which the sole (adult) epistemic authority provides knowledge to passive children, the potential benefits of relational or collaborative learning in the classroom are negated. In this situation, the learning process is distorted for all participants such that we are left with a one-way transmission of ideas instead of a mutual process of discovery and knowledge creation (as we find in communities of inquiry). In this sense, forms of misrecognition that directly impact the lives of children can also have negative, if indirect, repercussions for adult teachers and the broader educational community.

RESPONDING TO CHILD MISRECOGNITION

Philosophical encounters with children have the potential to help ameliorate the negative impacts of misrecognition on children and adults. As discussed earlier, adults leading philosophy sessions in schools can structure their interactions such that students receive *philosophical recognition*. When conducting group discussions, we can demonstrate both through pedagogical actions (using child-centered discussion prompts and building dialogue from student questions and interests) and words (providing verbal support and constructive feedback as students grapple with philosophical concepts and questions) that participating children are central to and codeterminants of the educational experience.

During our own sessions with precollege students, we intentionally refer to them as *philosophers* as a way to recognize them as persons deserving of being heard by peers and teachers and capable of contributing to their own education. In light of our discussion of misrecognition in particular, this is a significant act, as it—along with broader, sustained pedagogical and interpersonal strategies—gives us (and students) a means to engage children in a different light; namely, as persons possessed of experiences and insights that can form a foundation for the co-construction of knowledge in philosophical dialogue.

Moreover, the performance of philosophical recognition requires an additional skill set: *active listening*. If we recognize the extant forms of prejudice that can impact children's self-conceptions, and the adult-child power dynamics that place youth in positions of epistemic disadvantage, then we should not begin our educational interactions under the assumption that all children are fully prepared (or willing) to share their voices in the classroom. Acknowledging these background conditions requires that we do more than simply remain open to *hearing* children's voices. Rather, we must be proactive and employ a method of active listening that creates the conditions for their voices to be heard.

Clark, McQuail, and Moss (2003) describe this form of listening as "an active process of communication involving hearing, interpreting, and constructing meanings" (13). Understood in this way, listening is not limited to a one-off sensorial act, but rather, is enacted through a set of embedded practices by which we create a "culture of listening" (Clark, McQuail, and Moss, 2003, 7). These practices include hearing children's spoken words, along with taking steps through additional listening strategies—including play, artwork, and numerous experiential, child-centered activities—to set the ground for alternative forms of adult-child communication. In this sense, active listening is generative in nature; it is both a disposition and a series of actions that facilitate successful communication with children.

In the classroom, in addition to approaching the child as a competent person with insights and knowledge to share (through acts of philosophical recognition), active listening will also involve a reflexive awareness on the part of adults such that we are aware of power relations and differences in social status that can impact adult-child relationships. Haynes and Murris (2012) describe this awareness as an "ethics of listening":

> An ethics of listening in education must be pursued with a sensitive political will on the part of adults: through relinquishing authority and unlearning assumptions routinely made about children, through dialogue and conversation with children, through giving them the responsibility of thinking together for themselves and the power of decision-making, through individual reflection, through addressing their rights, and through explicit attention to relationships and communication in schools. (228)

Upon this backdrop we can engage children as participants in dialogue (in communities of inquiry) and also create opportunities for them to express themselves beyond the written and spoken word (especially in the case of young children). To do this, we can move beyond traditional discussion-based methods in precollege philosophy and include additional modes of expression, including the creation of artwork, the use of cameras and digital media, and games, as alternative means for children to represent their knowledge, questions, and curiosities. These additional means of communication can make the child's voice *visible* in significant ways (Rinaldi, 1996; Clark and Moss, 2001), serve as additional bases for philosophical practice, and assist the adults in learning to listen.[5]

None of this is to say that active listening and philosophical recognition can fully address or ameliorate problems associated with child misrecognition and prejudice or related adult-child power dynamics in schools. These problems include structural as well as interpersonal elements that we cannot fully address here. However, moving forward from these discussions, and grounded in our own fieldwork with children, we contend that there are additional outcomes that should be considered in practicing, researching, and determining the success of precollege philosophy. In addition to *skill-based* outcomes (such that we structure our practice and assessments to promote children's advancement in making judgments, reasoning, philosophical awareness, or other relevant skills) and *topic-based* outcomes (such that we focus our lessons around philosophical themes and concepts like *justice*, *equality*, or *fairness* and determine the success of our work by evaluating the children's understanding of the relevant theme/ concept), we can also consider *recognition-based* outcomes. We might think of these outcomes as akin to what Dewey references when he speaks of the "indirect and vital moral education" that can come from the interactions and relationships of students, teachers, and the "school community" (Dewey, 1936, 4).

We can develop forms of pedagogy and listening—which are caring, responsive, and inclusive—that promote important forms of self-regard in children. These forms of self-regard underlie and support the exercise of the same skill sets and forms of agency that are so vital in other, traditional forms of education. Here, for example, we are thinking about the importance of self-esteem and self-confidence for children (and adults for that matter) to be capable of forming and standing up for a belief, to have the courage to speak up in class, and more generally, *to regard one's self* as valuable and deserving of respectful treatment. Given the importance of recognition for children, we suggest that sustained attention be given to the potential for developing and assessing precollege philosophy curricula, classroom practices, and research to foster recognition-based outcomes that support children's positive identity formation and relations-to-self.

NOTES

1. Honneth describes the development of a "relation-to-self" as a "process in which children gradually internalize the patterns of interaction they learn in their successive encounters with their mother, father, siblings, and finally, peers. The organization of the psyche thus occurs as an interactive process" (Honneth, 2012, 198).

2. For Honneth, the recognition of developing children by caretakers (in the form of love, care, and supported independence) is of foundational importance as "this relationship of

recognition prepares the ground for a type of relation-to-self in which subjects mutually acquire basic confidence in themselves, [and] . . . is both conceptually and genetically prior to every other form of reciprocal recognition" (Honneth, 1995, 107).

3. For more on forms of prejudice against children (sometimes referred to as "childism"), see Pierce and Allen (1975), Young-Bruehl (2013), and Webb (2004).

4. In chapter 10 we discuss the potential impact of the social identities of students—including race, ethnicity, class, and gender—in more detail, along with consideration of associated power relations among students and between students and teacher in the classroom.

5. We discuss alternatives to the traditional whole-class discussion in more depth in the chapter 10.

Chapter 10

Children's Philosophical Encounters: Taking Seriously the Role of Privilege in Classrooms

The classroom, with all its limitations, remains a location of possibility.

—bell hooks

SPACE FOR ALL CHILDREN'S VOICES

We have argued that philosophical recognition of young people should be one of the fundamental aims of philosophical practice in schools. This demands an appreciation for children's philosophical insights and unique perspectives, involving pedagogical and interpersonal strategies that manifest a commitment to making space for all children's voices. We explored in earlier chapters the ways in which development of a robust community of philosophical inquiry involves children and adults listening to one another, being open to multiple perspectives, and being able to disagree respectfully.

We described the importance of an intellectually safe learning environment, one that is dependent on the strength of the classroom community, requiring trust, openness, and respect, but which does not rest on feelings of comfort or complacency. But also essential to an environment in which every child's voice can be heard is an awareness of the different positions that various students occupy in the classroom and in the world and the ways in which these diverse vantage points can affect whether and how students contribute to philosophical discussions.

This chapter considers the ways that certain children's voices can be privileged in a classroom, and others' disadvantaged—because of, for example, race, ethnicity, class, or gender—and investigates strategies for cultivating an intellectually safe environment for philosophical inquiry in which every voice matters. Throughout this book, we've argued that philosophical inquiry in schools requires the creation of a space in which children's questions and ideas are at the center of the intellectual enterprise, in which they are able to explore the topics that matter to them. Engaging in open discussions with their peers and becoming aware of the variety of life experiences and points of view at work in the classroom encourages students to become active participants in our diverse democratic society.

This demands the expansion of our understanding of philosophy, involving an awareness of children's perspectives as an important part of the philosophical land-scape, and requires an integrity of practice that works to bring all children's voices into the conversation. This commitment necessarily involves an awareness of the vari-ous social and political power relations at play in the classroom.

In the previous chapter, we explored epistemic injustices done to children more generally—that is, the ways in which children's abilities to convey knowledge to oth-ers and to make sense of their own experiences can be undermined by child-focused prejudice. There are also particular forms of epistemic injustice that are experienced, for example, by children of color, children from low-income backgrounds, and girls from all races and backgrounds.

Children who experience unequal social conditions can hold views of the world that differ from those of socially advantaged students (and, of course, from each other's views as well). The classroom often reflects the privilege that certain groups—white, male, heterosexual, etc.—continue to hold within the larger social system, and stu-dents who belong to more marginalized groups find that their perspectives go unad-dressed or dismissed, that they are unrecognized.

There are many examples of the way that this plays out. Male students often dominate classroom discussion, especially in classrooms beyond elementary school, while studies show that girls become increasingly reticent about speaking out (Julé, 2004; Sadker and Sadker, 1994). White children come to expect their images and experiences to be reflected in classroom materials, while children of color become accustomed to the absence of their images and points of view in the texts they read in school. Many upper- and middle-class children take for granted the ability of their families to be involved in their schools, while children from low-income backgrounds frequently find such expectations bewildering, given their families' lack of time and money for such participation. Many children struggle to make sense of the contrast between their lives outside of school and the world of the classroom.

The ways in which children approach school in general, and philosophical inquiry in particular, depends in large part on their life experiences. Each of us has developed a set of background ideas about the meaning of such concepts as truth, knowledge, beauty, and goodness, and our experiences play a significant role in the ways we both substantively understand and procedurally investigate these concepts.

To ensure that every child's approach to philosophical thinking is valued requires a clear awareness of the dangers of setting up any "voice of authority" (whether that voice be adult, white, male, middle class, etc.) that can shut down a student's ability to be heard and/or inhibit a student's willingness to express honestly his or her point of view. Educational institutions often mirror the power dynamics of the larger soci-ety, and it is imperative that part of philosophical inquiry includes questioning those dynamics and the perspectives of those who benefit from them.

Children's questions and ideas can be powerful opening points for examining issues of race, class, gender, ethnicity, and political and social inequalities. Too often, the adults in their lives are uncomfortable having such exchanges, and end up shutting down children when they initiate these exchanges. Darren Chetty has noted that there is little in the current precollege philosophy literature about addressing topics of race and racism (Chetty, 2014, 1). And when it comes to addressing issues of class, gender, and social inequalities generally, precollege philosophy literature has also been relatively silent. But children want to talk about these issues, and a commitment to a classroom sensitive to the diverse needs and experiences of its students involves taking up student questions and thoughts about the ethical, social, and political implications of social inequalities. When facilitators are willing to engage with children in discussions about race, gender, and class, we signal to the children that their questions matter and that these are important topics to address.

Because students in positions of greater disadvantage are more likely to be the focus of stereotypes that obscure their perspectives, it is particularly important that teachers cultivate a space in which it is clearly understood by the group that the greater the diversity of ideas and approaches, the richer the philosophical exchange. Fostering such spaces demands a kind of enhanced epistemological modesty—the acknowledgment that all members of the group are fallible and hold views that could end up being mistaken—that includes the awareness that everyone's perspectives are profoundly influenced by their own experiences of privilege and/or disadvantage and that cultivates an openness to our views being called into question. This involves being "open to what we have not heard before" and committed to "resist[ing] the urge to translate what [we] hear into what is familiar" (Murris, 2013, 251). Students learn that enlarging their own understanding of the world depends on being open to listening to ideas and viewpoints that are unfamiliar and can sometimes be uncomfortable.

INTERPRETING AND EXPRESSING ONE'S OWN EXPERIENCES

In order to develop an understanding of themselves and their lives, it is crucial for children to be able to express their attempts to make sense of their experiences. Adult condescension and skepticism about children's reflective capacities can hinder children's abilities to do so. Children from socially marginalized groups face even greater obstacles than other children in general when they attempt to articulate the way they see the world. For example, ordinary classroom interactions that seem innocuous to white teachers and students can be experienced by students of color as alienating (Pollock, 2008, 227), as when a teacher or a white student asks the only black student in the class to express the African-American perspective on a particular issue, or when the Somali child is asked to explain Islam. Girls of all races and ethnicities are often more reticent to contribute to classroom discussions, in part because, as studies have shown, teachers call on boys more often than they call on girls, and girls are more likely to be given positive feedback for their social skills while boys are praised for intellectual proficiency (Julé, 2004; Sadker and Sadker, 1994).

In chapter 2, we considered the importance of questioning and the ways in which precollege philosophy discussions prioritize student questions. Philosophy sessions frequently involve a paradigm shift, as children's authentic questions take center stage. For some children, adapting to this shift is challenging. All students are not equally at ease articulating and expressing their questions. Particular children—for example, intellectually confident, white, male, fluent English speakers—can dominate questioning.

Studies show that students from higher-income families are more likely to be encouraged to ask questions in school, while students from more modest-income backgrounds are urged to be deferential to authority, perhaps in order to protect these children from getting into trouble (Calarco, 2014; Berger, 2014, 58–59). A flourishing philosophical community, therefore, involves the facilitator's attentiveness to the questions asked in philosophy sessions, and in particular to who asks them and how they are asked, and an appreciation for differing cultural norms and individual confidence in asking questions. A variety of strategies can be used to encourage children to express their questions freely (see the discussion of instructional strategies below). When philosophical practice emphasizes openness to all student questions and awareness of the power dynamics that can inform student participation, the students who feel least comfortable in school may become the most deeply engaged.

Teachers often express surprise at what particular students, who may in the past have shown little interest in what goes on in the classroom, contribute to philosophy discussions. Time after time, teachers who begin philosophy programs in their classrooms comment on the way that the sessions engage many learners who struggle in other school contexts. We believe that this can be largely explained by the nature of philosophical discussions—involving questions and ideas controlled for the most part by the students—coupled with the open environment of the community of inquiry, where any idea can be offered so long as the speaker can articulate reasons for its consideration. The subjects explored come from the students' interests, and there is no set agenda for the content of the discussions (other than that they have philosophical significance and integrity). Students actively shape the content and structure of their classroom's philosophical inquiry, which supports student agency and independent thinking, and this breathes life into many students' attitudes about school.

In this framework, students will raise questions about justice and fairness, unequal social and political power, and oppression and exploitation. The facilitator must be prepared to address these issues with students. We want students to develop the skills and confidence to become actively engaged members of a diverse society. Philosophy has a unique role to play in helping students develop these skills—including critical and creative thinking, awareness of multiple perspectives, and the ability to ask good questions and adeptly articulate their views—and key to the success of this role is the creation of a space for the candid exchange of ideas among peers with a wide range of viewpoints. It is imperative, then, that the philosophy community be committed to inclusiveness and attentiveness to the expression of all perspectives,[1] so that it is clear that every child's contributions are valuable to the group.

ENSURING INCLUSIVE PHILOSOPHICAL EXPLORATION: CULTURALLY RESPONSIVE PEDAGOGY AND SILENCE

Much work has been done in recent years on the importance of developing culturally responsive teaching practices. "Culturally responsive pedagogy" can be understood as situated in a framework that recognizes the rich and varied cultural wealth, knowledge, and skills that students from diverse groups bring to schools, and seeks to develop dynamic teaching practices, multicultural content, multiple means of assessment, and a philosophical view of teaching that is dedicated to nurturing student academic, social, emotional, cultural, psychological, and physiological well being. (Howard, 2010, 67–68)

It is beyond the scope of this chapter to examine the enormous range of work in this area, but the practices advocated by many educators as essential for cultivating an inclusive philosophical community include the following:

1. Developing a knowledge base about cultural diversity, which includes understanding the cultural characteristics of various ethnic groups;
2. Designing culturally relevant curricula;
3. Building a learning community conducive to learning for diverse students;
4. Accommodation of the communication styles of different ethnic groups by developing classroom interactions that reflect these styles; and
5. Providing a wide range of instructional strategies to meet the needs of a diverse student body (Gay, 2002, 106–14).

As described in chapter 5, a philosophical community of inquiry is a shared experience that aims at creating possibilities for *all* members of the classroom community to learn from one another. Cultivating a robust learning community requires paying attention to the cultural framework of the classroom and working to ensure that what goes on in the classroom is socially meaningful and appreciative of students' multiple perspectives.

One of the vital features of a culturally responsive pedagogy in philosophy sessions is the accommodation of diverse communication and learning styles. The traditional model for precollege philosophy sessions involves whole-class engagement in verbal communication, in the form of a large group discussion, often held in a circle. While this method of conducting philosophy sessions has much to offer, not every student will be immediately comfortable with this approach. The larger the class size, for example, the more challenging this model can be for many students, especially at the inception of a philosophy program.

Alternatives to large group discussions inspire more students to engage in philosophy sessions. Often teachers can start a philosophy discussion with small-group work or "turn and talk" exchanges (in which pairs of students share their reactions to a prompt with each other). The use of "silent discussions" (see chapter 6) allows students to contribute solely in writing, giving students who are less comfortable with the give-and-take of a fast-moving verbal philosophical discussion access to a philosophical exchange that proceeds more slowly and deliberately. The use of art, music, movement, and games is also valuable for reaching a wide variety of learners.

For many students, it takes time to become comfortable speaking in a large group. For others, silence can be an important element of engagement. What constitutes participation in a philosophy session? How do we expand our concept of participation? Are there avenues for students to participate silently? Can active listening count as participation? How do we view the silence of students?

Silence holds multiple meanings for individuals within and across racial, ethnic and cultural groups and at any given moment in a classroom interaction. In schools, however,
silence is often assigned a limited number of meanings. Silence is most often thought
of only as the absence of talk, and almost always as problematic rather than potentially
powerful. Student silence is typically interpreted either as a result of his or her group
membership, or as a result of individual characteristics, rather than as a combination of
stances toward participation. Teachers either tend to read classroom silences through
individual lenses, assuming that a student is shy or reticent to speak, or understand student
silences through group lenses, assuming that the student's group membership (i.e., as an
Asian American) translates into a particular style of participation or silence in class. . . .
To avoid these pitfalls, educators should explore the multiple meanings silence holds for
students. (Pollock, 2008, 218–19)

When a student is silent, there are likely to be multiple reasons for that silence—personal, social, and cultural. Given this, rather than making assumptions for why a particular student is not participating verbally in discussions, the facilitator can approach
silence as an inevitable aspect of philosophy sessions and ensure that the range of
options for participation demonstrates attentiveness to the multiplicity of student communication styles.

Three approaches in particular can be useful for responding to silence. First, the
group can understand silence as a powerful aspect of a philosophical discussion.
When the facilitator allows silence to linger, this makes space for students who are
not the first to jump in to fill that space with speech and allows for the development of
a collective comfort with silence as part of inquiry. Second, the nature of silence can
be a subject for philosophical investigation with students. For example, after holding
a silent discussion (see chapter 6), ask students about how and when participation can
occur through silence, the meaning of silence, and the differences between choosing
silence and being silenced. Finally, silence, involving listening and reflection, can be
understood as one form of participation in the classroom experience.

When silence is accepted as a form of participation, space opens up for more students to engage with philosophical topics. A student recently commented, "This is the
first class I've ever been in where I didn't feel uncomfortable about being quiet most
of the time and where I really wanted to speak when I did."[2] When students who need
more time for reflection before speaking have a choice whether to participate verbally, this allows them to take that time. This does not mean, however, that we allow
students to disengage from what is happening or that we accept student invisibility.

Silence as a form of participation must be coupled with related strategies that
encourage and support a wide range of participation styles, including the kinds of
small-group practices mentioned earlier in the chapter. Another effective strategy
is to employ writing as a regular part of philosophical inquiry, particularly in third
grade and up, while utilizing art in earlier grades. Students can write questions and
ideas that come to their minds as they are listening to the prompt, for example, or can
draw examples that illustrate how they think about the philosophical question being
examined.

The use of philosophy journals as places for students to record their questions
and reflect about texts and class discussions is an effective way to take into account
varying student communication styles. Writing provides a comfortable means of

expression for students less comfortable with speaking in large groups, with the classroom's dominant language, and/or with the pace of fast-moving philosophical discussions. The quiet space that journal writing creates gives students time to grow comfortable with the give-and-take of a philosophy discussion.

All students can take a quiet few moments to write down any questions they have after the prompt is read or after the activity has begun, and then those who want to share those questions verbally with the larger group can do so (or all students can do so in "turn and talk" exchanges or small groups). At the end of a session, students can be asked to write a reflection in response to a question that emerges from the discussion that has just taken place. From time to time, the philosophy teacher can collect the journals and respond in writing to students directly, providing another means of developing trust and furthering philosophical conversation with individual students.

THE POWER OF THE TEXT

One of the crucial moments in a philosophy session is the choice of text (when texts are used) to prompt philosophical inquiry. Along with seeking philosophically suggestive texts, it is crucial for philosophy teachers to be sensitive to the opportunities and/ or barriers that might be constructed through use of particular kinds of texts. Do the texts reflect a wide variety of experiences? Do the authors possess diverse racial and ethnic backgrounds? How are the characters presented? The texts used in philosophy sessions are central to a pedagogy that is sensitive to the classroom's and/or the society's diversity. Students need, appreciate, and respond to texts that reflect their life experiences. A wide variety of multicultural and gender-sensitive books can shape the classroom environment in general and philosophical inquiry in particular.

Along with presenting a variety of perspectives, it is important that some of the texts be used to interrogate social power dynamics. As observed earlier, children are very aware of issues of inequality and oppression, and will raise these issues when they are not discouraged from doing so. Questions about race and gender issues start early. Young children notice differences in skin color (see Tatum, 2003, 31–51) and differences, for example, in the way boys and girls of all races are expected to dress. Often, teachers and other adults are hesitant about engaging children's questions about race and gender.

Frequently, this reluctance to engage stems from an attempt to provide an inclusive environment for diverse groups of students and a sense that discussion of these issues might not be comfortable for some students. In our experience, however, it is generally not the children who are uncomfortable, but the adults. In a supportive environment that values respect for children's points of view and recognizes that students come from backgrounds with varying levels of social power, it is important that educators not shy away from these issues.

Sometimes adults will say of young children, "I don't want them to have to develop a racial awareness yet." This is almost always said by white adults about white children, because children of color are cognizant of their racial identities very early, and, moreover, this comment fails to recognize that, at least in the United States, virtually everyone, even white children in communities where there are few or no people of color, becomes aware of racial differences early in their lives (Tatum, 2003, 32–37). In the twenty-first century, the ability to work with people from different racial and ethnic groups is as essential as the possession of technological skills, and it is important that we help all children learn to work closely with people whose race, religion, class, or culture may be different from their own.

The educator bell hooks has written that a transformative educational environment depends on community and a shared commitment to learning in the classroom (hooks, 1994, 40). For hooks, this means shifting our paradigms for what classroom learning requires, becoming aware of the "narrow boundaries that have shaped the way knowledge is shared in the classroom" and being willing to experience the disquiet that can be involved when our ways of understanding the world are challenged (hooks, 1994, 40–44).

As we noted in chapter 5, an intellectually safe community does not promise comfort or certainty, but rather helps its members examine difficult and contestable issues. Philosophical inquiry involves a willingness to be vulnerable—in expressing our own views, we risk them being challenged, and in listening to others, we risk being changed by what we hear. Grappling with difficult issues can be uncomfortable, but part of the work of making sense of the world for ourselves involves rethinking what we have assumed we already know. In our experience, children can be fearless in their attempts to do this, and it is our responsibility to support them.

One of the ways we can encourage student discussions of race, gender, and other social inequalities is to bring in texts that raise these issues competently and compellingly. Once the text is read, the topics explored will then be up to the students. As in any philosophy session, student questions shape the inquiry. Thus it is important both that we not silence student attempts to tackle difficult issues and that we not push particular discussions on students laden with our own agendas.

The facilitator's role is to support the children's explorations of the questions of interest to them, and to help maintain the trust, respect, and openness to others' ideas that are the hallmarks of a community of philosophical inquiry, while also being cognizant of the power dynamics that can influence who is (and is not) heard in the classroom. This doesn't mean that we promote our personal, political, or social positions, but it does mean that when issues of social inequality, injustice, and oppression emerge from children's questions and comments, we follow their lead. It also means that we pay attention to the manifestation of social inequalities in the classroom that can hinder the voice(s) of students.

Many picture books broach questions about social inequalities, discrimination, and exploitation.[3] In chapter 6, we discussed a number of books that are effective starting points for explorations of racism, social class, and gender issues. In, for example, *The Other Side* by Jacqueline Woodson and *Freedom Summer* by Deborah Wiles, the inequality of blacks and whites is the fundamental theme. Children discussing these books raise questions about who has the authority to exclude others, the power imbalances between the black and white characters, the oppression of the African-American communities depicted in the stories, and the injustices implicit in a racist society. *Amazing Grace* by Mary Hoffman fosters thinking about both race and gender, and *The Paper Bag Princess* by Robert Munsch has been used successfully to examine gender issues with students of all ages. In Monica Gunning's *A Shelter in Our Car*, issues of poverty, homelessness, and social class differences are at the heart of the story. For middle- and high-school students, there is a wealth of literature and nonfictional works that raise questions about social inequalities.

THE ROLE OF THE FACILITATOR

We live in a world of fast-changing demographics. The Pew Research Center estimates that by 2050, almost one in five Americans will be an immigrant, and demographers predict that by 2035, students of color will constitute a majority of the US student population (Howard, 2010, 36–40). At the same time, the vast majority of teachers are white and native English speakers, and there is no sign that this is changing (Howard, 2010, 41). Most teachers are white, middle-class women, and the far majority of academics engaged in precollege philosophy in the United States are also white and middle class. Those of us engaged in this work share both a collective responsibility and individual obligations to ensure that we can successfully educate and work with diverse groups of students.

Cultural competence is a contemporary concept that involves a framework for supporting a culturally responsive pedagogy. The National Center for Cultural Competence lists five elements necessary for cultural competence (2008): (1) valuing diversity; (2) having the capacity for self-assessment; (3) being aware of the dynamics of cultural interaction; (4) acquiring institutionalized cultural knowledge; and (5) having the ability to adapt to cultural diversity. The underlying principle of this framework is that working successfully with diverse populations requires an ongoing dedication on the part of educators to learn from the wide range of different cultural frameworks and values. This involves both learning about the ways that cultural knowledge is developed and maintained and reflecting about our own frameworks of knowledge and values.

Tyrone Howard observes, "[I]t is not uncommon for students of color to have deep-seated mistrust or suspicion of teachers who come from racially privileged groups. Teachers have a tremendous responsibility and obligation to earn the trust of students from diverse backgrounds" (Howard, 2010, 120). Part of this obligation, Howard asserts, is the development of racial awareness, which recognizes not just the social, political, and economic consequences of being a member of a racially marginalized group but also the unearned opportunities and advantages that come with being a member of a racially privileged group, and involves a commitment to advocating for social justice. If we are to inspire and support diverse groups of young people to come together to explore essential questions about life and the human condition, it is imperative that we develop an awareness of our own prejudices, unconscious beliefs, and ways of thinking, so that we can minimize their impact on our ability to reach students with very different frameworks. This can mean being willing to look at the subtle and sometimes unconscious ways that we might respond to students differently, depending on their race, sex, and/or class (see, e.g., Christie, 2007), including paying attention to who we call on, the language we use, and other manifestations of our own perspectives and biases.

Awareness of our own limited perspectives and mistaken assumptions is difficult work, and this demands honesty and an openness to seeing the world differently and acknowledging one's own epistemic limitations. But if we are serious about working to keep certain children's voices from being privileged in a classroom, and other children's voices correspondingly silenced or diminished, we have to acknowledge and maintain awareness of our own racial identities and privileged positions in the classroom—as adult educators with institutional authority, as whites, as males, as upper or middle class, as native English speakers, etc. This requires an acknowledgment that the way we see students is distorted by our particular cultural lens, that our students have a great deal to teach us, and that the world is a rich and complex place about which we always have more to learn.

An authentic and potentially transformative community of philosophical inquiry depends on the voices of every participant. Each time a voice goes silent, we lose a valuable perspective that can improve our understanding of the world. Further, if we are not attentive to the potential impact of prejudice, inequality, and related power dynamics in the classroom, we can inadvertently contribute to silencing already-marginalized students. As part of our commitment to fashion spaces open to the perspectives of these and all students, we must address, personally and collectively, the issues that deter many students from participating fully in the community. We owe it to our students to work as hard and as courageously as they do to make sense of the world and ourselves.

NOTES

1. It is worth noting that a commitment to the expression of all perspectives does not mean that students are entitled to utter, for example, hate speech, as the focus on every voice being heard comes within a context that is aimed at developing a respectful and intellectually safe community of philosophical inquiry.

2. Class at University of Washington, Seattle, Washington, fall 2014.

3. In his article "The Elephant in the Room: Picturebooks, Philosophy for Children and Racism" (2014), Darren Chetty notes that a number of picture books recommended by precollege philosophy educators for discussions of racism and diversity are, in fact, more celebrations of difference than prompts that inspire authentic discussions about race. By contrast, Woodson's *The Other Side* and Wiles' *Freedom Summer* are both examples of children's books that address the systematic oppression central to racism.

Chapter 11

Philosophy and Transforming Precollege Education

RESPECT FOR CHILDREN

At the heart of this book and our work in precollege philosophy is a dedication to cultivating and demonstrating respect for children. Although children are often told how important it is to "respect others," it is rare that respect *for children* is prioritized. Search "respect" and "children" online, and you will find pages and pages about ways to teach children how to respect others, and very little about respect for children themselves. So many aspects of young people's lives fail to generate respect from adults—their agency, their time, their work, their bodies, their thoughts and ideas, their questions.

When we empower children's voices and take seriously their articulated points of view, we begin to build a classroom structure that is committed to respect for children. Respect for children's ideas and intellects is embedded in the very concept of talking philosophically with children. A child's effort to grapple honestly with complex concepts and questions is an activity that is in itself worthy of recognition. Thinking about philosophical issues with children involves appreciating their attempts to attain understanding and intellectual self-determination, as well as evaluating the ideas they suggest with the same respect accorded to adult reflection.

This involves taking children seriously *as children*; we're not pretending that children are adults, but we acknowledge the ideas and perspectives of children as worthy of attention and consideration. Further, we recognize children's ability to teach, while also learning from, receptive adults. It's empowering for children to have their ideas recognized by others as having substance and meriting recognition from others.

As we have noted elsewhere in this book, according children's ideas genuine consideration provides reciprocal rewards. Children gain the experience of conversing in a genuine way with adults, which enhances their ability to communicate, advocate for their beliefs, and express their thoughts coherently. In turn, adults benefit from children's novel and imaginative insights about philosophical questions and issues raised in collaborative dialogue. Matthews writes,

219

Children are people, fully worthy of both the moral and intellectual respect due persons. They should be respected for what they are, as well as for what they can become. Indeed, we can learn from them and let them enrich our lives as, much more obviously, they learn from us and let us enrich their lives. The parent or teacher who is open to the perspectives of children and to their forms of sensibility is blessed with gifts that adult life otherwise lacks. (Matthews, 1994, 122–23)

Indeed, the sensibility of children can help us adults step away from the comfortable insulation of our long-held beliefs and reawaken our awareness of the philosophical concerns inherent in everyday life.

People frequently remark that it's important to them that children learn to "think for themselves." However, children are told what to think far more often than they are encouraged to think independently. In order to develop competence at "thinking for themselves," children need practice doing it. Few areas provide better practice for acquiring the habit of independent thinking than philosophy. Uncertainty and questions are at its core, and delving into philosophical wondering leads to an ability to identify a core concept, distinction, or assumption when discussing an issue, to recognize the deeper questions involved, and to creatively consider potential responses and solutions. Thinking for oneself involves asking searching questions, evaluating situations independently, and coming up with one's own answers. These skills are crucial to children being able to build their own future, and should be at the heart of precollege education.

THE BIGGER PICTURE

Over the past fifty years, there have been ongoing efforts to reform the public education system in the United States. While a full exploration of these policy efforts is beyond the scope of this chapter, we offer some reflections about the role that philosophical practice has the potential to play in improving schools.

Education reform efforts have largely fallen into three categories: (1) attempts to increase equity and decrease discrimination so that all students have the opportunity for an enriched and meaningful education; (2) a focus on parental choice, including charter schools and public funds for religious and private school education; and (3) the use of standards and tests to determine what students should know and measure whether they have learned it. The Common Core is the most recent example of this third reform movement. All of these movements have had successes and setbacks, and none of them have been completely effective at what they intended to do—that is, to transform education in the United States.

What all of these movements have in common is that none of them have had the experiences and voices of students at the center of their efforts to improve education. How do students experience schooling? What do students believe they need? Why do students go to school? What does it mean to be educated? Of course, many factors, including the quality of teachers, the way in which education is funded, the home lives of the students, and the various challenges students face, are all important factors in answering these questions. But the question, we believe, that lies at the heart of education and is essential to any effort to change schools in a positive way is in some ways a simple one: What makes learning meaningful to students?

In our view, what matters most in thinking about education is how students are experiencing what is going on in the classroom. Is it relevant to their lives? Does it help them to resolve the issues that matter to them? How does the classroom curriculum help them to make sense of the world? Educator Deborah Meier asserts that "teaching is mostly listening" (Meier, 2002, xiii). Yet much of education seems to function on the basis of the belief that teaching is telling, and that if someone is at the front of the room teaching, someone must be learning. But, both from experience and recent research, we know this isn't necessarily true (see, e.g., Hattie, 2011).

Education is meaningful for students when the subjects being taught matter to them, when they recognize their importance and care about understanding their content. When students are engaged, they begin to cultivate certain habits of mind, or what we think of as philosophical dispositions, that are central to becoming educated. We categorize these dispositions as follows: (1) critical and flexible thinking; (2) imaginative problem-solving, including a willingness to explore new ideas; (3) an ability to listen carefully and communicate clearly; (4) a propensity to ask questions and search for assumptions; (5) a commitment to seek and evaluate reasons; (6) intellectual humility, honesty, and carefulness; and (7) a comfort with uncertainty. These habits of mind are, for the most part, difficult if not impossible to assess in a standardized test; however, in our view, they are at the core of education, and their essence is the ability to think well.

In learning how to think well, more important than knowing the answers is knowing how to ask and address questions to which you don't have the answers. The questions that are the subject of investigation in a community of philosophical inquiry are, by definition, questions for which we do not have the answers. When these questions come from the students, and are important to them, students begin to become aware of the connections between who they are, the subjects they study in school, and their everyday experiences. They learn to trust their own ideas and questions and to be unafraid of questions to which they don't know the answers. They learn, in other words, to think for themselves, which, we assert, should be education's preeminent goal. After all, as one second-grade philosophy student put it, "It's what you think that makes you who you are."[1]

PHILOSOPHY AND THE SPIRIT OF EDUCATION

Philosophy remains at the margins of education in the United States. The subject is unfamiliar to most educators, broadly understood as an "adults-only" subject, and seen by most people as an abstract academic endeavor reserved for very few scholars. This view is reinforced by current educational policy and curricula that do not explicitly include space for the practice of philosophy in schools. The reasons for this are complex; they include a lack of public understanding of the nature and value of philosophy (given that much of the population is never introduced to philosophy in their schooling), a current lack of advocacy by philosophers at the level of educational policy, and an imprecise fit between contemporary educational strategies and philosophical practice (i.e., there is not an obvious correspondence between philosophical question-ing and pedagogy and the aims of much standardized test-based instruction).[2]

Yet, walk into an elementary school classroom where there are regular philosophy sessions, and you will see students alive with thinking and talking about deep and seri-ous subjects. Listen to ordinary conversations among teenagers, and you will observe exchanges about what's "right" and "wrong," identity, truth, fairness, and justice. Contrary to the common view of philosophy as specialized and esoteric, philosophy involves questions that are part of our common heritage and everyday lives—ques-tions about morality, knowledge, reality, social and political conditions, art, and beauty. Philosophical thinking is an activity we engage in every time we ask ourselves about the meaning of our lives, the importance of friendship, the nature of love, or the obligations we have to the environment. Further, and as demonstrated by a growing body of educational research (see, e.g., Topping and Trickey, 2004, 2007), philosophi-cal instruction leads to the advancement of numerous academic skills at the heart of recent motivations for education reform in public schooling. The rigorous intellectual demands of philosophical practice help students to develop proficiencies in speaking and listening, analytic reasoning, writing and argumentation, and clear and creative thinking. Given these benefits and the receptivity of children to philosophical prac-tice, we believe it is time for a reconsideration of the role that philosophy can play in improving educational experience and outcomes in our schools.

For all of these reasons it's important that we encourage children and young people to participate in philosophy, develop their philosophical sensitivity, and inquire with each other about complex philosophical topics. Students hunger for engagement with issues that matter to them, and the unsettled nature of philosophical questions furnishes students with space to explore without the constriction of looking for a single, settled answer. The broad and foundational topics of philosophy can help shape classroom learning communities to foster meaning, understanding, and awareness of the connec-tions between students' work in schools and their life experiences. Students engaged in exploring philosophical issues have opportunities, as Katherine Simon put it,

> to develop a host of invaluable *intellectual* and moral skills, traits and sensibilities: a hunger for deeper understanding and the stamina to seek it out, a sense of connection with the human beings throughout history who have struggled with similar questions, the ability to see shades of gray in conflicts and to articulate nuanced opinions, the habit of seeking out multiple points of view, the habit of collaborating to explore complex issues, the willingness to change one's mind when that is warranted, and even the capacity for empathy. (Simon, 2001, 3) (emphasis in original)

When young people engage in philosophical practice, there is a coming together of an educational experience that puts student questions and ideas in the forefront and a learning enterprise that builds essential thinking, listening, and communication skills.

As we have noted elsewhere in this book, philosophical issues are at play in virtually every school subject—from mathematics, science, history, and language arts through art, music, and so on. Although structured time set aside for philosophical inquiry is essential, building philosophy into the curriculum does not require the creation of wholesale philosophy classes. Philosophy stretches across disciplines, as its areas of investigation include ethics, social and political issues, aesthetics, philosophy of literature, philosophy of science, philosophy of mathematics, and the like. Philosophy can take place, for example, in a regular science class to examine the issue of objectivity or the kind of evidence necessary to accept a theory, or in a history class to explore the basis for political and civil rights or the moral issues implicated by immigration, and so on. As exemplified by many of the lesson plans in part III, philosophical investigation and discussion is a natural fit for almost any subject matter taught in schools.

Philosophical questions can serve a foundational role in the study of various topics. For instance, a study of the Holocaust and genocide can be framed around questions such as: What is a community and what shapes its identity? What do we owe members of our communities? Is indifference morally wrong? What is courage? (Goering, Shudak and Wartenberg, 2013, 152–67). Introductory chemistry classes can highlight such issues as what it means for something to be an element, what constitutes a scientific explanation, and so on (see, e.g., Kennedy and Kennedy, 2011). There is frequent reference in educational circles to the importance of utilizing essential questions, generally described as important, foundational, and open-ended questions that provoke inquiry (see, e.g., McTighe and Wiggins, 2013). Many such questions are, of course, philosophical. Considering such questions serves to deepen student understanding and can provide a meaningful context for the topics being studied.

The challenges for introducing philosophy into precollege classrooms stem primarily not from the inaccessibility of philosophy's subject matter—as we have observed, philosophical topics abound in everyday life and in most school subject areas—but from the widespread conception of philosophy, particularly in the United States, as an esoteric academic enterprise unrelated to precollege education. Connected to this view is the absence of an appreciation for children's philosophical capacities and the value of philosophical practice with young people. Introducing philosophy into schools on a large scale would require demonstrating—through education and research—the benefits of philosophy as a core subject in education, as well as training precollege educators to develop philosophical sensitivity and a related facility with philosophical problems and discussion. This involves working both at the grassroots level with educators, students, and administrators, as well as broad advocacy, research, and educational efforts to influence policy-makers and intellectual leaders.

A CONCLUDING NOTE

We have attempted in this book to analyze many of the theoretical and policy issues implicated in efforts to bring philosophical inquiry into schools, as well as to offer practical resources and support for educators already engaged or interested in engaging in the work of developing communities of philosophical inquiry in classrooms. Given the importance of this work and the real challenges facing it, it is important to acknowledge that the policy and practical issues associated with advocating for philosophy in schools call for evaluating the best approaches to policy-makers, educators, and administrators, as well as an associated long-term investment of resources to develop training programs for teachers, particularly in Colleges of Education, that would lead to more precollege philosophy educators.

We caution, too, that seeking wholesale policy changes (e.g., pushing for a state board of education to make philosophy a mandatory subject in that state) before the requisite groundwork has been laid involves serious potential drawbacks, not the least of which is requiring a subject that few have the requisite training and experience to teach. It might be that the best way forward entails a combination of introducing philosophy one classroom or school at a time, connecting already practicing precollege philosophy teachers with one another, and working with Colleges of Education and philosophy departments at colleges and universities to develop additional research projects, philosophy in schools programs, and more teacher education in philosophy. Our comments here are meant to be provisional, as a contribution to, and a catalyst for continuing a much-needed conversation about the best way forward for precollege philosophy and education.

In our experience, the most powerful way to illustrate the merits of philosophical inquiry with young people is to allow people to see it in action. In countless workshops and classrooms over the years, we have seen educators and parents captivated by the experience of seeing children participating in rich, deep, and complex philosophical conversations. One first-grade teacher commented, for example:

> Philosophy in my first grade classroom has been a powerful means through which my students have been able to wrestle with questions and express their thoughts in a safe yet challenging environment. Their sense of justice and right or wrong is revealed, along with their reasoning skills and the ability to engage with one another in respectful and mature dialogue. The language of "I agree/disagree with so-and-so because" has trickled into other class discussions in all subjects. Hearing them talk, it's hard to believe they're only six and seven year olds! (Carrie Lam, first-grade teacher, John Muir Elementary School, Seattle, Washington, 2013)

Children are far more competent than adults think. We underestimate children's interest in examining complex intellectual topics, as well as their abilities to do so. Too often, we approach serious issues with children with too much assurance that we know what's best for them and too little confidence that they possess the potential for figuring things out for themselves.

Providing young people with a forum for examining their own questions and ideas, in a structured and rigorous framework, is empowering—for children, for adults, and for schools. Bringing philosophy into schools may seem at first a small act—one more subject to teach. But this apparently small act can in fact be deeply significant. Founded on children thinking for themselves, philosophical practice generates recognition of children's intellectual capacities, appreciation for the contributions children can make to thinking about large and complex problems, and respect for children's experiences and ideas. This, we believe, can be transformative for education.

NOTES

1. Class at John Muir Elementary School, Seattle, Washington, winter 2012.

2. A related issue for the advancement of philosophy in schools includes relevant teacher training in philosophy and, further, the creation of job opportunities for trained philosophy teachers. As long as philosophy is not supported at the level of educational policy, Colleges of Education will not include philosophy as a core subject for preservice teacher education.

Appendix

SELECTED BOOKS FOR TEENAGERS AND ADULTS

The Universe and Dr. Einstein, by Lincoln Barnett
Three Dialogues between Hylas and Philonous, by George Berkeley
Lying: Moral Choice in Public and Private Life, by Sissela Bok
Labyrinths, by Jorge Luis Borges
The Stranger, by Albert Camus
The Alchemist, by Paulo Coelho
Mrs. Bridge, by Evan Connell
Meditations on First Philosophy, by Descartes
Pilgrim at Tinker Creek, by Annie Dillard
Middlemarch, by George Eliot
Invisible Man, by Ralph Ellison
The Campaign, by Carlos Fuentes
The Mind's I: Fantasies and Reflections on the Self and Soul, composed and arranged by
    Daniel C. Dennett and Douglas R. Hofstadter
The Brothers Karamazov, by Fyodor Dostoevsky
Sophie's World, by Jostein Gaarder
In a Different Voice, by Carol Gilligan
Engaging Philosophy, by Mitch Green
Siddhartha, by Hermann Hesse
Their Eyes Were Watching God, by Zora Neale Hurston
Brave New World, by Aldous Huxley
"A White Heron," in *The Country of the Painted Firs and Other Stories*, by Sarah Orne Jewett
The Trial, by Franz Kafka
Fear and Trembling and The Sickness Unto Death, by Soren Kierkegaard
Philosophical Fragments, by Soren Kierkegaard
The Ones Who Walk Away from Omelas, by Ursula LeGuin (short story)
A Sand County Almanac, by Aldo Leopold
The Time of the Hero, by Mario Vargas Llosa
The Book of Laughter and Forgetting, by Milan Kundera
One Hundred Years of Solitude, by Gabriel Garcia Marquez
Tar Baby, by Toni Morrison

What Does It All Mean?, by Thomas Nagel
The Examined Life, by Robert Nozick
Tell Me a Riddle, by Tillie Olsen
Animal Farm, by George Orwell
A Dialogue on Personal Identity and Immortality, by John Perry
The World of Silence, by Max Picard
Republic, by Plato
Ishmael: An Adventure of the Mind and Spirit, by Daniel Quinn
A Theory of Justice, by John Rawls
The Problems of Philosophy, by Bertrand Russell
The Catcher in the Rye, by J. D. Salinger
Nausea, by Jean-Paul Sartre
No Exit, by Jean-Paul Sartre
Walden, by Henry David Thoreau
The Death of Ivan Illyich, by Leo Tolstoy
A Young Person's Guide to Philosophy, edited by Jeremy Weate
Mrs. Dalloway, by Virginia Woolf

JOURNALS AND MAGAZINES

Analytic Teaching
Childhood and Philosophy
Journal of Philosophy in Schools
Philosophy Now
Questions: Philosophy for Young People
Teaching Philosophy

SELECTED ONLINE RESOURCES

Harvard University's Justice with Michael Sandel: http://www.justiceharvard.org
LEARN NC K-12 philosophy resources: http://www.learnnc.org/lp/editions/philosophy-resources
Philosophy Bites: http://www.philosophybites.com
Philosophy for Kids: http://www.philosophyforkids.com
Philosophy Talk: http://www.philosophytalk.org
PLATO (Philosophy Learning and Teaching Organization): http://plato-apa.org
Teaching Children Philosophy: http://www.teachingchildrenphilosophy.org
The P4C Cooperative: www.p4c.com
University of Washington Center for Philosophy for Children: http://depts.washington.edu/nwcenter
What's the Big Idea? Introducing Middle School Students to Philosophy Through Film: http://whatsthebigideaprogram.com
Wondering Aloud: A Blog About Philosophy With Young People: http://philosophyforchildren.blogspot.com

Bibliography

Alexander, R. *Towards Dialogic Teaching: Rethinking Classroom Talk*. Cambridge: Dialogos, 2006.

Allen, Blake and Branton Shearer. "The Scale for Existential Thinking." *International Journal of Transpersonal Studies* 31.1 (2012): 21–37.

Appalachia Educational Laboratory. *Questioning and Understanding to Improve Learning and Thinking (QUILT): The Evaluation Results*. A proposal to the National Diffusion Network (NDN) documenting the effectiveness of the QUILT professional development program. ERIC Document Reproduction Service No. ED403230, 1994.

Applebee, Arthur N. *Curriculum as Conversation: Transforming Traditions of Teaching and Learning*. Chicago: University of Chicago Press, 1996.

Aristotle. *Metaphysics*. (W. D. Ross, trans.). Princeton, NJ: Princeton University Press, 1984.

———. *Nicomachean Ethics*. (Terence Irwin, trans.). Indianapolis, IN: Hackett Publishing., 1999.

Armstrong, Thomas. *Multiple Intelligences in the Classroom*. Washington DC: Association for Supervision and Curriculum Development, 2009.

Benware, C. and Deci, E. L. "Quality of Learning with an Active Versus Passive Motivational Set." *American Educational Research Journal* 21 (1984): 755–65.

Berger, Warren. *A More Beautiful Question*. New York: Bloomsbury Publishing, 2014.

Biggeri, Mario and Marina Santi. "The Missing Dimensions of Children's Well-being and Well-becoming in Education Systems: Capabilities and Philosophy for Children." *Journal of Human Development and Capabilities: A Multi-Disciplinary Journal for People-Centered Development* 13.3 (2012): 373–95.

Burbules, Nicholas, C. "The Limits of Dialogue as a Critical Pedagogy." In Peter Trifonas (ed.), *Revolutionary Pedagogies: Cultural Politics, Instituting Education and the Discourse of Theory*, New York: Routledge, 2000.

Butnor, Ashby. "Critical Communities: Intellectual Safety and the Power of Disagreement." *Educational Perspectives* 44.1–2 (2012): 29–31.

Calarco, Jessica McCrory. "Coached for the Classroom: Parents' Cultural Transmission and Children's Reproduction of Educational Inequalities." *American Sociological Review* 79.4 (2014): 1–23.

Chetty, Darren. "The Elephant in the Room: Picturebooks, Philosophy for Children and Racism." *Childhood and Philosophy* 10.19 (2014): 11–31.

Christie, Alice. "Recognizing (Almost) Invisible Gender Bias in Teacher Student Interactions." Retrieved from http://www.alicechristie.org/pubs/Christie-Gender.pdf (2007).

Clark, Alison and Peter Moss. *Listening to Young Children: The Mosaic Approach*. London: Jessica Kingsley Publishers, 2011.

Clark, Alison, Susan McQuail, and Peter Moss. *Exploring the Field of Listening to and Consulting with Young Children*. Nottingham: Department for Education and Skills, 2003.

Claxton, Guy. *Teaching to Learn: A Direction for Education,* London: Cassell Publishing, 1990.

Cobb, Edith. *The Ecology of Imagination in Childhood*. Dallas: Spring Publications, 1993.

Cohen, Jonathan. "Social, Emotional, Ethical, and Academic Education: Creating a Climate for Learning, Participation in Democracy, and Well-Being." *Harvard Educational Review* 76.2 (2006): 201–37.

Cole, David A. "Change in Self-Perceived Competence as a Function of Peer and Teacher Evaluation." *Developmental Psychology* 27.4 (1991): 682–88.

Cole, David A., Farrah M. Jacquez, and Tracy L. Maschman. "Social Origins of Depressive Cognitions: A Longitudinal Study of Self-Perceived Competence in Children." *Cognitive Therapy and Research* 25.4 (2001): 377–95.

Coles, Robert. *The Spiritual Life of Children*. Boston: Houghton Mifflin Company, 1990.

———. *Children of Crisis*. Boston, MA: Little, Brown and Co., 2003.

Costello, Peter (ed.). *Philosophy in Children's Literature*. Lanham, MD: Lexington Books, 2012.

Daniels, Denise H. and Kathryn E. Perry. "'Learner-Centered' According to Children." *Theory into Practice* 42.2 (2003): 102–08.

Darling-Hammond, Linda. "Reframing the School Reform Agenda: Developing Capacity for School Transformation." *Phi Delta Kappan* 74.10 (1993): 752–61.

Delfos, Martine F. *Are You Listening to Me?: Communicating with Children from Four to Twelve Years Old*. Uitgeverij SWP BV, 2001.

Denham, Susanne A. and Roger P. Weissberg. "Social-Emotional Learning in Early Childhood: What We Know and Where to Go From Here." In Elda Chesebrough, Patricia King, and Thomas P. Gullotta (eds.), *A Blueprint for the Promotion of Prosocial Behavior in Early Childhood*, 13–50. New York: Kluser Academic/Plenum Publishers, 2004.

Dewey, John. *How We Think*. Buffalo, New York: Prometheus Books, 1933.

———. *Moral Principles in Education*. Carbondale: Southern Illinois University Press, 1936.

———. *Experience and Education*. New York: Simon & Schuster, 1938.

———. *Democracy and Education*. Hollywood, FL: Simon & Brown, 2011.

Dotson, Kristie. "How Is This Paper Philosophy?" *Comparative Philosophy* 3.1 (2012): 3–29.

Edmonds, David and Nigel Warburton. *Philosophy Bites*. London: Oxford University Press, 2010.

Fisher, David. "Dialogic Teaching: Developing Thinking and Metacognition through Philosophical Discussion." *Early Child Development and Care* 177.6–7 (2007): 615–31.

Freire, Paulo. *Pedagogy of the Oppressed* (rev. ed.). New York: Continuum, 1993.

Fricker, Mirana. *Epistemic Injustice: Power and the Ethics of Knowing*. Oxford, UK: Oxford University Press, 2007.

Friquegnon, Marie-Louise. "What is a Child." *Thinking: The Journal of Philosophy for Children* 13.1 (1997): 12–16.

Gardner, Howard. *Changing Minds: The Art And Science of Changing Our Own And Other People's Minds*. Boston: Harvard Business Review Press, 2006a.

———. *Frames of Mind: The Theory of Multiple Intelligences*. New York: Basic Books, 1993.

———. *Intelligence Reframed*. New York: Basic Books, 1999.

———. *Multiple Intelligences: New Horizons*. New York: Basic Books, 2006b.

Gardner, Susan. "Inquiry is no Mere Conversation (or Discussion or Dialogue): Facilitation of Inquiry is Hard Work." *Critical and Creative Thinking: The Australasian Journal of Philosophy for Children* 13.2 (1995): 38–49.

Garrison, D. Randy. *E-Learning in the 21st Century: A Framework for Research and Practice.* New York: Routledge, 2011.

Gay, Geneva. "Preparing for Culturally Responsive Teaching." *Journal of Teacher Education* 53.2 (2002): 106–16.

Gendler, Tamar. *Intuition, Imagination and Philosophical Methodology.* Oxford: Oxford University Press, 2010.

Goering, Sara, Nicholas Shudak, and Thomas Wartenberg. *Philosophy in Schools: An Introduction for Philosophers and Teachers.* New York: Routledge, 2013.

Gopnik, Alison. *The Philosophical Baby.* New York: Farrar Straus and Giroux, 2009.

Gregory, Maughn. "A Framework for Facilitating Classroom Dialogue." *Teaching Philosophy* 30.1 (2007): 59–84.

Haslanger, Sally. *Resisting Reality: Social Construction and Social Critique.* Oxford, UK: Oxford University Press, 2012.

Hattie, John. *Visible Learning for Teachers: Maximizing Impact on Learning.* London: Routledge, 2011.

Haynes, Joanna. *Children as Philosophers.* London: Routledge, 2002.

— — — and Karin Murris. *Picturebooks, Pedagogy and Philosophy.* London: Routledge, 2012.

Heschel, Abraham. *God in Search of Man: A Philosophy of Judaism.* New York: Farrar, Strauss and Giroux, 1955.

Hill Collins, Patricia. *Another Kind of Public Education: Race, Schools, the Media, and Democratic Possibilities.* Boston: Beacon Press, 2009.

Holt, John. *How Children Fail.* New York: Merloyd Lawrence, 1982.

Honneth, Axel. *The Struggle for Recognition: The Moral Grammar of Social Conflicts* (Joel Anderson, trans.). Cambridge, MA: The MIT Press, 1995.

Honneth, Axel. *The I in We: Studies in the Theory of Recognition* (Joseph Ganahl, trans.). Cambridge, UK: Polity Press, 2012.

hooks, bell. *Teaching to Transgress.* New York: Routledge, 1994.

Howard, Tyrone C. *Why Race and Culture Matter in Schools.* New York: Teachers College Press, 2010.

Jackson, Thomas E. "The Art and Craft of Gently Socratic Inquiry." In Arthur L. Costa (ed.), *Developing Minds: A Resource Book for Teaching Thinking.* Alexandria, VA: Association for Supervision and Curricular Development, 2001: 459–62.

Jenks, Chris. *Childhood* (2nd ed.). New York: Routledge, 2005.

Julé, Allyson. *Gender, Participation and Silence in the Language Classroom: Sh-Shushing the Girls.* New York: Palgrave Macmillan, 2004.

Kennedy, Nadia and David. "Community of Philosophical Inquiry as a Discursive Structure, and its Role in School Curriculum Design." *Journal of Philosophy of Education* 45.2 (2011): 265–83.

Kozol, Jonathan. *Savage Inequalities. Children in America's Schools.* New York: Broadway Books, 1991.

Kuhn, Deanna. *Education for Thinking.* Cambridge: Harvard University Press, 2005.

Levin, Tamar and Ruth Long. *Effective Instruction.* Washington DC: Association for Supervision and Curriculum Development, 1981.

Lipman, Matthew. "Philosophy for Children: Some Assumptions and Implications." In Eva Marsal, Takara Dobashi, and Barbara Weber (eds.), *Children Philosophize Worldwide.* Frankfurt: Peter Lang, 2009.

— — —. *Philosophy Goes to School.* Philadelphia: Temple University Press, 1988.

———, Ann Margaret Sharp and Frederick S. Oscanyan. *Philosophy in the Classroom*. Philadelphia: Temple University Press, 1980.

———. *Thinking in Education*. Cambridge: Cambridge University Press, 2003.

Lone, Jana Mohr. "Philosophical Sensitivity." *Metaphilosophy* 44.1–2 (2013): 171–86.

———.*The Philosophical Child*. New York: Rowman & Littlefield, 2012.

——— and Roberta Israeloff (eds.). *Philosophy and Education: Introducing Philosophy to Young People*. Cambridge: Cambridge Scholars Publishing, 2012.

Matthews, Gareth. *Dialogues with Children*. Cambridge: Harvard University Press, 1992.

———. "Holiness." In Eva Marsal, Takara Dobashi, and Barbara Weber (eds.), *Children Philosophize Worldwide*. Frankfurt: Peter Lang, 2009.

———. *Philosophy and the Young Child*. Cambridge: Harvard University Press, 1980.

———. *Philosophy of Childhood*. Cambridge: Harvard University Press, 1994.

McCall, Catherine C. *Transforming Thinking: Philosophical Inquiry in the Primary and Secondary Classroom*. London: Routledge, 2009.

McCombs, Barbara L. and Jo Sue Whisler. *The Learner-Centered Classrooms and School: Strategies for Increasing Student Motivation and Achievement. The Jossey-Bass Education Series*. San Francisco, CA: Jossey-Bass Publishers, 1997.

McDowell, John. "Deliberation and Moral Development in Aristotle' Ethics." In Stephen Engstrom and Jennifer Whiting (eds.), *Aristotle, Kant, and the Stoics: Rethinking Happiness and Duty*. Cambridge: Cambridge University Press, 1998.

McIntyre, Lee. Making Philosophy Matter-or Else". *The Chronicle of Higher Education*, December 11, 2011.

McTighe, Jay and Grant Wiggins. *Essential Questions: Opening Doors to Student Understanding*. Washington DC: Association for Supervision and Curriculum Development, 2013.

Measelle, Jeffrey R., Jennifer C. Ablow, Philip A. Cowan, and Carolyn P. Cowan. "Assessing Young Children's Views of Their Academic, Social, and Emotional Lives: An Evaluation of the Self-Perception Scales of the Berkeley Puppet Interview." *Child Development* 69.6 (1998): 1556–76.

Meece, Judith. "Applying Learner-Centered Principles to Middle School Education." *Theory Into Practice* 42.2 (2003): 109–16.

Meir, Deborah. *The Power of Their Ideas: Lessons for America from a Small School in Harlem*. Boston: Beacon Press, 2002.

Mercer, Neil and Karen Littleton. *Dialogue and the Development of Children's Thinking: A Sociocultural Approach*. London: Routledge, 2007.

Morehouse, R. and M. Williams. "Report on Student Use of Argument Skills." *Critical and Creative Thinking* 6.1 (1998): 14–20.

Murdoch, Iris. *Metaphysics as a Guide to Morals*. New York: Penguin Books, 1993.

Murphy, P. K., A. O. Soter, I. A. Wilkinson, M. N. Hennessey, and J. F. Alexander. "Examining the Effects of Classroom Discussion on Students' Comprehension of Text: A Meta-Analysis." *Journal of Educational Psychology* 101.3 (2009): 740–64.

Murris, Karin. *Teaching Philosophy with Picture Books*. Newport, UK: Infonet Publications, 1992.

———. "The Epistemic Challenge of Hearing Child's Voice," *Studies in Philosophy and Education* 32 (2013): 245–59.

Nagel, Thomas. *What Does It All Mean?* Oxford, UK: Oxford University Press, 1987.

Nelson, Larry J., Craig H. Hart, Cortney A. Evans, Robert J, Coplan, Susanne Olsen Roper, and Clyde C. Robinson. "Behavioral and Relational Correlates of Low Self-Perceived Competence in Young Children." *Early Childhood Research Quarterly* 24 (2009): 350–61.

Nelson, Larry J., K. H. Rubin, and N. A. Fox. "Social Withdrawal, Observed Peer Acceptance, and the Development of Self-Perceptions in Children Ages 4 to 7 Years." *Early Childhood Research Quarterly* 20 (2005): 185–200.

Noddings, Nel. *Caring: A Relational Approach to Ethics and Moral Education*. Oakland, CA: University of California Press, 2013.

Nussbaum, Martha. *Love's Knowledge*. New York: Oxford University Press, 1990.

Nystrand, R. *Opening Dialogue: Understanding Dynamics of Language and Learning in the English Classsroom*. New York: Teacher College Press, 1997.

Opdal, Paul Martin. "Curiosity, Wonder and Education seen as Perspective Development." *Studies in Philosophy and Education* 20 (2001): 331–44.

Paley, Vivian Gussin. *You Can't Say You Can't Play*. Cambridge: Harvard University Press, 2009.

Peters, R. S. *Ethics and Education*. London: Allen and Unwin, 1966.

Piaget, Jean. *Judgement and Reasoning in the Child*. New York: Routledge, 2002.

Plato. *Laws*. (Trevor J. Saunders, trans.). New York: Penguin Books, 1970.

———. *Republic*. (C. D. C. Reeve, trans.). Indianapolis: Hackett Publishing, 2004.

Pollock, Mica (ed.). *Everyday Antiracism: Getting Real About Race in School*. New York: The New Press, 2008.

Proust, Marcel. *Swann's Way*. (Lydia Davis, trans.). New York: Viking, 2002.

Reznitskaya, Alina. "Dialogic Teaching: Rethinking Language Use During Literature Discussions." *The Reading Teacher* 65.7 (2012): 446–56.

Rinaldi, Carlina. *In Dialogue with Reggio Emilia: Listening, Researching, and Learning*. London: Routledge, 2006.

Rosenthal, Robert and Lenore Jacobson. *Pygmalion in the Classroom: Teacher Expectation and Pupils' Intellectual Development*. New York: Irvington Publishers, 1992.

Rothstein, Dan and Luz Santana. *Make Just One Change: Teach Students to Ask Their Own Questions*. Boston: Harvard Education Press, 2011.

Russell, Bertrand. *The Problems of Philosophy*. New York: Oxford University Press, 1997.

Sadker, Myra and David. *Failing at Fairness: How America's Schools Cheat Girls*. New York: Charles Scribners Sons, 1994.

Schapiro, Tamar. "Childhood and Personhood." *Arizona Law Review* 45.3 (2003): 575–94.

———. "What is a child?" *Ethics* 109.4 (1999): 715–38.

Schrader, Dawn E. "Intellectual Safety, Moral Atmosphere, and Epistemology in College Classrooms." *Journal of Adult Development* 11.2 (2004): 87–101.

Sellars, Wilfrid. "Philosophy and the Scientific Image of Man." In *Science, Perception and Reality*. London: Routledge & Kegan Paul, 1963: 35–78.

Shapiro, David. *Plato Was Wrong! Footnotes on Doing Philosophy with Young People*. Lanham, Maryland: Rowman & Littlefield, 2012.

Shor, Ira, and Paulo Freire. "What is the 'Dialogical Method' of Teaching?" *Journal of Education* 169.3 (1987): 11–31.

Simon, Katherine G. *Moral Questions in the Classroom: How to Get Kids to Think More Deeply About Real Life and Their Schoolwork*. New Haven and London: Yale University Press, 2003.

Skidmore, David. "Pedagogy and Dialogue." *Cambridge Journal of Education* 36.4 (2006): 503–514.

Solomon, Robert. "'What is Philosophy?' The Status of World Philosophy in the Profession." *Philosophy East and West* 51.1 (2001): 100–04.

Sprod, Tim. "Improving Scientific Reasoning through Philosophy for Children: An Empirical Study." *Thinking* 13.2 (1997): 11–16.

Tallis, Raymond. *In Defence of Wonder and Other Philosophical Reflections*. Durham, UK: Acumen Publishing, 2012.

Tatum, Beverly Daniel. *Why Are All the Black Kids Sitting Together in the Cafeteria?* New York: Basic Books, 2003.

Taylor, Charles. "The Politics of Recognition." In Amy Gutmann (ed.), *Multiculturalism: Examining the Politics of Recognition*, 25–73. Princeton, NJ: Princeton University Press, 1994.

Trickey, S. and K. J. Topping. "'Philosophy with Children': A Systematic Review." *Research Papers in Education* 19.3 (2004): 365–80.

———. "Collaborative Philosophical Enquiry for School Children: Cognitive Effects at 10–12 Years." *British Journal of Educational Psychology* 77 (2007): 271–88.

———. "Collaborative Philosophical Enquiry for School Children: Socio-Emotional Effects at 11 to 12 Years." *School Psychology International* 27.5 (2006): 599–614.

United Nations Educational, Scientific, and Cultural Organization. *Teaching Philosophy in Europe and North America.* Paris, France, 2011.

Vygotsky, Lev. *Thought and Language.* Cambridge, MA: MIT Press, 1962.

Wagner, Tony. *The Global Achievement Gap.* New York: Basic Books, 2008.

Walker, Caren M., Thomas E. Wartenberg, and Ellen Winner. "Engagement in Philosophical Dialogue Facilitates Children's Reasoning About Subjectivity." *Developmental Psychology* 49.7 (2013): 1338–47.

Wall, John. *Ethics in Light of Childhood.* Washington DC: Georgetown University Press, 2010.

Wartenberg, Thomas. *A Sneetch is a Sneetch and Other Philosophical Discoveries: Finding Wisdom in Children's Literature.* Malden, MA: Wiley-Blackwell, 2013.

———. *Big Ideas for Little Kids.* New York: Rowman & Littlefield, 2009.

Watkins, Chris. "Classrooms as Learning Communities." *Research Matters Series No. 24.* London: Institute of Education School Improvement Network, 2004.

Weimer, Maryellen. *Learner-Centered Teaching: Five Key Changes to Practice.* Hoboken, NJ: John Wiley & Sons, 2002.

White, David. *Philosophy for Kids: 40 Fun Questions That Help You Wonder About Everything!* Austin, Texas: Prufrock Press, 2000.

White, John. "The Roots of Philosophy." In A. Phillips Griffiths (ed.), *The Impulse to Philosophize*, 73–88. Cambridge: Cambridge University Press, 1992.

Wilen, William W. *Questioning Skills for Teachers* (3rd ed.). Washington DC: National Education Association, 1991.

Winnicott, D.W. *Playing and Reality.* New York: Routledge, 2010.

Zophy, Jonathan. "On Learner-Centered Teaching." *Society for History Education* 15.2 (1982): 185–96.

Index

About the Authors

Jana Mohr Lone is the founder and director of the University of Washington Center for Philosophy for Children. Since 1995 she has taught philosophy in classrooms from preschool to college, as well as taught college students, K-12 teachers, parents, and others about ways to bring philosophy into the lives of young people. She is the author of *The Philosophical Child*, which explores ways that parents, grandparents, and other adults can stimulate philosophical conversations about children's questions, *Philosophy and Education: Introducing Philosophy to Young People* (coeditor with Roberta Israeloff), which examines various issues involved in teaching philosophy to young people, and many articles about K-12 philosophy. She writes the blog *Wondering Aloud: Philosophy with Young People*. A frequent speaker about precollege philosophy, Jana is the president of PLATO (Philosophy Learning and Teaching Organization), the founding editor-in-chief of the journal *Questions: Philosophy for Young People*, and from 2009 to 2015 was the chair of the American Philosophical Association Committee on Pre-College Instruction in Philosophy.

Michael D. Burroughs is assistant director of the Rock Ethics Institute and senior lecturer in philosophy at the Pennsylvania State University. For over a decade, he has been working to provide greater access to precollege philosophy in the United States. Michael has taught philosophy at numerous academic levels, including K-12 and college classes, as well as conducted workshops for precollege teachers and university professors. In 2008, Michael cofounded *Philosophical Horizons*, a precollege philosophy program dedicated to introducing the history and practice of philosophy to children in Memphis city schools (K-12). Michael also served as outreach coordinator for the Philosophy Department at the University of North Carolina (UNC) at Chapel Hill. During his tenure at UNC-Chapel Hill, he taught university courses on precollege philosophy and collaborated with local educators and philosophy and education graduate students to begin numerous elementary-, middle-, and high-school philosophy programs. Michael serves as the incoming vice-president on the board of directors of PLATO (Philosophy Learning and Teaching Organization) and has presented and written extensively on issues pertaining to precollege philosophy, including chapters in *Philosophy in Schools: An Introduction for Philosophers and Teachers* (Routledge, 2013) and *Ethics in Youth Sport: Policy and Pedagogical Applications* (Routledge, 2013).